CAPITAL PUNISHMENT
CRUEL AND UNUSUAL?

ISSN 1538-6678

CAPITAL PUNISHMENT
CRUEL AND UNUSUAL?

Mei Ling Rein

INFORMATION PLUS® REFERENCE SERIES
Formerly published by Information Plus, Wylie, Texas

Detroit • New York • San Francisco • San Diego • New Haven, Conn. • Waterville, Maine • London • Munich

Capital Punishment: Cruel and Unusual?

Mei Ling Rein

Project Editor
Ellice Engdahl

Editorial
Beverly Baer, Paula Cutcher-Jackson, Pamela A. Dear, Kathleen Edgar, Debra Kirby, Prindle LaBarge, Elizabeth Manar, Kathleen Meek, Charles B. Montney, Heather Price

Permissions
Margaret Abendroth, William Sampson, Sheila Spencer

Composition and Electronic Prepress
Evi Seoud

Manufacturing
Keith Helmling

LIBRARY OF CONGRESS CATALOGING-IN-PUBLICATION DATA

ISBN 0-7876-5103-6 (set)
ISBN 0-7876-7518-0
ISSN 1538-6678

Printed in the United States of America
10 9 8 7 6 5 4 3 2 1

TABLE OF CONTENTS

This chapter traces the history of capital punishment in the United States from the colonial period to the present day. Crimes punishable by death, constitutional legality of the death penalty, clemency, and worldwide trends are also covered.

Is the death penalty cruel and unusual? This chapter attempts to answer that question by presenting Supreme Court rulings and opinions given by various justices. Also discussed are the proper imposition of the death penalty, requirement of flexible guidelines for judges and jurors, and sentencing by judge instead of by jury.

This chapter presents court cases and legal decisions regarding the death penalty and mitigating circumstances, "comparative proportionality review," the right to counsel, harmless error (including coerced confessions and presumption of malice), evidence and appeals, and victim impact statements.

This chapter investigates court cases and legal decisions regarding minors and the death sentence, the role of psychiatrists (including validity of testimony, a prisoner's right to an examination, and proving insanity), the competency standard, consideration of race, and methods of execution. Information about the execution of insane and mentally retarded persons and the Antiterrorism Act of 1996 is also included.

As of 2002, 38 states authorized the death penalty. The first section of Chapter 5 defines the different types of capital offenses and discusses statutory changes and challenges to state death penalty laws. The second section details the minimum age for execution, the execution of mentally retarded persons, and death penalty methods. The last section discusses public and private executions. This chapter also contains a section about witnessing executions.

From 1930 to 2000 approximately 4,600 executions were conducted under civil authority in the United States. This chapter supplies statistics on the number and location of executions; the gender, race and ethnicity of death row inmates; crimes warranting the death penalty; and methods of execution.

From 1973 to 2002 approximately 7,000 people had received the death sentence. The first part of the chapter discusses the death sentence in terms of geographic distribution, race, gender, and characteristics of death row inmates. The second section gives information about getting off death row, the capital appeals process, legal resources, and exoneration. The last section covers execution moratoriums, DNA testing, federal studies of racial and ethnic bias, state studies of their death penalty systems, and costs of administering the death penalty.

This chapter presents public opinion surveys regarding capital punishment. Areas covered include support for the death penalty, acceptable penalties for murder, crimes deserving the death penalty, death penalty versus life imprisonment without parole, reasons for supporting capital punishment, rate of imposition, and the death penalty as a deterrent.

Capital punishment is controversial in many countries of the world. This chapter presents United Nations resolutions regarding capital punishment, opinions on capital punishment by retentionist (those that use the death penalty) and abolitionist (those that do not use the death penalty) countries, and views on minors and the death penalty.

In this chapter can be found statements dating from 1972–2002 which argue that the system of capital punishment should be maintained.

PREFACE

Capital Punishment: Cruel and Unusual? is one of the latest volumes in the Information Plus Reference Series. The purpose of each volume of the series is to present the latest facts on a topic of pressing concern in modern American life. These topics include today's most controversial and most studied social issues: abortion, capital punishment, care for the elderly, crime, health care, the environment, immigration, minorities, social welfare, women, youth, and many more. Although written especially for the high school and undergraduate student, this series is an excellent resource for anyone in need of factual information on current affairs.

By presenting the facts, it is Gale's intention to provide its readers with everything they need to reach an informed opinion on current issues. To that end, there is a particular emphasis in this series on the presentation of scientific studies, surveys, and statistics. These data are generally presented in the form of tables, charts, and other graphics placed within the text of each book. Every graphic is directly referred to and carefully explained in the text. The source of each graphic is presented within the graphic itself. The data used in these graphics are drawn from the most reputable and reliable sources, in particular from the various branches of the U.S. government and from major independent polling organizations. Every effort has been made to secure the most recent information available. The reader should bear in mind that many major studies take years to conduct, and that additional years often pass before the data from these studies are made available to the public. Therefore, in many cases the most recent information available in 2004 dated from 2001 or 2002. Older statistics are sometimes presented as well if they are of particular interest and no more recent information exists.

Although statistics are a major focus of the Information Plus Reference Series, they are by no means its only content. Each book also presents the widely held positions and important ideas that shape how the book's subject is

discussed in the United States. These positions are explained in detail and, where possible, in the words of their proponents. Some of the other material to be found in these books includes: historical background; descriptions of major events related to the subject; relevant laws and court cases; and examples of how these issues play out in American life. Some books also feature primary documents, or have pro and con debate sections giving the words and opinions of prominent Americans on both sides of a controversial topic. All material is presented in an even-handed and unbiased manner; the reader will never be encouraged to accept one view of an issue over another.

HOW TO USE THIS BOOK

Few topics are as controversial as capital punishment. Capital punishment has been debated since the colonial period in America and is currently a worldwide issue. This book includes the history of capital punishment plus discussions of numerous court cases, legal decisions, and historical statistics. Also included is information about execution methods, minors and the death penalty, public attitudes, and capital punishment around the world.

Capital Punishment: Cruel and Unusual? consists of eleven chapters and three appendices. Each of the chapters is devoted to a particular aspect of capital punishment. For a summary of the information covered in each chapter, please see the synopses provided in the Table of Contents at the front of the book. Chapters generally begin with an overview of the basic facts and background information on the chapter's topic, then proceed to examine subtopics of particular interest. For example, Chapter Seven: Under Sentence of Death begins with a discussion of the increasing number of prisoners on death row. It then details the race, gender, and characteristics of prisoners awaiting execution, and the criminal history of death row inmates. Also covered are methods of getting off death row, including the appeals process, legal resources, exoneration, moratoriums, and DNA testing. Federal and state studies of the death penalty and costs of administering the death penalty are also included. Readers can find their way through a chapter by looking for the section and sub-section headings, which are clearly set off from the text. They can also refer to the book's extensive index if they already know what they are looking for.

Statistical Information

The tables and figures featured throughout *Capital Punishment: Cruel and Unusual?* will be of particular use to the reader in learning about this issue. These tables and figures represent an extensive collection of the most recent and important statistics on capital punishment and related issues—for example, graphics in the book cover capital offenses; federal laws providing for the death penalty; methods of execution; number of prisoners executed; number of persons under sentence of death; death row exoneration; support for capital punishment; and countries retaining the death penalty. Gale believes that making this information available to the reader is the most important way in which we fulfill the goal of this book: to help readers to understand the issues and controversies surrounding capital punishment in the United States and reach their own conclusions.

Each table or figure has a unique identifier appearing above it for ease of identification and reference. Titles for the tables and figures explain their purpose. At the end of each table or figure, the original source of the data is provided.

Appendices

In order to help readers understand these often complicated statistics, all tables and figures are explained in the text. References in the text direct the reader to the relevant statistics. Furthermore, the contents of all tables and figures are fully indexed. Please see the opening section of the index at the back of this volume for a description of how to find tables and figures within it.

In addition to the main body text and images, *Capital Punishment: Cruel and Unusual?* has three appendices. The first is the Important Names and Addresses directory. Here the reader will find contact information for a number of government and private organizations that can provide information on capital punishment. The second appendix is the Resources section, which can also assist the reader in conducting his or her own research. In this section, the author and editors of *Capital Punishment: Cruel and Unusual?* describe some of the sources that were most useful during the compilation of this book. The final appendix is the detailed Index, which facilitates reader access to specific topics in this book.

ADVISORY BOARD CONTRIBUTIONS

The staff of Information Plus would like to extend their heartfelt appreciation to the Information Plus Advisory Board. This dedicated group of media professionals provides feedback on the series on an ongoing basis. Their comments allow the editorial staff who work on the project to make the series better and more user-friendly. Our top priority is to produce the highest-quality and most useful books possible, and the Advisory Board's contributions to this process are invaluable.

The members of the Information Plus Advisory Board are:

- Kathleen R. Bonn, Librarian, Newbury Park High School, Newbury Park, California

- Madelyn Garner, Librarian, San Jacinto College—North Campus, Houston, Texas

- Anne Oxenrider, Media Specialist, Dundee High School, Dundee, Michigan

- Charles R. Rodgers, Director of Libraries, Pasco-Hernando Community College, Dade City, Florida

- James N. Zitzelsberger, Library Media Department Chairman, Oshkosh West High School, Oshkosh, Wisconsin

COMMENTS AND SUGGESTIONS

The editors of the Information Plus Reference Series welcome your feedback on *Capital Punishment: Cruel and Unusual?* Please direct all correspondence to:

Editors
Information Plus Reference Series
27500 Drake Rd.
Farmington Hills, MI 48331-3535

ACKNOWLEDGMENTS

The editors wish to thank the copyright holders of material included in this volume and the permissions managers of many book and magazine publishing companies for assisting us in securing reproduction rights. We are also grateful to the staffs of the Detroit Public Library, the Library of Congress, the University of Detroit Mercy Library, Wayne State University Purdy/Kresge Library Complex, and the University of Michigan Libraries for making their resources available to us.

Following is a list of the copyright holders who have granted us permission to reproduce material in Capital Punishment: Cruel and Unusual? *Every effort has been made to trace copyright, but if omissions have been made, please let us know.*

For more detailed source citations, please see the sources listed under each individual table and figure.

Amnesty International Publications: Table 9.1, Table 9.2, Table 9.3, Table 9.4, Table 9.5

Death Penalty Information Center: Figure 6.1, Table 6.2, Figure 7.2, Figure 7.3

Gale Group: Table 5.4

The Gallup Organization: Figure 8.1, Figure 8.2, Table 8.2, Table 8.3

Judicial Conference of the United States, Committee on Defender Services, Subcommittee on Federal Death Penalty Cases: Table 7.11, Table 7.12

NAACP Legal Defense and Educational Fund, Inc.: Table 6.3, Table 7.2

Ohio Northern University, The Claude W. Pettit College of Law: Table 5.3, Table 6.4, Table 6.5, Table 7.3

U.S. Department of Justice: Table 7.10

U.S. Department of Justice, Bureau of Justice Statistics: Table 5.1, Table 5.2, Table 5.5, Table 6.1, Table 6.6, Table 6.7, Figure 7.1, Table 7.1, Table 7.4, Table 7.5, Table 7.6, Table 7.7, Table 7.8, Table 8.1

U.S. Senate Committee on the Judiciary: Table 7.9

CHAPTER 1
A CONTINUING CONFLICT—
A HISTORY OF CAPITAL PUNISHMENT IN AMERICA

THE COLONIAL PERIOD

Since the first European settlers arrived in America, the death penalty has been accepted as just punishment for a variety of offenses. The English Penal Code, which applied to the British colonies, listed 14 capital offenses, but actual practice varied from colony to colony. In the Massachusetts Bay Colony 12 crimes warranted the death penalty—idolatry, witchcraft, blasphemy, rape, statutory rape, kidnapping, perjury in a trial involving a possible death sentence, rebellion, murder, assault in sudden anger, adultery, and buggery (sodomy). In the statute each crime was accompanied by quotations from the Old Testament of the Bible justifying capital punishment. Later arson, treason, and grand larceny were added.

In 1608 the first recorded execution in the new colonies occurred in the Jamestown colony of Virginia. Captain George Kendall, one of the original leaders of the colony, was convicted of mutiny by a jury of his peers and sentenced to death by shooting. In 1632 Jane Champion, a slave, became the first woman to be put to death in the new colonies. She was hanged in James City, Virginia, for the murders of her master's children.

In contrast to the Massachusetts Bay Colony, the Quakers adopted much milder laws. The Royal Charter for South Jersey (1646) did not permit capital punishment for any crime, and there was no execution until 1691. In Pennsylvania William Penn's Great Act of 1682 limited the death penalty to treason and murder. Most states, however, followed the much harsher British codes. For example, in New York, hitting one's parent was punishable by death.

THE FIRST ABOLITIONISTS OF THE DEATH PENALTY

Although the Founding Fathers commonly accepted the death penalty, many early Americans opposed capital punishment. In the late 18th century Dr. Benjamin Rush

(1745–1813), a physician considered to be the founder of the American abolition movement, decried capital punishment. He attracted the support of Benjamin Franklin (1706–90), and it was at Franklin's home in Philadelphia that Rush became one of the first Americans to propose a "House of Reform," a prison where criminals could be detained until they changed their antisocial behavior. Consequently, in 1790 the Walnut Street Jail, the primitive seed from which the American penal system grew, was built in Philadelphia.

Dr. Rush published numerous pamphlets, the most notable of which was *Inquiry into the Justice and Policy of Punishing Murder by Death* (1792). Rush argued that the biblical support given to capital punishment was questionable and that the threat of hanging did not deter crime. Influenced by the philosophy of the Enlightenment (the Age of Reason in the mid- to-late 1700s), Rush believed the state exceeded its granted powers when it executed a citizen. In addition to Franklin, Rush attracted many other Pennsylvanians to his cause, including William Bradford, Pennsylvania's attorney general. Bradford suggested the idea of different degrees of murder, some of which did not warrant the death penalty. As a result, in 1794 Pennsylvania repealed the death penalty for all crimes except first-degree murder, defined as "willful, deliberate, and premeditated killing or murder committed during arson, rape, robbery, or burglary."

THE ABOLITIONIST MOVEMENT

Dr. Rush's proposals attracted many followers, and numerous petitions aiming to abolish all capital punishment were presented in Ohio, New Jersey, New York, and Massachusetts. No state, however, reversed its laws.

The second quarter of the 19th century was a time of reform in America. Capital punishment opponents rode the tide of righteousness and indignation created by anti-saloon and antislavery advocates. Abolitionist societies sprang up, especially along the Atlantic coast. In 1845 the American Society for the Abolition of Capital Punishment was founded.

In the late 1840s Horace Greeley (1811–72), the editor and founder of the *New York Tribune* and a leading advocate of most abolitionist causes, led the crusade against the death penalty. In 1846 Michigan became the first state to abolish the death penalty for all crimes except treason (until 1963), making it, for all practical purposes, the first English-speaking jurisdiction in the world to abolish the death penalty for common crimes. (Common crimes, also called ordinary crimes, are crimes committed during peacetime. Ordinary crimes that could lead to the death penalty include murder, rape, and, in some countries, robbery or embezzlement of very large sums of money. In comparison, exceptional crimes are military crimes committed during exceptional times, mainly wartime. Examples are treason, spying, or desertion [leaving the armed services without permission].) The law took effect on March 1, 1847. In 1852 and 1853 Rhode Island and Wisconsin, respectively, became the first two states to outlaw the death penalty for all crimes. Most states began limiting the number of capital crimes. Outside the South, murder and treason became the only acts punishable by death.

Opponents of the death penalty initially benefited from abolitionist sentiment, but as the Civil War (1861–65) neared, concern about the death penalty was lost amid the growing antislavery movement. It was not until after the Civil War that Maine and Iowa abolished the death penalty. Almost immediately, however, their legislatures reversed themselves and reinstated the death penalty. In 1887 Maine again reversed itself and abolished capital punishment. It has remained an abolitionist state ever since. Colorado abolished capital punishment in 1897, a decision apparently against the will of many of its citizens. At least twice, these citizens lynched convicted murderers. In response, the state restored the death penalty in 1901.

Meanwhile, the federal government, following considerable debate in the U.S. Congress, reduced the number of federal crimes punishable by death to treason, murder, and rape. In no instance was capital punishment to be mandatory.

A DECLINE IN ABOLITIONIST FORTUNES

At the start of the 20th century, death penalty abolitionists again took advantage of American reformism as the Progressives (liberal reformers) tried to correct the deficiencies of the American system. Between 1907 and 1917 nine states (Arizona, Kansas, Minnesota, Missouri, North Dakota, Oregon, South Dakota, Tennessee, and Washington) and Puerto Rico, a U.S. territory, abolished capital punishment. However, the momentum did not last. By 1921, of the nine states, just Minnesota and North Dakota,

remained abolitionist. The Prohibition Era (1920–33), characterized by frequent disdain for law and order, almost destroyed the abolitionist movement, as many Americans began to believe that the death penalty was the only proper punishment for gangsters who committed murder.

The movement's complete collapse was only prevented by the determined efforts of the famed Clarence Darrow, the "attorney for the damned"; Lewis E. Lawes, the abolitionist warden of Sing Sing Prison in New York; and the American League to Abolish Capital Punishment (founded in 1927). Nonetheless, of the 16 states and jurisdictions that outlawed capital punishment after 1845, only 7—Maine, Michigan, Minnesota, North Dakota, Rhode Island, Wisconsin, and Puerto Rico—had no major death penalty statute at the beginning of the 1950s. Between 1917 and 1957 no state abolished the death penalty.

The abolitionist movement made a mild comeback in the mid-1950s, and the issue was discussed in several state legislatures. In 1957 the U.S. territories of Alaska and Hawaii abolished the death penalty. In the states, however, the movement's singular success in Delaware (1958) was reversed three years later (1961), a major disappointment for death penalty opponents.

The abolitionists were able to recover during the civil rights movement of the 1960s. In 1963 Michigan, which in 1847 had abolished capital punishment for all crimes except treason, finally outlawed the death penalty for that crime as well. Oregon (1964), Iowa (1965), and West Virginia (1965) all abolished capital punishment, while many other states sharply reduced the number of crimes punishable by death. Oregon reinstated capital punishment in 1978. In 1995 New York became the 38th state to reinstate the death penalty, ending its 18-year ban on capital punishment. At year-end 2002, 38 states, the federal government, and the U.S. military had the death penalty.

FEDERAL DEATH PENALTY

The federal government no longer lists rape as one of the crimes punishable by death, but it continues to impose the death penalty for murder, treason, and espionage. Over the years, the federal government has added to the number of federal offenses punishable by death. In 1790 Thomas Bird became the first inmate executed under the federal death penalty. He was hanged in Maine for murder. Between 1790 and 1963 the federal government put to death 336 men and four women. On February 15, 1963, Victor Feguer was hanged in Iowa for kidnapping and murder. This was the last execution by the federal government until nearly 40 years later. On June 11, 2001, federal execution resumed when the U.S. government carried out Timothy McVeigh's death sentence. McVeigh was sentenced to death in 1997 for bombing the Alfred P. Murrah Federal Building in Oklahoma City, Oklahoma, on April 19, 1995, killing 168 people.

Antidrug, Violent Crime, and Antiterrorism Laws

In 1988 Congress reinstated the death penalty by enacting the Anti-Drug Abuse Act (Public Law 100-690), which included a drug-kingpin provision allowing the death penalty for murder resulting from large-scale illegal drug dealing. The act did not provide for the method of federal execution. In 1993 then President George H. W. Bush authorized the use of lethal injection under this law. As of November 20, 2003, three inmates were under sentence of death pursuant to this law.

In 1994 the Violent Crime Control and Law Enforcement Act (Public Law 103-322; also known as the Federal Death Penalty Act of 1994) added more than 50 crimes punishable by death. Among these federal crimes are murder of certain government officials, kidnapping resulting in death, murder for hire, fatal drive-by shootings, sexual abuse crimes resulting in death, carjacking resulting in death, and other crimes not resulting in death, such as running a large-scale drug enterprise. The method of execution will be the same as that used in the state where the sentencing occurs. If the state does not allow the death penalty, the judge would choose a state with the death penalty. Under the act, 15 persons have been sentenced to death, including Timothy McVeigh.

Antiterrorism legislation came about in the wake of the Oklahoma City bombing in 1995. In 1996 Congress passed the Antiterrorism and Effective Death Penalty Act (AEDPA; Public Law 104-132). The act, signed into law on April 24, 1996, just after the first anniversary of the Oklahoma City bombing by Timothy McVeigh, was intended "to deter terrorism, provide justice for victims, [and] provide for an effective death penalty." The law also restricts death row inmates' use of *habeas corpus* petitions, federal appeals by which state and federal inmates request a federal court to determine whether they are being held in violation of their constitutional rights. The law requires death row inmates to file their *habeas corpus* petitions in the appropriate district courts within six months of the final state appeal. Prior to the enactment of this law, no filing deadline existed. Under the 1996 law, a defendant who fails to challenge his or her conviction or sentence within the time specified cannot file another petition unless approved by a three-judge appellate court. The AEDPA further dictates that federal judges will have to defer to the rulings of the state courts, unless the rulings violate the Constitution or the laws of the United States or contradict "the Supreme Court's recognition of a new federal right that is made retroactively applicable."

Another capital crime was added on June 25, 2002, as part of the Terrorist Bombings Convention Implementation Act of 2002 (Public Law 107-197). The law makes punishable by death the bombing of places of public use, government facilities, public transportation systems, and infrastructure facilities with the intent to cause death or serious physical injury or with intent to cause destruction resulting in major economic loss.

In 1992 the Administrative Office of the United States Court established the Federal Death Penalty Resource Counsel Project (FDPRCP) to serve as a clearinghouse for information helpful to defense attorneys appointed in federal death penalty cases. According to the FDPRCP, between 1988, when the Anti-Drug Abuse Act was signed into law, to November 10, 2003, the U.S. attorney general authorized the government to seek the death penalty in 305 cases. In 42 percent of cases, the defendants either entered a plea agreement, the government withdrew the request for the death penalty, or the government dismissed the charges. One person received clemency, and two were found innocent. Juries and judges chose the death sentence 33 times and rejected it 61 times. Sixty-eight inmates were on trial or awaiting trial. Three inmates had been executed.

Federal prisoners used to be imprisoned in the state where the trial was held, but between 1993 and 1996 the U.S. Bureau of Prisons built a 50-cell federal death house in Terre Haute, Indiana, to accommodate the condemned. It started housing death row inmates in 1999.

Federal Government Resumes Executions

After being sentenced to death for conspiracy and murder in 1997, Timothy McVeigh received an execution date of May 16, 2001. U.S. Attorney General John Ashcroft, however, delayed the execution following the discovery that the Federal Bureau of Investigation (FBI) failed to turn over more than 3,000 documents to the defense and prosecution during the trial. McVeigh appealed for a second stay of execution, but the U.S. Court of Appeals for the Tenth Circuit denied his request, affirming a U.S. District Court's ruling that there was no evidence that the federal government intentionally hid the FBI files from the defense. On June 11, 2001, the execution was carried out.

Eight days later, on June 19, 2001, Texas drug boss Juan Raul Garza became the second federal prisoner to be executed since 1988. He was the first person to be executed under the Anti-Drug Abuse Act of 1988 for murders resulting from a drug enterprise. Garza received the death sentence in 1993 for the 1990 murders of three associates.

Garza was initially scheduled to be executed in August 2000. In July 2000 the Clinton administration granted a four-month reprieve (a stay of execution for a short time to resolve an issue) to allow the Justice Department to establish clemency guidelines by which a death row inmate could plead for his life after exhausting all appeals. Some critics noted that the administration, which had been running the government for seven years, should have previously taken the time to put in place a clemency protocol for capital cases. Others claimed the government could have applied to capital cases the clemency guidelines that it uses for noncapital cases. It should be noted that, even with no formal guidelines in place, Garza could have pleaded for clemency.

On September 13, 2000, Garza asked President Clinton to commute his death sentence to life imprisonment without parole. Garza's lawyer argued that the Justice Department study of the federal death penalty system, released the day before, showed the federal capital punishment is "plagued by systemic bias, disparity and arbitrariness." Defense counsel claimed that it would be unfair to put Garza to death because the federal death penalty discriminates against members of minorities and is administered unevenly geographically. (Of the 18 men on federal death row at that time, 16 were minorities, and 6 had been convicted in Texas.) Again, the president delayed the execution, this time to December 12, 2000. It took another six months for the U.S. government to carry out Garza's death penalty. Newly elected President George W. Bush, formerly the governor of Texas, refused to stay the execution.

Louis Jones, Jr., a retired soldier, was executed by the U.S. government on March 18, 2003. In 1995 Jones was convicted of killing a female soldier. He admitted kidnapping Tracie Joy McBride from an air force base in Texas. The federal government prosecuted Jones because his crime originally occurred at a U.S. military facility.

Federal Capital Punishment in Non–Death Penalty States

Since taking office in February 2001, U.S. Attorney General John Ashcroft has authorized the death penalty in several non–death penalty states, such as Iowa, Massachusetts, Michigan, Vermont, and West Virginia. According to Justice Department policy, federal criminal law can be enacted in any state.

Federal law can also be enacted in any U.S. territory. In 2000 federal prosecutors in Puerto Rico sought the death penalty against two men for kidnapping and murder. Puerto Rico had its last execution in 1927 and had banned the death penalty in 1929. In August 2003 a federal jury voted to acquit the defendants.

Massachusetts outlawed capital punishment in 1975, but in 2000 the federal government sought the death penalty in the case of Kristen Gilbert in Massachusetts, a non–death penalty state. Gilbert allegedly killed four patients at the Veterans Affairs Medical Center in Northampton, a federal hospital. The jury found Gilbert guilty of first-degree murder but was deadlocked on the death sentence. As a result, Judge Michael Ponsor sentenced the defendant to life imprisonment without the possibility of parole.

On March 16, 2002, Michigan became the first non–death penalty state in which a federal jury sentenced a man to death. Marvin Gabrion received the death penalty for killing Rachel Timmerman in 1997 on federal property in Manistee National Forest. No execution date has been set. Michigan has not executed an inmate since it became a state in 1837. The last execution was that of Stephen Simmons, on September 24, 1830. Simmons was hanged in Detroit for killing his wife.

In September 2003 Massachusetts was once again the scene of a federal death penalty case. The Federal Death Penalty Act of 1994 allowed federal prosecutors to seek the death penalty in the case of Gary Lee Sampson, who killed two men in separate carjacking incidents in 2001. Before the trial phase began, Sampson pleaded guilty to the crimes. The case proceeded to the penalty phase, in which a federal jury sentenced him to death. As with other death penalty cases, Sampson's case will undergo several appeals.

Federal Government Designates Virginia for First Sniper Trial

The Washington, D.C., area was terrorized by sniper shootings between October 2 and October 22, 2002. Ten people were shot to death and three others wounded as they went about their daily activities. Two suspects—John Allen Muhammad and Lee Boyd Malvo—were later arrested. The federal government, which had initially taken custody of the men, decided to turn them over to the state of Virginia, where several of the murders occurred. Although six murders occurred in Montgomery County, Maryland, U.S. Attorney General John Ashcroft considered Virginia's record on the death penalty since it was restored in 1976—89 executions, compared to Maryland's 3, Furthermore, Maryland had a moratorium on the death penalty. Unlike Maryland, Virginia also allows the death penalty for juveniles as young as 16. Malvo was 17 years old at the time of the crimes.

The government first tried the case against 42-year-old Muhammad on October 14, 2003. The defendant was charged with the shooting death of Dean Harold Meyers of Maryland at a gas station in Manassas, Virginia, on October 9, 2002. Muhammad faced the death penalty under two Virginia laws—committing multiple murders in a three-year-period and killing Meyers as part of a terrorist plan to intimidate the public in order to extort $10 million from the government. On November 17, 2003, Muhammad was convicted of both capital charges. He was also convicted of conspiracy to commit murder and the illegal use of a firearm. A week later the jury sentenced him to die.

Lee Boyd Malvo, Muhammad's accused accomplice, had been charged with capital murder in the shooting of Linda Franklin outside a Home Depot store in Falls Church, Virginia, on October 14, 2002. He was also charged with an act of terrorism in killing Franklin. In December 2003 Malvo was convicted of the two counts of capital murder and sentenced to life without parole.

THE U.S. MILITARY

The U.S. military has its own death penalty law—the Uniform Code of Military Justice (UCMJ) found under United States Code, Title 10, Chapter 47. Lethal injection is the method of execution. For crimes that occurred on or after November 17, 1997, the UCMJ provides the alternative sentence of life without the possibility of parole. As commander-in-chief, the president of the United States can write regulations and procedures to implement the UCMJ provisions. The military needs the president's approval to implement a death sentence.

According to the Bureau of Justice Statistics of the U.S. Justice Department, the military executed 160 inmates between 1939 and 1961. As of July 1, 2003, seven men were on the military death row—five blacks, one white, and one Asian. All were convicted of premeditated murder or felony murder (murder that occurs during the commission of another serious crime, such as arson). The military's death row at the U.S. Disciplinary Barracks is located at Fort Leavenworth, Kansas.

The first American soldier to be executed since the Civil War was Army Private Edward "Eddie" Slovik. In 1944 he was charged with desertion while assigned to the European theater during World War II (1939–45). Although Slovik was just one of hundreds of American soldiers who were convicted of desertion and sentenced to death, he was the only one executed. It is believed that, among other reasons, the military wanted to use his case as a deterrent to future desertions. Slovik died by firing squad on January 31, 1945, in France. Since then no other soldier has been executed for desertion. The last military execution occurred on April 13, 1961, when Army Private John A. Bennett was hanged for the 1955 rape and murder of an 11-year-old girl.

NATIVE AMERICANS

The U.S. government has let Native American nations use their own discretion regarding the death penalty. Most of the tribes have decided against using the death penalty, though according to the NAACP Legal Defense Fund & Educational Fund, Inc. (New York, NY), as of July 1, 2003, there were 39 Native Americans on state death rows.

RESOLVING THE CONSTITUTIONAL ISSUES

Until the 1960s there was legally no question that the death penalty was acceptable under the U.S. Constitution. Then, in 1963 U.S. Supreme Court Justice Arthur J. Goldberg (joined by Justices William O. Douglas and William J. Brennan), dissenting from a rape case in which the defendant had been sentenced to death (*Rudolph v. Alabama,* 375 U.S. 889), raised the question of the legality of the death penalty. The filing of a large number of lawsuits in the late 1960s led to an implied moratorium (a temporary suspension) on executions.

The moratorium lasted until 1977, when the state of Utah executed Gary Gilmore. Gilmore had been convicted of killing Ben Bushnell, a motel manager in Provo, Utah, on July 20, 1976. Authorities had also charged him with the July 19 murder of Max Jensen, a gas station attendant, in Orem, Utah. Gilmore received the death penalty for the Bushnell murder. He refused to appeal his case, demanding that his sentence be carried out swiftly. Gilmore requested the state supreme court to grant his wish because he did not want to spend his life on death row. The court granted his wish, but interventions by his mother, as well as by anti–death penalty organizations, resulted in several stays of execution. These organizations were concerned that the defendant's refusal to appeal his case and the court's agreement to carry out his wish might establish a precedent that would hurt the cause of other inmates. After several suicide attempts, Gilmore finally got his wish and died by firing squad on January 17, 1977.

Since 1972, with *Furman v. Georgia* (408 U.S. 238) and the accompanying cases, the Supreme Court has been defining and refining what is and is not acceptable under the U.S. Constitution. With the replacement of Chief Justice Earl Warren by Chief Justice Warren Burger, and his later replacement by Chief Justice William Rehnquist, the Court majority has generally interpreted the death penalty as worthy of extra attention because of the seriousness of the consequences, though it is most assuredly considered an acceptable punishment for murder.

CHANGES IN CAPITAL PUNISHMENT IN THE UNITED STATES

Limiting Federal Appeals

Habeas corpus review, which affords state and federal prisoners the chance to challenge the constitutionality of their convictions or sentences, has long been considered an important safeguard in all criminal trials, especially those involving the death penalty. Some people fear that the limitations on federal *habeas corpus* petitions required by the Antiterrorism and Effective Death Penalty Act of 1996 (AEDPA) may contribute to the execution of innocent persons. In addition, they believe that the unclear language of the AEDPA has allowed for varying interpretations in federal appeals courts. For the first time, in 2000, in *(Terry) Williams v. Taylor* (529 U.S. 362) and *(Michael) Williams v. Taylor* (529 U.S. 420), the U.S. Supreme Court addressed the lower courts' interpretation of the AEDPA.

Some States Consider Restoring the Death Penalty

Several states without the death penalty have considered reinstating it. In 2003 Hawaii, Massachusetts, Minnesota, and Wisconsin lawmakers introduced bills that would reinstitute the death penalty. However, none of the legislation passed.

Massachusetts carried out its last executions in 1947 when two inmates were electrocuted for abduction and murder. In 1984 the state abolished the death penalty. Over the years lawmakers tried to bring back capital punishment. In 1997 a bill to reinstate the death penalty was defeated by just one vote. Again, in 1999 and 2001 reinstatement bills failed to pass by a large margin. In September 2003 Massachusetts governor Mitt Romney announced that he had formed a panel of legal and forensics experts to help him write a bill that would reinstate the death penalty. Governor Romney, a proponent of capital punishment, believes that "[j]ust as science can be used to free the innocent, it can be used to identify the guilty." Death penalty opponents argue that no system, even one based on the latest science and technology, could be without errors. The governor's council is expected to present the death penalty bill in 2004.

Some States Retain the Death Penalty

Several states executed more prisoners in 2001 than in 2000. They included Delaware, Missouri, North Carolina, and Oklahoma. In 2001 Oklahoma executed 18 inmates versus 11 in 2000. North Carolina's executions rose from one to five, and those of Delaware increased from one to two. Missouri put seven inmates to death in 2000, compared to six in 2001. On November 6, 2001, New Mexico executed its first inmate since 1960. Terry Clark was executed for the 1986 murder of a nine-year-old girl, whom he had also raped. In 2002 Texas carried out 33 death sentences, nearly double its 17 executions in 2001. For the first time since 1989, Mississippi executed an inmate. Tracy Hansen was put to death for 1987 murder of police officer David Bruce Ladner.

In May 2000 the New Hampshire legislature became the first state legislature to pass a bill abolishing the death penalty. Governor Jeanne Shaheen, however, vetoed the bill. A similar bill introduced in the House of Representatives in January 2001 was defeated three months later. Although the death penalty is in the statute books, New Hampshire has not sentenced anyone to death since reinstating capital punishment in 1991. The state had not had an execution since 1939. As of July 1, 2003, New Hampshire had no inmates on death row.

New Rules on How States Impose Death Sentences

In June 2002 the U.S. Supreme Court ruled on two cases, restricting the ways states impose death sentences. In *Atkins v. Virginia* (536 U.S. 304), the Court held that executing mentally retarded persons violates the Eight Amendment's ban on cruel and unusual punishment. The Court, however, did not define mental retardation but left it to each state to formulate its own definition.

In *Ring v. Arizona* (536 U.S. 584), the Court ruled that a death sentence violates the Sixth Amendment right to a trial by jury when a judge and not a jury determines the facts required for imposing the death penalty. The *Ring* decision immediately affected Arizona, Idaho, and Montana, where a single judge made the final decision to impose a death sentence. Since *Ring,* these three states have passed legislation requiring jury sentencing in capital cases. Colorado and Nebraska, which used a three-judge panel to determine the death sentencing, also amended their laws to allow for jury sentencing. Prior to the *Ring* ruling, judges in Alabama, Delaware, Florida, and Indiana determined the punishment after juries made a recommendation. Since the *Ring* decision, Delaware and Indiana have passed laws requiring a unanimous vote by jurors in imposing the death penalty. As of November 30, 2003, Alabama and Florida had not amended their capital laws to comply with the Supreme Court ruling.

The Supreme Court did not indicate whether *Ring* would apply retroactively to inmates who have used up all their appeals. Experts say that, were *Ring* to be applied retroactively in the aforementioned nine states, inmates in other states might also be affected by the high court ruling. For example, in states such as Missouri and Nevada, judges are allowed to sentence the defendant if the jury fails to reach a unanimous vote during the penalty phase.

COURT RULES THAT *RING V. ARIZONA* IS NOT RETROACTIVE. Following the *Ring* ruling, four Arizona death row inmates who had exhausted their appeals filed a petition with the state supreme court, claiming that the ruling applies retroactively. About 90 inmates on Arizona's death row have completed all appeals. On February 26, 2003, the Arizona Supreme Court held in *State v. Towery* (No. CR-02-0031-PC) that *Ring* does not apply retroactively to final cases. The court added,

> [A]pplying *[Ring]* retroactively would greatly disrupt the administration of justice.... [C]ourts must protect a victim's rights by ensuring a "prompt and final conclusion of the case after the conviction and sentence." [Arizona Constitution] ... Conducting new sentencing hearings, many requiring witnesses no longer available, would impose a substantial and unjustified burden on Arizona's administration of justice.

ARIZONA SUPREME COURT AGREES TO HEAR ACTIVE APPEALS. On April 3, 2003, the Supreme Court of Arizona issued an opinion saying it will review 27 cases involving inmates who had not exhausted their appeals. The opinion, *State v. Ring* (No. CR-97-0428-AP), was issued in light of *Ring v. Arizona* (2002) in which the U.S. Supreme Court remanded Timothy Ring's case to the state supreme court. Timothy Ring was among the 27 inmates whose case was not yet final. All inmates had previously either pled guilty to, or had been found guilty of, first-degree premeditated murder or felony murder. In each case a judge had handed down the death sentence. The court announced that it will review the cases for "harmless error" only on the impact of *Ring* on the death sentences of each of the defendants. A "harmless error" is one that did not affect the verdict in the case.

As a result of the April 2003 state supreme court ruling, Timothy Ring's case was heard by that court on September 5, 2003. The court remanded his case to the lower court for resentencing.

FEDERAL APPEALS COURT RULES *RING V. ARIZONA* IS RETROACTIVE. On September 2, 2003, the U.S. Court of Appeals for the Ninth Circuit, in *Summerlin v. Stewart* (No. 98-99002), ruled 8–3 that in light of *Ring v. Arizona,* Warren Summerlin's death sentence should be vacated. The court let stand Summerlin's conviction for the sexual assault and murder of Brenna Bailey, a bill collector, in Arizona in 1981. The appellate court held that the ruling should apply retroactively, even to those inmates who have exhausted their appeals.

The Ninth Circuit Court addressed the state's argument that an earlier Supreme Court ruling, *Teague v. Lane* (488 U.S. 289, 1989), bars inmates who have exhausted their appeals from filing petitions for a federal *habeas corpus* review. The circuit court explained that *Teague* does not apply to Arizona cases because it refers to new Supreme Court rulings that make a procedural change in the law.

Ring, however, has made a substantive change in the law. The court added that, alternatively, there is a *Teague* exception that allows for a retroactive application of a procedural rule if it is a "watershed rule ... that ... alters our understanding of the bedrock procedural elements essential to the fairness of a particular conviction." The Ninth Circuit concluded that the *Ring* ruling satisfies both conditions. Judge Sidney R. Thomas, writing the majority opinion, added:

> The Supreme Court's decision in *Ring* affects the structure of every capital trial and has rendered unconstitutional every substantive statute in conflict with its dictates....*Ring's* effect on capital murder cases is akin to that of *Furman,* which declared that death penalty statutes vesting complete discretion in the judge or in the jury, like Arizona's, were unconstitutional. *Furman,* as already noted, was given full retroactive effect for the purposes of federal *habeas* review.

The *Summerlin* decision, therefore, technically overturned the death sentence of more than 100 inmates in Arizona, Idaho, and Montana, who were under the jurisdiction of the Ninth Circuit. On December 1, 2003, the U.S. Supreme Court agreed to decide whether *Ring* should be applied retroactively. The case, *Schriro v. Summerlin* (No. 03-526), which was appealed by the state of Arizona, will be heard in 2004.

Experts observe that if the high court affirmed the appellate court's ruling, resentencing would involve millions of dollars. The process could also be prolonged by having to recreate each case, revisit old evidence, and assemble witnesses, some of whom might not be available. In her dissenting opinion in *Ring v. Arizona,* Justice Sandra Day O'Connor predicted that *Ring* would overburden the appeals courts. The Court decision affects not only Arizona but also at least eight other jurisdictions, including Idaho and Montana (judge as a sole sentencer); Colorado and Nebraska (a three-judge panel as sentencer); and Alabama, Delaware, Florida, and Indiana (an advisory jury with the judge as the ultimate sentencer). Nearly 700 inmates are on death row in these nine states.

ARIZONA JURORS IMPOSE MORE DEATH SENTENCES. Reporter Jim Walsh of the *Arizona Republic* (November 12, 2003) reported that, since the new state sentencing law was first used on November 2002, jurors have been handing down death sentences. Within a one-year period (November 2002 to November 2003), jurors in Maricopa County sentenced seven of eight defendants to death. Statewide, jurors imposed a total of 10 death sentences out of 15 cases heard. In comparison, between 1995 and 1999, Maricopa County judges imposed death sentences in 11 of 75 (14.7 percent) cases. Statewide, within that four-year period, judges sentenced 29 of 143 (20.3 percent) defendants to death.

In 2002, after the U.S. Supreme Court issued the *Ring*) ruling, some experts noted that states where judges ultimately made the life-or-death decision would see fewer death sentences. Many claimed that judges, who are elected public figures, may be driven by political ambitions to issue death sentences. Some observers prefer to wait and see before concluding that the large number of death sentences imposed in Arizona is the start of a trend.

SEVERAL FIRSTS

Judges Declare Federal Death Penalty Unconstitutional

On July 1, 2002, in the first ruling of its kind, Judge Jed Rakoff of the U.S. District Court in Manhattan, New York, declared in *United States v. Quinones* (205 F. Supp. 2d [S.D.N.Y. 2002]) that the Federal Death Penalty Act of 1994 (Public Law 103-322) is unconstitutional and, therefore, could not be sought in the case before him. Ten defendants, of whom Alan Quinones was one, faced capital punishment on federal charges of a drug-related murder they committed in 1999. In his ruling, Judge Rakoff stated:

> [T]o this Court, the unacceptably high rate at which innocent persons are convicted of capital crimes, when coupled with the frequently prolonged delays before such errors are detected (and then often only fortuitously or by application of newly developed techniques), compels the conclusion that execution under the Federal Death Penalty Act, by cutting off the opportunity for exoneration, denies due process and, indeed, is tantamount to foreseeable, state-sponsored murder of innocent human beings.

On December 10, 2002, the U.S. Court of Appeals for the Second Circuit, in *United States v. Quinones* (313 F.3d 49 [2nd Cir. 2002]), reversed Rakoff's ruling. The appeals court noted that past Supreme Court rulings clearly rejected the district court's thesis that an individual has the "fundamental right to the opportunity for exoneration over the course of [his] natural life." The court added that, although the Supreme Court realized that innocent people may be put to death before obtaining evidence to prove their innocence, it has not found capital punishment to be inherently unconstitutional.

The defendants filed a petition for rehearing, claiming that the appeals court misunderstood their argument, the ruling of the district court, as well as the opinions of various Supreme Court cases. On February 6, 2003, the U.S. Court of Appeals for the Second Circuit denied the petition.

On September 24, 2002, a second federal judge declared the Federal Death Penalty Act of 1994 unconstitutional. U.S. District Judge William Sessions III, in *United States v. Fell* (217 F. Supp. 2d 469 [2nd. Cir. 2002]), found that the "relaxed evidentiary standards" used in the penalty phase of federal death penalty cases violate due process. The court gave as an example the government's intent to present to the penalty jury a statement allegedly made by the defendant's co-accomplice, who had since died.

Nation's First Execution Resulting from a DNA "Cold Hit"

The state of Virginia executed James Earl Patterson on March 14, 2002, for the 1987 rape and murder of Joyce Aldridge. Patterson was the first person in the nation to be executed based on a DNA "cold hit." States collect biological samples, such as blood and saliva, from criminal offenders and store these DNA profiles in a database. When DNA evidence collected at a crime scene matches a DNA sample already in the database, the match in the unsolved case is called a "cold hit."

In the Patterson case in 1999, he was in prison for another rape when the "cold hit" occurred—DNA from the Aldridge crime scene was found to match his DNA in the database. He confessed to the Aldridge crime in 2000 and was sentenced to death. Patterson waived his appeals in order to let his execution proceed as scheduled.

Earlier, in 1994, Virginia had become the first state to execute a person who was convicted as a result of DNA evidence. The defendant, Timothy Spencer, was convicted in 1988 for several rapes and murders he committed starting in 1984.

First Death Row Inmate Is Freed by DNA Testing

Kirk Bloodsworth of Maryland was the nation's first death row inmate to be exonerated based on postconviction DNA testing. Bloodworth was convicted for the rape and murder of a nine-year-old girl in 1984. He was sentenced to death in 1985. On retrial, Bloodworth received two life terms. DNA testing in 1992 excluded him from the crime. Finally in 1993 Bloodworth was released from prison. In 1999 the state paid Bloodworth $300,000 for wrongful conviction and imprisonment, including time on death row.

A CALL FOR MORATORIUM

Illinois

On January 31, 2000, Illinois became the first state to declare a moratorium on the death penalty. Governor George H. Ryan, a death penalty supporter, suspended all executions because he believed the state's death penalty system was "fraught with errors." The *Chicago Tribune* had issued a report showing that 13 inmates in Ryan's state had been released from death row since 1976. The reasons for the exoneration of these inmates ranged from DNA evidence showing innocence to false testimonies by jailhouse informants to coercion of so-called witnesses by prosecution and police.

Governor Ryan then appointed a commission to investigate the 13 cases, as well as all capital cases in Illinois. On April 15, 2002, the *Report of the Governor's Commission on Capital Punishment* was released. The 14-member panel issued 85 recommendations it thought would help reform the state's death penalty process. The recommended reforms included videotaping of capital suspects during interrogation at police facilities, banning the death penalty in cases where the conviction is based on a single-eyewitness testimony, and thorough examination of a jailhouse-informant testimony at a pretrial hearing to determine whether to use that testimony during trial.

John J. Kinsella, First Assistant State's Attorney of DuPage County, Illinois, was asked to appear before the U.S. Senate Judiciary Committee in 2002 to express his views as a prosecutor concerning Governor Ryan's moratorium and his Commission on capital punishment. Kinsella noted that the governor had only one active prosecutor among the 14 commission members. While many of the commission recommendations involve how the police should perform their jobs, not one police officer was invited to be a part of the commission. No victim rights groups were also represented. Furthermore, most of the members were death penalty opponents.

MARYLAND

In July 2001 a *de facto* (in practice, as opposed to *de jure,* meaning in law) moratorium occurred in Maryland pending the resolution by the state's high court of an appeal by inmate Steven Oken challenging the constitutionality of Maryland's capital punishment laws. Oken was sentenced to death in 1991 for the 1987 murder of Dawn Marie Garvin. He had also received life sentences for killing his sister-in-law and a motel desk clerk in Maine.

In May 2002 Maryland's governor, Parris Glendening, imposed a moratorium to allow for the completion of a study on capital punishment. Newly elected governor Robert Ehrlich, Jr., lifted the ban on executions in January, 2003.

Maryland again imposed a moratorium in February 2003 after the state's highest court stayed the execution of Oken, who was scheduled to die the following month. The Maryland Court of Appeals granted the temporary reprieve to hear Oken's case at a future date. On May 1, 2003, during his fourth review by the state's appellate court, Oken argued that the state's death penalty is unconstitutional in light of the 2000 Supreme Court ruling, *Apprendi v. New Jersey* (530 U.S. 466), which held that jurors must use the higher standard of "beyond a reasonable doubt" in considering evidence during the sentencing phase of a trial.

The Maryland Court of Appeals (*Oken v. State,* No. 117, November 17, 2003) upheld the death sentence of Steven Oken. The court did not address Oken's *Apprendi* argument and ruled only on his claim that *Ring v. Arizona* implicated the state's death penalty law. The court rejected that claim. Oken could still appeal his case to the U.S. Supreme Court.

CLEMENCY

The power of clemency may rest solely with a state's governor, with the clemency board, or with the governor and a board of advisers. In federal cases the president alone has clemency power. All states provide for clemency, which may take the form of a reprieve, a commutation, or a pardon. A reprieve, which typically involves a stay of execution, is just a temporary measure to allow further investigation of a case. A commutation involves the reduction of a criminal sentence after a criminal conviction. In the context of capital punishment, a commutation typically means replacing the death sentence with a lesser sentence, such as life without parole. Neither a reprieve nor a commutation removes a person's responsibility for the crime. A pardon, however, frees from punishment a person convicted of a crime, as well as removes his or her criminal record as if the conviction never happened.

As of November 30, 2003, the Death Penalty Information Center (Washington, D.C.), reported that since the reinstatement of the death penalty in 1976, 223 death row inmates had received a commutation of their death sentences. In 1999 five death row inmates received reprieve, the most notable being that of Darrell Mease, who was scheduled for execution on February 10, 1999. On January 28, 1999, as a tribute to Pope John Paul II, who requested clemency for Mease during the pope's visit to St. Louis, Missouri, Governor Mel Carnahan commuted Mease's sentence to life imprisonment without parole.

In 2000 Maryland and North Carolina each commuted the death sentence of a death row inmate to life without parole. Before leaving office in January 2001, President Bill Clinton commuted the death sentence of federal inmate David Ronald Chandler to life imprisonment without parole. Two other prisoners, one from Oklahoma and one from North Carolina, received commutations of their death sentences to life without parole in 2001.

On January 10, 2003, before leaving office, Governor George Ryan of Illinois pardoned four inmates who had been on death row at least 12 years. Governor Ryan claimed the men were innocent of the murders for which they had been convicted. He found that the police had tortured the men into making false confessions. Three of the men had been released. The fourth inmate remained in prison because of a separate conviction. The following day Governor Ryan commuted 167 death sentences to life imprisonment without the possibility of parole, emptying death row. The Illinois death row did not remain empty for long. In February 2003 Anthony Mertz was sent to death row for a 2001 rape and murder. *Death Row USA, Fall 2003* (NAACP Legal Defense and Educational Fund, Inc., New York, 2003) reported that as of October 1, 2003, eight inmates were under sentence of death in Illinois.

In May 2003 Louisiana Governor Mike Foster commuted the death sentence of Herbert Welcome to life without parole in light of the 2002 Supreme Court *Atkins v. Virginia* (536 U.S. 304) ruling, which prohibited the execution of those with mental retardation. Welcome had an IQ of between 50 and 57.

Following the Supreme Court's refusal to hear Kevin Stanford's appeal (*In re Stanford,* 123 S.Ct. 472, October 21, 2002), Kentucky Governor Paul Patton announced on June 19, 2003, that he would not sign Stanford's death warrant. The governor said, "I don't know what action that I will take on that case. But I will settle that case once and for all before I leave office." On his final day in office, December 8, 2003, Governor Patton commuted Stanford's death sentence to life without parole. In 1989 Stanford's case resulted in the Supreme Court ruling that allowed the execution of persons who were age 16 or 17 at the time of their crime.

Jerome Campbell of Ohio was scheduled to be executed on June 27, 2003, for the 1988 murder of 78-year-old John Turner. The day before the execution, Governor Bob Taft commuted Campbell's death sentence to life imprisonment without parole. The state's Pardon and Parole Board had recommended the clemency based on its belief that the jury would not have sentenced the defendant to death had they had information regarding the hearsay testimony of two jailhouse informants who received leniency in their punishment. DNA testing in 2002, which was not available during the trial, showed that the blood on Campbell's shoe was his and not the victim's.

SOME GOVERNMENT OFFICIALS ARE HAVING SECOND THOUGHTS

Some people believe that certain crimes are so brutal they deserve the ultimate punishment. Others fear that wrongly convicted persons may be executed. Various government officials advocate maintaining capital punishment in the United States. Yet others have voiced their doubts about the application of the death penalty. Still some have called for a moratorium on executions. In December 1998 retiring Florida Supreme Court Justice Gerald Kogan told the *Washington Post,* "There are several cases where I had grave doubts as to the guilt of a particular person."

On July 8, 2001, federal judge Michael Ponsor of the U.S. District Court of Massachusetts wrote about his experience presiding over the case of Kristen Gilbert (discussed earlier), the first death penalty case in Massachusetts since 1947 ("Life, Death, and Uncertainty," *Boston Globe*). Ponsor was the judge who sentenced the defendant to life imprisonment without the possibility of parole when the jury was deadlocked on the death sentence. In the newspaper article, Judge Posnor wrote that, having tried the case, he concluded that errors will eventually occur in the imposition of the death penalty because the legal system could not possibly carry out something that difficult perfectly in every instance.

The former attorney general of Virginia (1985–86), William G. Broaddus, under whose watch five inmates were executed, became a death penalty opponent. In 1996 he was co-counsel for Paraguayan Angel Francisco Breard, who was sentenced to death for a 1992 attempted rape and murder. Breard's case caused an international uproar when the Republic of Paraguay sued Virginia state officials for failure to notify the Paraguayan consulate of Breard's arrest in compliance with the Vienna Convention. In addition, the case was appealed to the highest court of the United Nations, the International Court of Justice, which asked for a stay of execution. The U.S. Supreme Court denied the stay and Breard was executed in 1998.

In October 2001 New Mexico Governor Gary Johnson, in a letter sent to people who wrote him regarding the imminent execution of Terry Clark, indicated that, while he had no intention of declaring a moratorium on executions, he believed that "eliminating the death penalty in the future may prove to be better public policy given the reality of the sentence today." He, therefore, was "open to a debate on this topic." On November 6, 2001, Clark was executed for the 1986 murder of a nine-year-old girl he had also raped. He was the first inmate put to death in New Mexico in nearly 42 years.

On July 1, 2003, Charles B. Blackmar, who served as senior judge of Missouri's supreme court from 1982 to 1992, wrote a letter to the editor of the *Kansas City Star.*

Judge Blackmar wrote that most countries with similar political and traditional practices as the United States have abolished capital punishment and that none of these countries is experiencing worse crime problems than the United States.

DIVERGENT VIEWS OF SUPREME COURT JUSTICES

On July 2, 2001, Supreme Court Justice Sandra Day O'Connor, a long-time supporter of the death penalty and the swing justice on the Court, expressed concern about capital punishment. She said in a speech before the Minnesota Women Lawyers (Minneapolis, MN) that "if statistics are any indication, the system may well be allowing some innocent defendants to be executed." On October 18, 2001, Justice O'Connor told the Nebraska Bar Association (Lincoln, NE) that, unless qualified lawyers are willing to work for indigent defendants who cannot afford counsel, innocent people may be sentenced to death. Justice O'Connor said, "More often than we want to recognize, some innocent defendants have been convicted and sentenced to death."

On April 9, 2001, Justice Ruth Bader Ginsburg had expressed similar concerns at a lecture at the University of the District of Columbia. Justice Ginsburg stated:

> I have yet to see a death case among the dozens coming to the Supreme Court on eve-of-execution stay petitions, in which the defendant was well represented at trial.... Public funding for the legal representation of poor people in the United States is hardly generous. In capital cases, state systems for affording representation to indigent defendants vary from adequate to meager.

At the Ninth Circuit Judicial Conference on July 18, 2002, Justice John Paul Stevens told the audience of judges and lawyers that the issue of executing offenders who were juveniles at the time of the crime might be the "next area for debate." However, he noted that this debate is more likely to be addressed by legislatures rather than the courts. He also said that the legislatures will have to address the issue of whether there should be an age limit of at least 18 years for the imposition of the death penalty.

On August 28, 2002, Justice Stevens echoed the same sentiment when the high court denied Toronto Patterson's appeal for a stay of execution. He was scheduled to be put to death in Texas that same day. The defendant petitioned the Court to consider the constitutionality of executing an inmate who was a minor during the commission of the crime. Patterson had been convicted of killing three relatives, including two children, in 1995 when he was 17 years old. Justice Stevens wrote the dissenting opinion (*In re Toronto M. Patterson,* 536 U.S. 984), saying that "Given the apparent consensus that exists among the States and in the international community against the execution of a capital sentence imposed on a juvenile offender, I think it would be appropriate for the Court to revisit the issue at the earliest opportunity. I would therefore grant a stay of this execution...." Justice Ginsburg, joined by Justice Stephen Breyer, also issued a statement, saying that in light of the Court's ruling that executing mentally retarded offenders constitutes cruel and unusual punishment (*Atkins v. Virginia,* 536 U.S. 304, 2002), the Court should revisit the issue of executing inmates who were juveniles at the time of the crime.

Justice Antonin Scalia has voiced a different view of the death penalty. In his speech at the Pew Forum on Religion and Public Life conference, "A Call for Reckoning: Religion & the Death Penalty" (The University of Chicago Divinity School, Chicago, IL, January 25, 2002), Justice Scalia explained that the Roman Catholic Church's current stand against capital punishment does not reflect historical Christian teaching. He added,

> ... [T]he core of [St. Paul's] message [in Romans 13:1–5, St. James version] is that government ... derives its moral authority from God. It is the minister of God with powers to revenge, to execute wrath, including even wrath by the sword, which is unmistakably a reference to the death penalty....

According to Justice Scalia, judges who consider the death penalty immoral should resign rather than sabotage the death penalty. He admitted that

> ... [T]he Constitution that I interpret and apply is not living, but dead; or as I prefer to call it, enduring. It means today not what current society, much less the Court, thinks it ought to mean, but what it meant when it was adopted. For me, therefore, the constitutionality of the death penalty is not a difficult, soul-wrenching question. It was clearly permitted when the Eighth Amendment was adopted—not merely for murder, by the way, but for all felonies....

CONTROVERSY OVER GREEN RIVER KILLER PLEA BARGAIN

A plea agreement between a serial killer and King County (Washington) prosecutor Norm Maleng has caused controversy over the fair application of the death penalty. Gary Leon Ridgway escaped the death penalty by agreeing to provide information about the 48 women he had murdered. Ridgway, known as the Green River Killer because he dumped the bodies of his victims, many of them prostitutes and runaways, along the Green River near Seattle, Washington, committed his crimes between 1980 and 1998. Authorities say this is the largest number of murders ever committed by a serial killer. In November 2001 authorities linked Ridgway's DNA to samples found on some of the victims. In December 2003 Ridgway received 48 consecutive life terms without the possibility of parole. He was also ordered to pay $10,000 for each victim.

Both sides of the death penalty issue have used the Green River killer case to bolster their causes. Opponents of the death penalty argue that if a case involving the largest number of serial killings did not warrant the death penalty, then others involving fewer murders certainly do not deserve the ultimate punishment. Some have noted that if the criminal justice system did not sentence a white mass murderer to death, then it should think twice about imposing the death penalty on a black person who has killed just one person or a few. Proponents of capital punishment use the case as an example of how murderers can manipulate the system, and they call for shortening the time between death sentencing and execution. Still others think the prosecutor took the right course by not acting on his initial plan to seek the death sentence. He believed that victims' families had the right to get more information from Ridgway about their loved ones so they could find closure.

In the *Seattle Times* (November 8, 2003), Washington Superior Court Judge David A. Nichols called for the abolition of the death penalty in his state. He pointed out that it is a "mockery of all reasonable notions of justice" that a mass murderer is able to avoid the death penalty because he has something to offer in exchange for the deal, while another murderer gets the death sentence because he has nothing to offer.

WORLDWIDE TREND

The *de facto* moratorium on the death penalty in the United States from 1967 to 1976 paralleled a general worldwide movement, especially among Western nations, toward the abolition of capital punishment. While the United States resumed executions in 1977, most of the Western world either formally or informally abolished capital punishment.

Today among the Western democratic nations (with which the United States traditionally compares itself), only the United States imposes the death penalty. There are technical exceptions: Israel, for example, maintains the death penalty in its statute books for "crimes against mankind" but has executed only Adolf Eichmann (1962). One of Nazi leader Adolf Hitler's SS officers, Eichmann was responsible for the murder of millions of Jews in occupied Europe during World War II (1939–45). Some countries still maintain the death penalty for treason—although no Western democracy has actually imposed it. One of the first acts of the parliaments of many of the eastern European countries after the fall of communism was to abolish capital punishment.

As of January 1, 2003, 83 countries and territories in the world continued to maintain and use the death penalty for ordinary crimes, or crimes committed during peacetime. Although many of these countries had not implemented the death sentence for many years, according to Amnesty International (London, United Kingdom), in 2002, 31 countries carried out 1,526 executions.

Extradition and Capital Punishment

An increasing number of countries refuse to extradite (surrender for trial) U.S. criminals who might face the death penalty. In March 2000 French authorities arrested fugitive James Charles Kopp, who was accused of murdering Buffalo, New York, abortion provider Dr. Barnett Slepian. It took months of negotiations before the French government sent Kopp back to New York for trial. The U.S. Justice Department had to agree in writing that the United States would not charge Kopp with capital murder. In spring 2001 the supreme courts of Canada and South Africa ruled that both nations would not extradite any criminal to the United States or any country that advocates capital punishment. In November 2001 Spain made a similar announcement, saying it will not extradite terrorist suspects to the United States unless the U.S. government agrees not to seek the death penalty.

A very controversial case also involving France concerned a fugitive convicted and sentenced to life imprisonment in absentia. Ira Einhorn was accused of murdering his girlfriend, Helen Maddux, in 1977. Her body was found in 1979, 18 months after she disappeared, in a closet in his apartment. Before his trial in 1981, Einhorn fled to Ireland, and eventually to France. The state of Pennsylvania held a trial without him, and he was convicted of Maddux's murder in 1993. In 1997, after French authorities arrested Einhorn, the United States requested his extradition. France, following rules of the European Convention on Human Rights, does not recognize verdicts handed down in trials in absentia or verdicts that result in the death penalty. As such, France refused to extradite the fugitive. Four years later, on July 20, 2001, France finally turned Einhorn over to U.S. officials after receiving assurances that he would be retried and not face the death penalty, forcing the Pennsylvania General Assembly to create a new law allowing for a condemned man to have another trial. On October 17, 2001, Einhorn was convicted of first-degree murder and sentenced to life imprisonment without parole.

CHAPTER 2

SUPREME COURT RULINGS—CRUEL AND UNUSUAL?

In 1967 a coalition of anti–death penalty groups sued Florida and California, the states with the most inmates on death row at that time, challenging the constitutionality of state capital punishment laws. An unofficial moratorium (temporary suspension) of executions resulted, pending Supreme Court decisions on several cases on appeal. The defendants in these cases claimed that the death penalty is "cruel and unusual punishment" in violation of the Eighth Amendment to the U.S. Constitution. Moreover, they alleged that the death penalty also violated the Fourteenth Amendment, which prevents states from denying anyone "equal protection of the laws." This moratorium lasted until January 17, 1977, when convicted murderer Gary Gilmore, virtually at his own request, was executed by the state of Utah.

"AS THE STATUTES ARE ADMINISTERED"

On June 29, 1972, a split 5–4 Supreme Court reached the landmark decision in *Furman v. Georgia* (408 U.S. 238, which included *Jackson v. Georgia* and *Branch v. Texas*), holding that "as the statutes are administered ... the imposition and carrying out of the death penalty [constitute] cruel and unusual punishment in violation of the Eighth and Fourteenth Amendments." In other words, the justices did not address whether capital punishment as a whole is unconstitutional. Rather, they chose to consider capital punishment in the context of its application in state statutes. The justices, whether they were of the majority opinion or of the dissenting opinion, could not agree on the arguments explaining why they opposed or supported the death penalty. As a result, the decision consisted of nine separate opinions, the lengthiest ruling in court history to date.

Justice William O. Douglas, in his concurring majority opinion, quoted former Attorney General Ramsey Clark's observation in his book, *Crime in America* (1970): "It is the poor, the sick, the ignorant, the powerless, and the hated who are executed." Douglas added,

We deal with a system of law and of justice that leaves to the uncontrolled discretion of judges or juries the determination whether defendants committing these crimes should die or be imprisoned. Under these laws no standards govern the selection of the penalty. People live or die, dependent on the whim of one man or of 12.... Thus, these discretionary statutes are unconstitutional in their operation. They are pregnant with discrimination, and discrimination is an ingredient not compatible with the idea of equal protection of the laws that is implicit in the ban on "cruel and unusual" punishments.

Justice William J. Brennan stated,

At bottom, ... the Cruel and Unusual Punishments Clause prohibits the infliction of uncivilized and inhumane punishments. The State, even as it punishes, must treat its members with respect for their intrinsic worth as human beings. A punishment is "cruel and unusual," therefore, if it does not comport with human dignity.

Justice Potter Stewart stressed another point, saying,

These death sentences are cruel and unusual in the same way that being struck by lightning is cruel and unusual. For, of all the people convicted of rapes and murders in 1967 and 1968, many just as reprehensible as these, the petitioners are among a capriciously [unpredictably] selected random handful upon whom the sentence of death has in fact been imposed.

This did not mean that Justice Stewart would rule out the death penalty. He believed that the death penalty was justified but would like to see a more equitable (fair) system of determining who should be executed. He explained,

I cannot agree that retribution [punishment or vengeance for a wrong or injury] is a constitutionally impermissible ingredient in the imposition of punishment. The instinct for retribution is part of the nature of man, and channeling that instinct in the administration of criminal justice serves an important purpose in promoting the stability of a society governed by law. When people begin to believe that organized society is unwilling or unable to impose upon criminal offenders the punishment they "deserve," then there are sown the seeds of anarchy—of self help, vigilante justice, and lynch law.

Justice Byron White, believing that the death penalty was so seldom imposed that executions were ineffective deterrents to crime, chose instead to address the role of juries and judges in imposing the death penalty. He concluded that the cases before the courts violated the Eighth Amendment because the state legislatures, having authorized the application of the death penalty, left it to the discretion of juries and judges whether or not to impose the punishment.

Justice Thurgood Marshall thought that "the death penalty is an excessive and unnecessary punishment which violates the Eighth Amendment." He added that "even if capital punishment is not excessive, it nonetheless violates the Eighth Amendment because it is morally unacceptable to the people of the United States at this time in their history." Justice Marshall also noted that the death penalty was applied with discrimination against certain classes of people (the poor, the uneducated, and members of minority groups) and that innocent people had been executed before they could prove their innocence. He also believed that it hindered the reform of the treatment of criminals, and that it promoted sensationalism during trials.

Differing Opinions

Chief Justice Warren Burger, dissenting, observed that "the constitutional prohibition against 'cruel and unusual punishments' cannot be construed to bar the imposition of the punishment of death." Justice Harry A. Blackmun was disturbed by Justices Stewart's and White's remarks that as long as capital punishment was mandated for specific crimes, it could not be considered unconstitutional. Justice Blackmun feared "that statutes stricken down today will be re-enacted by state legislatures to prescribe the death penalty for specified crimes without any alternative for the imposition of a lesser punishment in the discretion of the judge or jury."

Justice Lewis Powell declared,

I find no support—in the language of the Constitution, in its history, or in the cases arising under it—for the view that this Court may invalidate a category of penalties because we deem less severe penalties adequate to serve the ends of penology....

This Court has long held that legislative decisions in this area, which lie within the special competency of that branch, are entitled to a presumption of validity.

In other words, the Court would not question the validity of a government entity properly doing its job unless its actions were way out of line.

Justice William H. Rehnquist agreed with Justice Powell, adding the following comment:

How can government by the elected representatives of the people co-exist with the power of the federal judiciary, whose members are constitutionally insulated from responsiveness to the popular will, to declare invalid laws duly enacted by the popular branches of government?

Therefore, only Justices Brennan and Marshall concluded that the Eighth Amendment prohibited the death penalty for all crimes and under all circumstances. Justice Douglas, while ruling that the death penalty statutes reviewed by the high court were unconstitutional, did not necessarily require the final abolition of the death penalty. Justices Stewart and White also did not rule on the validity of the death penalty, noting instead that, because of the capricious imposition of the sentence, the death penalty violated the Eighth Amendment. However, Justices Rehnquist, Burger, Powell, and Blackmun concluded that the U.S. Constitution allows capital punishment.

Consequently, most state legislatures went to work to revise their capital punishment laws. They strove to make these laws more equitable in order to swing the votes of Stewart and White (and later that of John Stevens, who replaced the retired Justice Douglas).

PROPER IMPOSITION OF THE DEATH PENALTY

Four years later, on July 2, 1976, the Supreme Court ruled decisively on a series of cases. In a 7–2 decision, the justices ruled that the death penalty was, indeed, constitutional as presented in some new state laws. With Brennan and Marshall dissenting, the Court stressed (just in case *Furman* had been misunderstood) that "the death penalty is not a form of punishment that may never be imposed, regardless of the circumstances of the offense, regardless of the procedure followed in reaching the decision." Furthermore, "the infliction of death as a punishment for murder is not without justification and ... is not unconstitutionally severe."

The ruling upheld death penalty statutes in Georgia (*Gregg v. Georgia,* 428 U.S. 153, the source of the aforementioned quote), Florida (*Proffitt v. Florida,* 428 U.S. 242), and Texas (*Jurek v. Texas,* 428 U.S. 262), but struck down laws in North Carolina (*Woodson v. North Carolina,* 428 U.S. 280) and Louisiana (*Roberts v. Louisiana,* 428 U.S. 40). It ruled that the latter two states' laws were too rigid in imposing mandatory death sentences for certain types of murder.

Citing the new Georgia laws in *Gregg v. Georgia,* Justice Stewart supported the bifurcated (two-part) trial system, in which the accused would first be tried to determine his or her guilt. Then, in a separate trial, the jury would consider whether the convicted person deserved the death penalty or whether mitigating factors (circumstances that may lessen responsibility for a crime) warrant a lesser sentence, usually life imprisonment. This system meets the requirements demanded by *Furman.* Noting how the Georgia statutes fulfilled these demands, Justice Stewart observed,

> These procedures [established by the Georgia statutes] require the jury to consider the circumstances of the crime and the criminal before it recommends sentence. No longer can a Georgia jury do as *Furman*'s jury did: reach a finding of the defendant's guilt and then, without guidance or direction, decide whether he should live or die. Instead, the jury's attention is directed to the specific "circumstances of the crime: Was it committed in the course of another capital felony? Was it committed for money? Was it committed upon a peace officer or judicial officer? Was it committed in a particularly heinous way or in a manner that endangered the lives of many persons?" In addition, the jury's attention is focused on the characteristics of the person who committed the crime: Does he have a record of prior convictions for capital offenses? Are there any special facts about this defendant that mitigate against imposing capital punishment (e.g., his youth, the extent of his cooperation with the police, his emotional state at the time of the crime)? As a result, while some jury discretion still exists, "the discretion to be exercised is controlled by clear and objective standards so as to produce non-discriminatory application."

In addition, the Georgia law required that all death sentences be automatically appealed to the state supreme court, an "important additional safeguard against arbitrariness and caprice." The two-part trial system has since been adopted in the trials of all capital murder cases.

In *Proffitt v. Florida,* the high court upheld Florida's death penalty laws that had a bifurcated trial system similar to Georgia's. In Florida, however, the sentence was determined by the trial judge rather than by the jury, who assumed an advisory role during the sentencing phase. The Court found Florida's sentencing guidelines adequate in preventing unfair imposition of the death sentence.

PREDICTABILITY OF FUTURE CRIMINAL ACTIVITY

In *Jurek v. Texas,* the issue centered on whether a jury can satisfactorily determine the future actions of a convicted murderer. The Texas statute required that during the sentencing phase of a trial, after the defendant had been found guilty, the jury would determine whether it is probable the defendant would commit future criminal acts of violence that would threaten society. While agreeing with Jurek's attorneys that predicting future behavior is not easy, Justice Stewart noted,

> The fact that such a determination is difficult, however, does not mean that it cannot be made. Indeed, prediction of future criminal conduct is an essential element in many of the decisions rendered throughout our criminal justice system. The decision whether to admit a defendant to bail, for instance, must often turn on a judge's

prediction of the defendant's future conduct. Any sentencing authority must predict a convicted person's probable future conduct when it engages in the process of determining what punishment to impose. For those sentenced to prison, these same predictions must be made by parole authorities. The task that a Texas jury must perform in answering the statutory question is thus basically no different from the task performed countless times each day throughout the American system of criminal justice.

Is the Testimony of a Psychiatrist Valid?

In 1978 Thomas Barefoot was convicted of murdering a police officer. During the sentencing phase of the trial, the prosecution put two psychiatrists on the stand. Neither psychiatrist had actually interviewed Barefoot, nor did either ask to do so. Both psychiatrists agreed that an individual with Barefoot's background and who had acted as Barefoot had in murdering the policeman represented a future threat to society. Partially based on their testimony, the jury sentenced Barefoot to death.

Barefoot's conviction and sentence were appealed numerous times, and in 1983 his case was argued before the U.S. Supreme Court. Barefoot's attorneys claimed that psychiatrists could not reliably predict that a particular offender would commit other crimes in the future and be a threat to society. They further argued that psychiatrists should also not be allowed to testify about an offender's future dangerousness in response to hypothetical situations presented by the prosecutor and without having first examined the offender.

In *Barefoot v. Estelle* (463 U.S. 880, 1983), the Supreme Court ruled 6–3 that local juries were in the best position to decide guilt and impose a sentence. The Court referred to *Jurek v. Texas,* which upheld the testimony of laypersons concerning a defendant's possible future actions. The Court, therefore, looked upon psychiatrists as just another group of people presenting testimony to the jury for consideration.

The high court dismissed a brief presented by the American Psychiatric Association (APA), indicating that psychiatric testimony was "almost entirely unreliable" in determining future actions. The Court countered that such testimony had been traditionally accepted. The high court also dismissed Barefoot's contention that the psychiatrists should have personally interviewed him. Such methods of observation and conclusion were quite normal in courtroom procedures, and the psychiatric observations had been based on established facts. Barefoot's appeal was denied.

FLEXIBLE GUIDELINES FOR JUDGES AND JURORS ARE REQUIRED

In *Woodson v. North Carolina,* the Supreme Court addressed for the first time the question of whether the jury's handing down of a death sentence under North Carolina's mandatory death penalty for all first-degree murders constituted cruel and unusual punishment within the meaning of the Eighth and Fourteenth Amendments. The justices held that North Carolina's new statute provided "no standards to guide the jury in its inevitable exercise of the power to determine which first-degree murderer shall live and which shall die." Furthermore, the North Carolina law did not let the jury consider the convicted defendant's character, criminal record, or the circumstances of the crime before the imposition of the death sentence.

The Louisiana mandatory death sentence for first-degree murder suffered from similar inadequacies. It did, however, permit the jury to consider lesser offenses such as second-degree murder. In *Roberts v. Louisiana,* the Supreme Court rejected the Louisiana law because it forced the jury to find the defendant guilty of a lesser crime in order to avoid imposing the death penalty. The jury did not have the option of first determining if the accused was indeed guilty of first-degree murder for the crime he or she had actually committed and then recommending a lesser sentence if there were mitigating circumstances to support it.

As a result of either *Furman* or *Gregg* or both, virtually every state's capital punishment statute had to be rewritten. These statutes would provide flexible guidelines for judges and juries so that they might fairly decide capital cases and consider, then impose, if necessary, the death penalty.

EXCLUSION FROM JURIES OF THOSE AGAINST CAPITAL PUNISHMENT

In *Witherspoon v. Illinois* (391 U.S. 510, 1968), the Supreme Court held that a death sentence cannot be carried out if the jury that imposed or recommended such punishment was selected by excluding prospective jurors simply because they are against the death penalty or have reservations against its infliction. The Court found that the prosecution excluded those who opposed the death penalty without determining whether their beliefs would compel them to reject capital punishment. The defendant argued that this selective process had resulted in a jury that was not representative of the community.

The justices could not definitively conclude that the exclusion of jurors opposed to the death penalty results in an unrepresentative jury. They, however, believed that a person who opposes the death penalty can still abide by his duty as a juror and consider the facts presented at trial before making his decision about the defendant's punishment. The Court observed,

> If the State had excluded only those prospective jurors who stated in advance of trial that they would not even consider returning a verdict of death, it could argue that

the resulting jury was simply "neutral" with respect to penalty. But when it swept from the jury all who expressed conscientious or religious scruples against capital punishment and all who opposed it in principle, the State crossed the line of neutrality. In its quest for a jury capable of imposing the death penalty, the State produced a jury uncommonly willing to condemn a man to die.

The Court specifically noted that their findings in *Witherspoon* did not prevent the infliction of the death sentence when the prospective jurors excluded had made it "unmistakably clear" that they would automatically vote against the death sentence without considering the evidence presented during the trial, or that their attitudes toward capital punishment would keep them from making a fair decision about the defendant's guilt. Consequently, based on *Witherspoon,* it has become the practice in most states to exclude prospective jurors who indicate that they could not possibly in good conscience return a death penalty.

In *Lockett v. Ohio* (438 U.S. 586, 1978), the defendant contended, among several things, that the exclusion of four prospective jurors violated her Sixth and Fourteenth Amendment rights under the principles established in *Witherspoon v. Illinois*. The Supreme Court upheld *Witherspoon* in this case because the prospective jurors told the prosecutor that they were so against the death penalty they could not be impartial about the case. They had also admitted that they would not take an oath saying they would consider the evidence before making a judgment of innocence or guilt.

Weakening *Witherspoon*

In *Wainwright v. Witt* (469 U.S. 412, 1985), a 7–2 Supreme Court decision eased the strict requirements of *Witherspoon*. Writing for the majority, Justice Rehnquist declared that the new capital punishment procedures left less discretion to jurors. Rehnquist indicated that potential jurors in capital cases should be excluded from jury duty in a manner similar to how they were excluded in noncapital cases.

No longer would a juror's "automatic" bias against imposing the death penalty have to be proved with "unmistakable clarity." A prosecutor could not be expected to ask all the questions necessary to determine if a juror would automatically rule against the death penalty or fail to convict a defendant if he or she were likely to face execution. Fundamentally, the question of exclusion from a jury should be determined by the interplay of the prosecutor and the defense lawyer and by the decision of the judge based on his or her initial observations of the prospective juror. Judges can see firsthand whether prospective jurors' beliefs would bias their ability to impose the death penalty.

In his dissent, Justice Brennan claimed that making it easier to eliminate those who opposed capital punishment from the jury created a jury not only more likely to impose the death sentence but also more likely to convict. He also attacked the majority interpretation that now treated exclusion from a capital case as being similar to exclusion from any other case.

IT DOES NOT MATTER IF "DEATH-QUALIFIED" JURIES ARE MORE LIKELY TO CONVICT

In *Lockhart v. McCree* (476 U.S. 162, 1986), the Supreme Court resolved the issue of a fair trial with a "death-qualified" jury. A death-qualified jury is a jury that is willing to sentence a person to death after hearing the evidence of the case. The prospective jurors typically go through a selection process in which the prosecution and the defense question them about their attitudes toward the death penalty.

Ardia McCree was convicted of murdering Evelyn Boughton while robbing her gift shop and service station in Camden, Arkansas. In accordance with Arkansas law, the trial judge removed eight prospective jurors because they indicated they could not, under any circumstances, vote for the imposition of the death sentence. The resulting jury then convicted McCree and, although the state sought the death penalty, sentenced the defendant to life imprisonment without parole.

McCree appealed, claiming that the removal of the so-called *Witherspoon*-excludables violated his right to a fair trial under the Sixth and Fourteenth Amendments. These amendments guaranteed that his guilt or innocence would be determined by an impartial jury selected from a representative cross-section of the community, which would include people strongly opposed to the death penalty. Both the federal district court and the federal court of appeals agreed with McCree, but in a 6–3 decision, the Supreme Court disagreed.

The high court majority did not accept the validity of the studies presented to show that those strongly opposed to the death penalty were less likely to convict and those who supported the death penalty were more likely to convict. Justice Rehnquist, speaking for the majority, argued that, even if the justices did accept the validity of these studies, "the Constitution does not prohibit the States from 'death qualifying' juries in capital cases." Justice Rehnquist further observed,

> The exclusion from jury service of large groups of individuals not on the basis of their inability to serve as jurors, but on the basis of some immutable [unchangeable] characteristic such as race, gender, or ethnic background, undeniably gave rise to an "appearance of unfairness."
>
> [Nevertheless], unlike blacks, women, and Mexican-Americans, "*Witherspoon*-excludables" are singled out for exclusion in capital cases on the basis of an attribute that is within the individual's control. It is important to remember that not all who oppose the death penalty are subject to removal for cause in capital cases; those who

firmly believe that the death penalty is unjust may nevertheless serve as jurors in capital cases so long as they state clearly that they are willing to temporarily set aside their own beliefs in deference to the rule of law. Because the group of "*Witherspoon*-excludables" includes only those who cannot and will not conscientiously obey the law with respect to one of the issues in a capital case, "death qualification" hardly can be said to create an "appearance of unfairness."

Writing in dissent, Justice Marshall observed that if the high court thought in *Witherspoon* that excluding those who opposed the death penalty meant that a convicted murderer would not get a fair hearing during the sentencing part of the trial, it would also logically mean that he or she would not get a fair hearing during the initial trial part. The Court minority generally accepted the studies showing "that 'death qualification' in fact produces juries somewhat more 'conviction-prone' than 'nondeath-qualified' juries."

JURY MAY CONSIDER A LESSER CHARGE

Along with an accomplice, Gilbert Beck entered the home of Roy Malone. While the pair were tying up the victim, Beck's accomplice unexpectedly struck and killed Malone. Beck admitted to the robbery, but claimed the murder was not part of the plan. Beck was tried under an Alabama statute for "robbery or attempts thereof when the victim is intentionally killed by the defendant."

Under Alabama law, the judge was specifically prohibited from giving the jury the option of convicting the defendant of a lesser included offense. Instead, the jury was given the choice of either convicting the defendant of the capital crime, in which case he possibly faced the death penalty, or acquitting him, thus allowing him to escape all penalties for his alleged participation in the crime. The judge could not have offered the jury the lesser alternative of felony murder, which did not deal with the accused's intentions at the time of the crime.

Beck appealed, claiming this law created a situation in which the jury was more likely to convict. The Supreme Court, in *Beck v. Alabama* (447 U.S. 625, 1980), agreed and reversed the lower court's ruling, thus vacating his death sentence. The high court observed that, while not a matter of due process, it was virtually universally accepted in lesser offenses that a third alternative be offered. The Court noted,

> That safeguard would seem to be especially important in a case such as this. For when the evidence unquestionably establishes that the defendant is guilty of a serious, violent offense—but leaves some doubt with respect to an element that would justify conviction of a capital offense—the failure to give the jury the "third option" of convicting on a lesser included offense would seem inevitably to enhance the risk of an unwarranted conviction.

According to the ruling, such a risk could not be tolerated in a case where the defendant's life was at stake. *Beck*, however, did not require a jury to consider a lesser charge in every case, but only where the consideration would be justified.

DOES THE BUCK STOP WITH THE JURY?

During the course of a robbery, Bobby Caldwell shot and killed the owner of a grocery store. He was tried and found guilty. During the sentencing phase of the trial, Caldwell's attorney pleaded for mercy, concluding his summation by emphasizing to the jury,

> I implore you to think deeply about this matter.... You are the judges and you will have to decide his fate. It is an awesome responsibility, I know—an awesome responsibility.

Responding to the defense attorney's plea, the prosecutor played down the responsibility of the jury, stressing that a life sentence would be reviewed by a higher court:

> [The defense] would have you believe that you're going to kill this man and they know ... that your decision is not the final decision.... Your job is reviewable.... [T]hey know, as I know, and as Judge Baker has told you, that the decision you render is automatically reviewable by the Supreme Court.

The jury sentenced Caldwell to death, and the case was automatically appealed. The Mississippi Supreme Court upheld the conviction, but split 4–4 on the validity of the death sentence, thereby upholding the death sentence by an equally divided court. Caldwell appealed to the U.S. Supreme Court.

In a 5–3 decision (Justice Powell took no part in the decision), the Supreme Court, in *Caldwell v. Mississippi* (472 U.S. 320, 1985), vacated (annulled) the death sentence. Writing for the majority, Justice Marshall noted,

> It is constitutionally impermissible to rest a death sentence on a determination made by a sentencer who has been led to believe that the responsibility for determining the appropriateness of the defendant's death rests elsewhere.... [This Court] has taken as a given that capital sentencers would view their task as the serious one of determining whether a specific human being should die at the hands of the State.

Furthermore, the high court pointed out that the appeals court was not the place to make this life-or-death decision. Most appellate courts would presume that the sentencing was correctly done, which would leave the defendant at a distinct disadvantage. The jurors, expecting to be reversed by an appeals court, might choose to "send a message" of extreme disapproval of the defendant's acts and sentence him or her to death to show they will not tolerate such actions. Should the appeals court fail to reverse the decision, the defendant might be executed when the jury only intended to "send a message."

The three dissenting judges believed "the Court has overstated the seriousness of the prosecutor's comments" and that it was "highly unlikely that the jury's sense of responsibility was diminished."

KEEPING PAROLE INFORMATION FROM THE JURY

In 1990 Jonathan Dale Simmons beat an elderly woman to death in her home in Columbia, South Carolina. The week before his capital murder trial began, he pleaded guilty to first-degree burglary and two counts of criminal sexual conduct in connection with two prior assaults on elderly women. These guilty pleas resulted in convictions for violent offenses, which made him ineligible for parole if convicted of any other violent crime.

At the capital murder trial, over the defense counsel's objection, the court did not allow the defense to ask prospective jurors if they understood the meaning of a "life" sentence as it applied to the defendant. Under South Carolina law, a defendant who was deemed a future threat to society and receiving a life sentence was ineligible for parole. The prosecution also asked the judge not to mention parole.

During deliberation, the jurors asked the judge if the imposition of a life sentence carried with it the possibility of parole. The judge told the jury,

> You are instructed not to consider parole or parole eligibility in reaching your verdict.... The terms life imprisonment and death sentence are to be understood in the [plain] and ordinary meaning.

The jury convicted Simmons of murder, sentencing him to death. On appeal the South Carolina Supreme Court upheld the sentence. The case was brought before the U.S. Supreme Court. The high court, in a 6–2 decision (*Simmons v. South Carolina* [512 U.S. 154, 1994]), overruled the South Carolina Supreme Court, concluding,

> Where a defendant's future dangerousness is at issue, and state law prohibits his release on parole, due process requires that the sentencing jury be informed that the defendant is parole ineligible. An individual cannot be executed on the basis of information which he had no opportunity to deny or explain.... Petitioner's jury reasonably may have believed that he could be released on parole if he were not executed. To the extent that this misunderstanding pervaded its deliberations, it had the effect of creating a false choice between sentencing him to death and sentencing him to a limited period of incarceration. The trial court's refusal to apprise the jury of information so crucial to its determination, particularly when the State alluded to the defendant's future dangerousness in its argument, cannot be reconciled with this Court's well-established precedents interpreting the Due Process Clause.

JUDGE SENTENCING

Florida

Under Florida's capital trial system, the jury decides the guilt or innocence of the accused. If the jury finds the defendant guilty, it recommends an advisory sentence of either life imprisonment or death. The trial judge considers aggravating and mitigating circumstances, weighs them against the jury recommendation, and then sentences the convicted murderer to either life or death.

A Florida jury convicted Joseph Spaziano of torturing and murdering two women. The jury recommended that Spaziano be sentenced to life imprisonment, but the trial judge, after considering the mitigating and aggravating circumstances, sentenced the defendant to death. In his appeal, Spaziano claimed the judge's overriding of the jury's recommendation of life imprisonment violated the Eighth Amendment's prohibition against cruel and unusual punishment. The Supreme Court, in a 5–3 decision in *Spaziano v. Florida* (468 U.S. 447, 1984), did not agree.

Spaziano's lawyers claimed juries, not judges, were better equipped to make reliable capital-sentencing decisions and that a jury's decision of life imprisonment should be inviolate (not questioned). They reasoned that the death penalty was unlike any other sentence and required that the jury have the ultimate word. This belief had been upheld, Spaziano claimed, because 30 out of 37 states with capital punishment had the jury decide the prisoner's fate. Furthermore, the primary justification for the death penalty was retribution and an expression of community outrage. The jury served as the voice of the community and knew best whether a particular crime was so terrible that the community's response must be the death sentence.

The high court indicated that, although Spaziano's argument had some appeal, it contained two fundamental flaws. First, retribution played a role in all sentences, not just death sentences. Second, a jury was not the only source of community input. "The community's voice is heard at least as clearly in the legislature when the death penalty is authorized and the particular circumstances in which death is appropriate are defined." That trial judges imposed sentences was a normal part of the judicial system. The Supreme Court continued,

> In light of the facts that the Sixth Amendment does not require jury sentencing, that the demands of fairness and reliability in capital cases do not require it, and that neither the nature of, nor the purpose behind, the death penalty requires jury sentencing, we cannot conclude that placing responsibility on the trial judge to impose the sentence in a capital case is unconstitutional.

The Court added that just because 30 of 37 states let the jury make the sentencing decision did not mean states that let a judge decide were wrong. The Court pointed out that there is no one right way for a state to establish its method of capital sentencing.

Writing for the dissenters, Justice Stevens indicated,

> Because of its severity and irrevocability, the death penalty is qualitatively different from any other punishment, and hence must be accompanied by unique safeguards to ensure that it is a justified response to a given offense.... I am convinced that the danger of an excessive response can only be avoided if the decision to impose the death penalty is made by a jury rather than by a single governmental official ... [because a jury] is best able to "express the conscience of the community on the ultimate question of life or death."

Justice Stevens also gave weight to the fact that 30 out of 37 states had the jury make the decision, attesting to the "high level of consensus" (a majority view) that communities strongly believe life-or-death decisions should remain with the people—as represented by the jury—rather than relegated to a single government official.

Alabama

Louise Harris asked a coworker, Lorenzo McCarter, with whom she was having an affair, to find someone to kill her husband. McCarter paid two accomplices one hundred dollars, with a vague promise of more money after they killed the husband. McCarter testified against Harris in exchange for the prosecutor's promise that he would not seek the death penalty against McCarter. McCarter testified that Harris had asked him to kill her husband so they could share in his death benefits. An Alabama jury convicted Louise Harris of capital murder. At the sentencing hearing witnesses testified to her good background and strong character. She was rearing seven children, held three jobs simultaneously, and was active in her church.

Alabama law gives capital sentencing authority to the trial judge, but requires the judge to "consider" an advisory jury verdict. The jury voted 7–5 to give Harris life imprisonment without parole. The trial judge then considered her sentence. He found one aggravating circumstance (the murder was committed for monetary gain), one statutory mitigating circumstance (Harris had no prior criminal record), and one nonstatutory mitigating circumstance (Harris was a hardworking, respected member of her church).

Noting that she had planned the crime, financed it, and stood to benefit from the murder, the judge felt that the aggravating circumstance outweighed the other mitigating circumstances and sentenced her to death. On appeal, the Alabama Supreme Court affirmed the conviction and sentence. It rejected Harris's arguments that the procedure was unconstitutional because Alabama state law did "not specify the weight the judge must give to the jury's recommendation and thus permits the arbitrary imposition of the death penalty."

On appeal, the U.S. Supreme Court upheld the Alabama court's decision (*Harris v. Alabama* [513 U.S. 504], 1995). Alabama's capital-sentencing process is similar to that of Florida (as discussed in the *Spaziano* case earlier). Both require jury participation during sentencing but give the trial judge the ultimate sentencing authority. Nevertheless, while the Florida statute requires that a trial judge must give "great weight" to the jury recommendation, the Alabama statute requires only that the judge "consider" the jury's recommendation.

As in *Spaziano,* the high court ruled that the Eighth Amendment does not require the state "to define the weight the sentencing judge must give to an advisory jury verdict." The Court stated,

> Because the Constitution permits the trial judge, acting alone, to impose a capital sentence ... it is not offended when a State further requires a judge to consider a jury recommendation and trusts the judge to give it the proper weight.

JURY SENTENCING

In 2002 the U.S. Supreme Court decided a case concerning death sentencing in Arizona. Timothy Stuart Ring was convicted of murder in the armed robbery of an armored-car driver in 1994. According to Arizona law, Ring's offense was punishable by life imprisonment or death, and he would only be eligible for the death penalty if the trial judge held a separate hearing and found that the aggravating factors warranted the death penalty.

One of Ring's accomplices, who negotiated a plea bargain in return for a second-degree murder charge, testified against him at a separate sentencing hearing without a jury present. The same judge who had presided at Ring's trial concluded that Ring committed the murder and that the crime was committed "in an especially heinous, cruel or depraved manner." Weighing the two aggravating circumstances against the mitigating evidence of Ring's minimal criminal record, the judge sentenced the defendant to death.

Ring appealed to the Arizona Supreme Court, claiming that the state's capital sentencing law violated his Sixth and Fourteenth Amendment rights because it allowed a judge, rather than a jury, to make the factual findings that made him death-eligible. The court put aside Ring's argument against the Arizona's judge-sentencing system in light of the U.S. Supreme Court's ruling in *Walton v. Arizona* (497 U.S. 639). In 1990 the U.S. Supreme Court held in *Walton* that Arizona's sentencing procedure was constitutional because "the additional facts found by the judge qualified as sentencing considerations, not as 'element[s] of the offense of capital murder.'" Next, the Arizona Supreme Court threw out the trial judge's finding of the heinous nature of the crime but concluded that Ring's minimal criminal record was not enough to out-

weigh the aggravating evidence of "planned, ruthless robbery and killing." The court affirmed the death sentence.

Timothy Ring took his case to the U.S. Supreme Court. On June 24, 2002, by a 7–2 vote (*Ring v. Arizona,* 536 U.S. 584), the Court ruled that only juries and not judges can determine the presence of aggravating circumstances that warrant the death sentence. The Court included a discussion of *Apprendi v. New Jersey* (530 U.S. 466, 2000), in which it held that "the Sixth Amendment does not permit a defendant to be 'expose[d] ... to a penalty *exceeding* the maximum he would receive if punished according to the facts reflected in the jury verdict alone.'" *Apprendi* involved a defendant in a noncapital case who received a prison term beyond the maximum sentence. This occurred because New Jersey law allowed sentencing judges to increase the penalty if they found that a crime was racially motivated. In *Apprendi,* the Court held that any fact other than a prior conviction that increases the punishment for a crime beyond the maximum allowed by law must be found by a jury beyond a reasonable doubt. The Court found *Walton* and *Apprendi* irreconcilable. The Court also overruled *Walton* "to the extent that it allows a sentencing judge, sitting without a jury, to find an aggravating circumstance necessary for imposition of the death penalty." Justice Ruth Bader Ginsburg, who delivered the opinion of the Court, wrote,

> The right to trial by jury guaranteed by the Sixth Amendment would be senselessly diminished if it encompassed the factfinding [sic] necessary to increase a defendant's sentence by two years [referring to *Apprendi*], but not the factfinding necessary to put him to death. We hold that the Sixth Amendment applies to both.

However, Justice Antonin Scalia, joined by Justice Clarence Thomas, pointed out in a separate concurring opinion that under *Ring,* states that let judges impose the death sentence may continue to do so by requiring the finding of aggravating factors necessary to the imposition of the death penalty during the trial phase.

Justice Sandra Day O'Connor, in her dissenting opinion, joined by Chief Justice Rehnquist, claimed that just as the *Apprendi* decision has overburdened the appeals courts, the *Ring* decision will cause more federal appeals. O'Connor observed that *Ring v. Arizona* also invalidates the capital sentencing procedure of four other states. These included Idaho and Montana, where a judge had the sole sentencing authority, as well as Colorado and Nebraska, where a three-judge panel made the sentencing decisions. The Court ruling also potentially affected Alabama, Delaware, Florida, and Indiana, where the jury rendered an advisory verdict, but the judge had the ultimate sentencing authority. In June 2002 nearly 700 inmates were on death row in these nine states.

As a result of the *Ring* decision, Arizona, Idaho, Colorado, Nebraska, Delaware, Indiana, and Montana passed legislation providing for jury sentencing. As of November 30, 2003, Florida and Alabama had not enacted any legislation amending its sentencing procedure.

DOES EXTENDED STAY ON DEATH ROW CONSTITUTE CRUEL AND UNUSUAL PUNISHMENT?

In 2002 Charles Kenneth Foster, a Florida inmate, asked the U.S. Supreme Court to consider whether his long wait for execution constitutes cruel and unusual punishment prohibited by the Eighth Amendment. Foster has been on death row since 1975 for a murder conviction. In 1981 and again in 1984 the defendant was granted a stay of execution to allow his federal *habeas corpus* petition.

Justice Breyer dissented from the Court's refusal to hear the case (*Foster v. Florida,* No. 01-10868, October 21, 2002). Justice Breyer pointed out that the defendant's long wait on death row resulted partly from Florida's repeated errors in proceedings. The justice added,

> ...Death row's inevitable anxieties and uncertainties have been sharpened by the issuance of two death warrants and three judicial reprieves. If executed, Foster, now 55, will have been punished both by death and also by more than a generation spent in death row's twilight. It is fairly asked whether such punishment is both unusual and cruel.

Concurring with the Court opinion not to hear Foster's case, Justice Thomas observed that the defendant could have ended the "anxieties and uncertainties" of death row had he submitted to execution, which the people of Florida believe he deserves.

DOUBLE JEOPARDY

In 1991 David Sattazahn was convicted for the 1987 murder of a restaurant manager in Berks County, Pennsylvania. Sattazahn and an accomplice killed the manager in the process of robbing him of the day's receipts. The state sought the death sentence and included an aggravating circumstance—the commission of murder while perpetrating a felony (a serious offense). During the sentencing phase the jury could not reach a verdict as to life or death. The trial judge considered the jury as hung and imposed an automatic sentence of life imprisonment as mandated by state law.

On appeal to the Pennsylvania Superior Court, Sattazahn was granted a new trial. The court held that the trial judge had erred in jury instructions relating to his offenses and reversed his murder conviction. During the second trial the state again sought the death penalty, this time adding a second aggravating factor—the defendants' history of felony convictions involving using or threatening violence to the victim. The jury convicted Sattazahn of first-degree murder and sentenced him to death.

Next, the Pennsylvania Supreme Court heard Sattazahn's case. The death row inmate claimed, among other things, that the Pennsylvania Constitution prohibits the imposition of the death penalty because it guarantees protection from double jeopardy. The Double Jeopardy Clause of the Fifth Amendment states that "[n]o person shall ... be subject for the same offence to be twice put in jeopardy of life or limb." In other words, no person can be tried or punished twice for the same crime.

Relying on its ruling in *Commonwealth v. Martorano* (1993), the Pennsylvania Supreme Court affirmed both Sattazahn's conviction and death sentence. In *Martorano,* the Court noted that the jury, as in Sattazahn's first trial, was deadlocked. The hung jury did not "acquit" the defendant of the death sentence. Therefore, there was no double jeopardy prohibition against the death penalty during the second trial.

On January 14, 2003, the U.S. Supreme Court, by a 5–4 vote, agreed with the ruling of the Pennsylvania Supreme Court (*Sattazahn v. Pennsylvania,* 537 U.S. 101). Justice Scalia, writing the majority opinion, concluded that double jeopardy did not exist in this case. According to the Court,

> [T]he touchstone [test of genuineness] for double-jeopardy protection in capital-sentencing proceedings is whether there has been an "acquittal." Petitioner here cannot establish that the jury or the court "acquitted" him during his first capital-sentencing proceeding. As to the jury: The verdict form returned by the foreman stated that the jury deadlocked 9-to-3 on whether to impose the death penalty; it made no findings with respect to the alleged aggravating circumstance. That result—or more appropriately, that non-result—cannot fairly be called an acquittal....

The Court added that the imposition of a life sentence by the judge did not "acquit" the defendant of the death penalty either because the judge was just following the state law. "A default judgment [the judge's] does not trigger a double jeopardy bar to the death penalty upon retrial."

Justice Ginsburg, writing for the dissent, was joined by Justices Stevens, Souter, and Breyer. The dissenters argued that jeopardy terminated after the judge imposed a final judgment of life imprisonment when the jury was deadlocked. Therefore, he was "acquitted" of the death penalty the first time, which means that the state could not seek the death penalty the second time. Justice Ginsburg also pointed out,

> [T]he Court's holding confronts defendants with a perilous choice.... Under the Court's decision, if a defendant sentenced to life after a jury deadlock chooses to appeal her underlying conviction, she faces the possibility of death if she is successful on appeal but convicted on retrial. If, on the other hand, the defendant loses her appeal, or chooses to forgo an appeal, the final judgment for life stands. In other words, a defendant in Sattazahn's position must relinquish either her right to file a potentially meritorious appeal, or her state-granted entitlement to avoid the death penalty.

CHAPTER 3

LEGAL DECISIONS—CIRCUMSTANCES, RIGHT TO COUNSEL, EVIDENCE, AND VICTIM IMPACT STATEMENTS

RAPE AND KIDNAPPING DO NOT WARRANT DEATH

On June 20, 1977, a 5–4 divided Supreme Court ruled, in *Coker v. Georgia* (433 U.S. 584) and in *Eberheart v. Georgia* (433 U.S. 917), that the death penalty may not be imposed for the crime of raping an adult woman that does not result in death. The Court stated,

> Rape is without doubt deserving of serious punishment, but in terms of moral depravity and of the injury to the person and to the public, it does not involve the unjustified taking of human life.... The murderer kills; the rapist, if no more than that, does not. Life is over for the victim of the murderers; for the rape victim, life may not be nearly so happy as it was, but it is not over and normally is not beyond repair. We have the abiding conviction that the death penalty, which is unique in its severity and irrevocability ... is an excessive penalty for the rapist who, as such, does not take human life.

Chief Justice Warren Earl Burger, joined by Justice William Rehnquist, dissented. The justices stated,

> ... A rapist not only violates a victim's privacy and personal integrity, but inevitably causes serious psychological as well as physical harm in the process.... Rape is not a mere physical attack—it is destructive of the human personality. The remainder of the victim's life may be gravely affected, and this in turn may have a serious detrimental effect upon her husband and any children she may have.... Victims may recover from the physical damage of knife or bullet wounds, or a beating with fists or a club, but recovery from such a gross assault on the human personality is not healed by medicine or surgery. To speak blandly, as the plurality does, of rape victims who are "unharmed," or to classify the human outrage of rape, as does Mr. Justice Powell, in terms of "excessively brutal," versus "moderately brutal," takes too little account of the profound suffering the crime imposes upon the victims and their loved ones.

The Court also held that kidnapping did not warrant the death penalty. While the victims usually suffered tremendously, they had not lost their lives. (If the kidnapped victim were killed, then the kidnapper would be tried for murder.) These high court decisions left only murder and treason as justifiable grounds for the imposition of the death penalty. So far, no cases involving the death penalty for treason have been brought to the Supreme Court.

MITIGATING CIRCUMSTANCES

Sandra Lockett was convicted for helping to plan and then driving the getaway car for a pawnshop robbery. Although it was unintended, the owner of the pawnshop was murdered. Lockett also hid her accomplices in her home. Later she was tried for the capital murder of the pawnshop owner. According to the Ohio death penalty statute, capital punishment had to be imposed on Lockett unless "(1) the victim induced or facilitated the offense; (2) it is unlikely that the offense would have been committed but for the fact that the offender was under duress, coercion, or strong provocation; or (3) the offense was primarily the product of the offender's psychosis or mental deficiency." Lockett was found guilty and sentenced to die.

Lockett appealed, claiming that the Ohio law did not give the sentencing judge the chance to consider the circumstances of the crime and the defendant's character and record as mitigating factors (factors that may lessen responsibility for a crime). In July 1978 the Supreme Court, in *Lockett v. Ohio* (438 U.S. 586), upheld Lockett's contention. Chief Justice Burger observed,

> A statute that prevents the sentencer in capital cases from giving independent mitigating weights to aspects of the defendant's character and record and to the circumstances of the offense ... creates the risk that the death penalty will be imposed in spite of factors that may call for a less severe penalty, and when the choice is between life and death, such risk is unacceptable and incompatible with the commands of the Eighth and Fourteenth Amendments.

Mitigating Circumstances Must Always Be Considered

In *Hitchcock v. Dugger* (481 U.S. 393, 1987), a unanimous Supreme Court further emphasized that all mitigating circumstances had to be considered before the convicted murderer could be sentenced. A Florida judge had instructed the jury not to consider, and he himself refused to consider, evidence of mitigating factors that were not specifically indicated in the Florida death penalty law. Writing for the Court, Justice Antonin Scalia stressed that a convicted person had the right "to present any and all relevant mitigating evidence that is available."

NOT BEING AT THE SCENE OF THE MURDER

On April 1, 1975, Sampson and Jeanette Armstrong, on the pretext of requesting water for their overheated car, tried to rob Thomas Kersey at home. Earl Enmund waited in the getaway car. Kersey called for his wife, who tried to shoot Jeanette Armstrong. The Armstrongs killed the Kerseys. Enmund was tried for aiding and abetting in the robbery-murder and sentenced to death.

In *Enmund v. Florida* (468 U.S. 782, 1982), a 5–4 split Supreme Court ruled that, in this case, the death penalty violated the Eighth and Fourteenth Amendments to the U.S. Constitution. The majority noted that only 9 of the 36 states with capital punishment permitted its use on a criminal who was not actually present at the scene of the crime. The exception was the case where someone paid a hit man to murder the victim.

Furthermore, over the years juries had tended not to sentence to death criminals who had not actually been at the scene of the crime. Certainly Enmund was guilty of planning and participating in a robbery, but murder had not been part of the plan. Statistically, since someone is killed in one out of two hundred robberies, Enmund could not have expected the Kerseys' murders during the robbery attempt. The Court concluded that, because Enmund did not kill or plan to kill, he should be tried only for his participation in the robbery. The Court observed,

> We have no doubt that robbery is a serious crime deserving serious punishment. It is not, however, a crime "so grievous an affront to humanity that the only adequate response may be the penalty of death" [from *Gregg v. Georgia,* 428 U.S. 153, 1976]. It does not compare with murder, which does involve the unjustified taking of human life.... The murderer kills; the robber, if no more than that, does not. Life is over for the victim of the murderer; for the [robbery] victim, life ... is not over and normally is not beyond repair.

Writing for the minority, Justice Sandra Day O'Connor concluded that intent is a complex issue. It should be left to the judge and jury trying the accused to decide intent, not a federal court far removed from the actual trial.

Enmund Reviewed

Just because a person had no intent to kill, however, does not mean that he or she cannot be sentenced to death. Crawford Bullock and a friend, Ricky Tucker, had been drinking at a bar. An acquaintance, Mark Dickson, offered them a ride home. During the drive an argument ensued over money Dickson supposedly owed Tucker.

Outside the car Bullock held Dickson while Tucker hit Dickson in the face with a whiskey bottle and punched him. When Dickson fell, Tucker smashed his head with a concrete block, killing him. Tucker and Bullock disposed of the body. The next day police spotted Bullock driving the victim's car. After his arrest Bullock confessed.

Under Mississippi law a person involved in a robbery that results in murder may be convicted of capital murder regardless of "the defendant's own lack of intent that any killing take place." The jury never was asked to consider whether Bullock in fact killed, attempted to kill, or intended to kill. He was convicted and sentenced to death as an accomplice to the crime. During the appeals process, the Mississippi Supreme Court confirmed that Bullock was indeed a participant in the murder.

In January 1986 a 5–4 divided U.S. Supreme Court, in *Cabana v. Bullock* (474 U.S. 376), modified the *Enmund* decision. It indicated that while *Enmund* had to be considered at some point during the judicial process, the initial jury trying the accused did not necessarily have to consider the *Enmund* ruling. The high court ruled that, while the jury had not been made aware of the issue of intent, the Mississippi Supreme Court had considered this question. Since *Enmund* did not require that intent be presented at the initial jury trial, only that it be considered at some time during the judicial process, the state of Mississippi had met that requirement.

The four dissenting justices claimed that it was difficult for any appeals court to determine intent from reading a typed transcript of a trial. Seeing the accused and others involved was important in helping determine who was telling the truth and who was not. This was why *Enmund* must be raised to the jury so it could consider the question of intent in light of what it had seen and heard directly.

A "Reckless Indifference to the Value of Human Life" Is Just as Bad as Pulling the Trigger

Gary Tison was a convicted criminal who had been sentenced to life imprisonment for murdering a prison guard during an escape from the Arizona State Prison in Florence, Arizona. Tison's three sons, his wife, his brother, and other relatives planned a prison escape involving Tison and a fellow prisoner, Randy Greenawalt, also a convicted murderer.

On the day of the planned escape, the three Tison sons smuggled guns into the prison's visitation area. After locking up the guards and visitors, the five men fled in a car. They later transferred to another car and waited in an abandoned house for a plane to take them to Mexico. When the plane did not come, the men got back on the road. The car soon had flat tires. One son flagged down a passing car. The motorist who stopped to help was driving with his wife, their 2-year-old son, and a 15-year-old niece.

Gary Tison then told his sons to go get some water from the motorist's car, presumably to be left with the family they planned to abandon in the desert. While the sons were gone, Gary Tison and Randy Greenawalt shot and killed the family. Several days later two of Tison's sons and Greenawalt were captured. The third son was killed, and Tison escaped into the desert, where he later died of exposure.

The Tison sons and Greenawalt were found guilty and sentenced to death. The sons, citing *Enmund,* appealed, claiming that they had neither pulled the triggers nor intended the deaths of the family who had stopped to help them. The 5–4 Supreme Court decision (*Tison v. Arizona,* 481 U.S. 137, 1987) upheld the death sentence, indicating that the Tison sons had shown a "reckless indifference to the value of human life [which] may be every bit as shocking to the moral sense as an 'intent to kill.'"

The Tison sons may not have pulled the triggers (and the Court fully accepted the premise that they did not do the shootings or directly intend them to happen), but they released and then assisted two convicted murderers. They should have realized that freeing two killers and giving them guns could very well put innocent people in great danger. Moreover, they continued to help the escapees even after the family was killed.

"These facts," concluded Justice O'Connor for the majority, "not only indicate that the Tison [sons'] participation in the crime was anything but minor, they also would clearly support a finding that they both subjectively appreciated that their acts were likely to result in the taking of innocent life." Unlike the situation in the *Enmund* case, they were not sitting in a car far from the murder scene. They were direct participants in the whole event. The death sentence would stand.

Writing for the minority, Justice William J. Brennan observed that had a prison guard been murdered (Gary Tison had murdered a prison guard in a previous escape attempt), then the Court's argument would have made sense. The murder of the family, however, made no sense and was not even necessary for the escape. The Tison sons were away from the murder scene getting water for the victims and could have done nothing to save them. While they were guilty of planning and carrying out an escape, the murder of the family who stopped to help them was an unexpected outcome of the escape.

Furthermore, the father had promised his sons that he would not kill during the escape, a promise he had kept despite several opportunities to kill during the actual prison escape. It was, therefore, not unreasonable for the sons to believe that their father would not kill in a situation that did not appear to warrant it. Justice Brennan concluded that "like Enmund, the Tisons neither killed nor attempted nor intended to kill anyone. Like Enmund, the Tisons have been sentenced to death for the intentional acts of others, which the Tisons did not expect, which were not essential to the felony, and over which they had no control."

AN "OUTRAGEOUSLY AND WANTONLY VILE" MURDER

During a heated dispute with his wife of 28 years, Robert Godfrey threatened her with a knife. Mrs. Godfrey, saying she was leaving her husband, went to stay with relatives. That same day she went to court to file for aggravated assault. Several days later she initiated divorce proceedings and moved in with her mother. During subsequent telephone conversations, the couple argued over the wife's determination to leave Godfrey permanently.

About two weeks later Robert Godfrey killed his wife and mother-in-law. Godfrey told police that his wife phoned him, telling him she expected all the money from the planned sale of their home. She also told Godfrey she was never reconciling with him. Godfrey confessed that he went to his mother-in-law's nearby trailer and shot his wife through a window, killing her instantly. He then entered the trailer, struck his fleeing 11-year-old daughter on the head with the gun, and shot his mother-in-law in the head, killing her. Godfrey believed his mother-in-law was responsible for his wife's reluctance to reconcile with him.

Godfrey was convicted of killing his wife and mother-in-law and of the aggravated assault of his daughter. The Georgia Code permits the imposition of the death penalty in the case of a murder that "was outrageously or wantonly vile, horrible, or inhuman in that it involved torture, depravity of mind, or an aggravated brutality to the victim." Aware of this law, the jury sentenced Godfrey to die. He appealed, claiming that the statute was unconstitutionally vague. After the Georgia Supreme Court upheld the lower court decision, the case was appealed to the U.S. Supreme Court.

The U.S. Supreme Court, in *Godfrey v. Georgia* (446 U.S. 420, 1980), noted that the victims were killed instantly (i.e., there was no torture), the victims had been "causing [Godfrey] extreme emotional trauma," and he acknowledged his responsibility. The high court concluded that, in this case, the Georgia law was unconstitutionally vague. Moreover, the Georgia Supreme Court did not attempt to narrow the definition of "outrageously and wantonly vile." In a concurring opinion, Justice Thurgood

Marshall, whom Justice William Brennan joined, found this an example of the inherently "arbitrary [subject to individual judgment] and capricious [unpredictable]" nature of capital punishment, since even the prosecutor in Godfrey's case observed numerous times that there was no torture or abuse involved.

"COMPARATIVE PROPORTIONALITY REVIEW"

Robert Harris and his brother decided to steal a car they would need for a getaway in a planned bank robbery. Robert Harris approached two teenage boys eating hamburgers in a car. He forced them at gunpoint to drive to a nearby wooded area. The teenagers offered to delay telling the police of the car robbery and even to give the authorities misleading descriptions of the two robbers. When one of the boys appeared to be fleeing, Harris shot both of them. Harris and his brother later committed the robbery, were soon caught, and confessed to the robbery and murders.

Harris was found guilty. In California, a convicted murderer could be sentenced to death or life imprisonment without parole only if "special circumstances" existed and the murder had been "willful, deliberate, premeditated, and committed during the commission of kidnapping and robbery." This had to be proven during a separate sentencing hearing.

The state showed that Harris was convicted of manslaughter in 1975; he was found in possession of a makeshift knife and garrote (an instrument used for strangulation) while in prison; he and other inmates sodomized another inmate; and he threatened that inmate's life. Harris testified that he had a very unhappy childhood, had little education, and his father had sexually molested his sisters. The jury sentenced Harris to death, and the judge concurred.

Harris claimed the U.S. Constitution, as interpreted in previous capital punishment rulings, required the state of California to give his case "comparative proportionality review" to determine if his death sentence was not out of line with that of others convicted of similar crimes. In "comparative proportionality review," a court considers the seriousness of the offense, the severity of the penalty, the sentences imposed for other crimes, and the sentencing in other jurisdictions for the same crime. Courts have occasionally struck down punishments inherently disproportionate and, therefore, cruel and unusual. Georgia, by law, and Florida, by practice, had incorporated such reviews in their procedures. Other states, such as Texas and California, had not.

When the case reached the U.S. Ninth Circuit Court of Appeals, the court agreed with Harris and ordered California to establish proportionality or lift the death sentence. The U.S. Supreme Court (*Pulley v. Harris*, 465 U.S. 37, 1984), in a 7–2 decision, did not agree. The Court noted that the California procedure contained enough safeguards to guarantee a defendant a fair trial and those convicted, a fair sentence. The high court added,

> That some [state statutes] providing proportionality review are constitutional does not mean that such review is indispensable.... To endorse the statute as a whole is not to say that anything different is unacceptable. Examination of our 1976 cases makes clear that they do not establish proportionality review as a constitutional requirement.

Justice Brennan, joined by Justice Marshall, dissented. He noted that the Supreme Court had thrown out the existing death penalty procedures during the 1970s because they were deemed arbitrary and capricious. He believed they still were, but the introduction of "proportionality" might "eliminate some, if only a small part, of the irrationality that currently surrounds the imposition of the death penalty."

INEFFECTIVE ASSISTANCE OF COUNSEL

In 1989 Kevin Eugene Wiggins received the death sentence for the 1988 drowning of an elderly Maryland woman in her home. The Maryland Court of Appeals affirmed his sentence in 1991. With the help of new counsel, Wiggins sought postconviction relief, challenging the quality of his initial lawyers. Wiggins claimed his lawyers failed to investigate and present mitigating evidence of his horrendous physical and sexual abuse as a child. The sentencing jury never heard that he was starved, that his mother punished him by burning his hand on the stove, and that after the state put him in foster care at age six, he suffered more physical and sexual abuse.

In 2001 a federal district court concluded that Wiggins' first lawyers should have conducted a more thorough investigation into his childhood abuse, which would have kept the jury from imposing a death sentence. However, the U.S. Court of Appeals for the Fourth Circuit reversed the district court decision, ruling that the original attorneys had made a "reasonable strategic decision" to concentrate their defense on raising doubts about Wiggins' guilt instead.

On June 26, 2003, the U.S. Supreme Court threw out the death sentence. In *Wiggins v. Smith* (123 S. Ct. 2527), the court ruled 7–2 that Wiggins' lawyers violated his Sixth Amendment right to effective assistance of counsel. The Court noted,

> Counsel's investigation into Wiggins' background did not reflect reasonable professional judgment.... Given both the nature and the extent of the abuse petitioner suffered, we find there to be a reasonable probability that a competent attorney, aware of this history, would have introduced it at sentencing in an admissible form.... We further find that had the jury been confronted with this considerable mitigating evidence, there is a reasonable probability that it would have returned with a different sentence....

WHEN DOES THE RIGHT TO COUNSEL END?

Joseph Giarratano was a Virginia prisoner under sentence of death. He went to court, complaining that, because he was poor, the state of Virginia should provide him with a lawyer to help prepare postconviction appeals. Virginia permitted the condemned prisoner the right to use the prison libraries to prepare an appeal, but it did not provide the condemned with his own personal attorney.

Virginia had "unit attorneys" who were assigned to help prisoners with prison-related legal matters. A unit attorney could give guidance to death row inmates but could not act as the personal attorney for any one particular inmate. This case became a class action in which the federal district court certified a class comprising "all current and future Virginia inmates awaiting execution who do not have and cannot afford counsel to pursue postconviction proceedings."

The federal district court and the federal court of appeals agreed with Giarratano, but the U.S. Supreme Court, in *Murray v. Giarratano* (492 U.S. 1, 1989), disagreed. Writing for the majority (Justices Byron White, O'Connor, and Scalia, with Justice Anthony Kennedy filing a concurring opinion), Chief Justice Rehnquist concluded that, while the Sixth and Fourteenth Amendments to the U.S. Constitution assured an indigent (poor) defendant the right to counsel at the trial stage of a criminal proceeding, they do not provide for counsel for postconviction proceedings, as the Court ruled in *Pennsylvania v. Finley* (481 U.S. 551, 1987). Since *Finley* had not specifically considered prisoners on death row, but all prisoners in general, the majority did not believe the decision needed to be reconsidered just because death row prisoners had more at stake.

Chief Justice Rehnquist agreed that those facing the death penalty have a right to counsel for the trial and during the initial appeal. During these periods, the defendant needs a heightened measure of protection because the death penalty is involved. Later appeals, however, involve more procedural matters that "serve a different and more limited purpose than either the trial or appeal."

In dissent, Justice John Stevens (joined by Justices Brennan, Marshall, and Harry A. Blackmun) indicated that he thought condemned prisoners in Virginia faced three critical differences from those considered in *Finley*. First, the Virginia prisoners had been sentenced to death, which made their condition different from a sentence of life imprisonment. Second, Virginia's particular judicial decision forbids certain issues to be raised during the direct review or appeal process and forces them to be considered only during later postconviction appeals. This means that very important issues may be considered without the benefit of counsel. Finally,

> Unlike the ordinary inmate, who presumably has ample time to use and reuse the prison library and to seek guid-

ance from other prisoners experienced in preparing ... petitions, a grim deadline imposes a finite limit on the condemned person's capacity for useful research.... [As the district court concluded,] an inmate preparing himself and his family for impending death is incapable of performing the mental functions necessary to adequately pursue his claims.

DOES THE RIGHT TO COUNSEL EXTEND TO CRIMES THAT HAVE NOT BEEN CHARGED?

In 1994 Raymond Levi Cobb confessed to burglarizing the home of Lindsey Owings the previous year. He claimed no knowledge, however, of the disappearances of Owings's wife and infant at the time of the burglary. The court subsequently assigned Cobb a lawyer to represent him in the burglary offense. With the permission of Cobb's lawyer, investigators twice questioned Cobb regarding the disappearance of the Owings family. Both times Cobb denied any knowledge of the missing pair.

In 1995, while free on bond for the burglary and living with his father, Cobb told his father he killed Margaret Owing and buried her baby, while still alive, with her. The father reported his son's confession to the police. Cobb was convicted of the murders and sentenced to death. On appeal, Cobb claimed that his confession, obtained in violation of his Sixth Amendment right to counsel, should have been suppressed.

The Texas Court of Criminal Appeals reversed Cobb's conviction, ordering a new trial. The court considered Cobb's confession to the murders inadmissible, holding that "once the right to counsel attaches to the offense charged [burglary], it also attaches to any other offense [in this case, murder] that is very closely related factually to the offense charged."

The state appealed to the U.S. Supreme Court. On April 2, 2001, in *Texas v. Cobb* (532 U.S. 162), the Court, in a 5–4 decision, stated,

> The Sixth Amendment right to counsel is ... "offense specific." It cannot be invoked once for all future prosecutions, for it does not attach until a prosecution is commenced, that is, at or after the initiation of adversary judicial proceedings—whether by way of formal charge, preliminary hearing, indictment, information, or arraignment [citing *McNeil v. Wisconsin,* 501 U.S. 171, 1991].

This means that Cobb's right to counsel did not extend to crimes with which he had not been charged. Since this right did not prohibit investigators from questioning him about the murders without first notifying his lawyer, Cobb's confession was admissible.

FEDERAL JUDGES CAN DELAY EXECUTIONS TO ALLOW *HABEAS CORPUS* REVIEWS

A Texas jury found Frank McFarland guilty of stabbing to death a woman he had met in a bar. The appellate court upheld his conviction, and two lower federal courts refused his request for a stay (postponement) of execution. The federal courts ruled that they did not have jurisdiction to stop the execution until McFarland filed a *habeas corpus* (a prisoner's petition to be heard in federal court; also referred to as *habeas*). The inmate argued that without the stay, he would be executed before he could obtain a lawyer to prepare the petition.

The Supreme Court granted a stay of execution. In a 5–4 decision (*McFarland v. Scott,* 512 U.S. 849, 1994), the Court ruled that federal law required governments to supply lawyers for poor defendants on death row who wanted to have *habeas* review. Once a defendant requested counsel, the federal court could postpone execution so the lawyer would have time to prepare an appeal. Justice Blackmun stated that "by providing indigent capital defendants with a mandatory right to qualified legal counsel in these proceedings, Congress has recognized that Federal *habeas corpus* has a particularly important role to play in promoting fundamental fairness in the imposition of the death penalty."

This case illustrated a problem in many states. For example, in 1994 there were 386 inmates on death row and only 118 lawyers with the Texas Resource Center, a federally financed legal office that handled capital cases. In 1993 judges in Texas set 100 execution dates. (State policy dictated that an execution must be scheduled about 45 days after the death sentence had been upheld on direct review.) If McFarland had drafted his own *habeas* petition, it would probably have been rejected as inadequate.

HARMLESS ERROR

Coerced Confessions

Oreste C. Fulminante called the Mesa, Arizona, police to report the disappearance of his 11-year-old stepdaughter, Jeneane Michelle Hunt. Fulminante was caring for the child while his wife, Jeneane's mother, was in the hospital. Several days later Jeneane's body was found in the desert east of Mesa with two shots to the head, fired at close range by a large-caliber weapon. There was a ligature (a cord used in tying or binding) around her neck. Because of the decomposed state of her body, it was not possible to determine whether she had been sexually assaulted.

Fulminante's statements about the child's disappearance and his relationship to her included inconsistencies that made him a suspect in her death. He was not, however, charged with the murder. Fulminante left Arizona for New Jersey, where he was eventually convicted on federal charges of unlawful possession of a firearm by a felon.

While incarcerated, he became friendly with Anthony Sarivola, a former police officer. Sarivola had been involved in loan-sharking for organized crime, but then became a paid informant for the Federal Bureau of Investi-

gation. In prison he masqueraded as an organized crime figure. When Fulminante was getting some tough treatment from the other inmates, Sarivola offered him protection, but only on the condition that Fulminante tell him everything.

Fulminante was later indicted in Arizona for the first-degree murder of Jeneane. In a hearing prior to the trial, Fulminante moved to suppress (remove from the record) the statement he had made to Sarivola in prison and then later to Sarivola's wife, Donna, following his release from prison. He maintained that the confession to Sarivola was coerced, and that the second confession was the "fruit" of the first one.

The trial court denied the motion to suppress, finding that, based on the specified facts, the confessions were voluntary. Fulminante was convicted of Jeneane's murder and subsequently sentenced to death.

In his appeal Fulminante argued, among other things, that his confession to Sarivola was coerced and that its use at the trial violated his rights of due process under the Fifth and Fourteenth Amendments to the U.S. Constitution. The Arizona Supreme Court ruled that the confession was coerced, but initially determined that the admission of the confession at the trial was a harmless error because of the overpowering evidence against Fulminante.

After Fulminante motioned for reconsideration, however, the Arizona Supreme Court ruled that the U.S. Supreme Court had set a precedent that prevented the use of harmless-error analysis in the case of a coerced confession. (The harmless-error standard, as stated in *Chapman v. California* [386 U.S. 18, 1967], held that an error is harmless if it appears "beyond a reasonable doubt that the error complained of did not contribute to the verdict obtained.") The Arizona Supreme Court reversed the conviction and ordered that Fulminante be retried without the use of his confession to Sarivola. Because of differences in the state and federal courts over the admission of a coerced confession with regard to harmless-error analysis, the U.S. Supreme Court agreed to hear the case.

In *Arizona v. Fulminante* (499 U.S. 279, 1991), Justice White, writing for the majority, stated that although the question was a close one, the Arizona Supreme Court was right in concluding that Fulminante's confession had been coerced. He further noted,

> The Arizona Supreme Court found a credible threat of physical violence unless Fulminante confessed. Our cases have [found] ... that a finding of coercion need not depend upon actual violence by a government agent; a credible threat is sufficient. As we have said, "coercion can be mental as well as physical, and ... the blood of the accused is not the only hallmark of an unconstitutional inquisition."

Justice White further argued that the state of Arizona had failed to meet its burden of establishing, beyond a reasonable doubt, that the admission of Fulminante's confession to Sarivola was harmless. He added,

> A defendant's confession is like no other evidence. Indeed, "the defendant's own confession is probably the most probative [providing evidence] that can be admitted against him.... [T]he admissions of a defendant come from the actor himself, the most knowledgeable and unimpeachable source of information about his past conduct. Certainly confessions have a profound impact on the jury, so much so that we may justifiably doubt its ability to put them out of mind even if told to do so."
> [From *Bruton v. United States,* 391 U.S. 123, 1968]

Presumption of Malice

Dale Robert Yates and Henry Davis planned to rob a country store in Greenville County, South Carolina. When they entered the store, only the owner, Willie Wood, was present. Yates and Davis showed their weapons and ordered Wood to give them money from the cash register. Davis handed Yates the $3,000 and ordered Wood to lie across the counter. Wood, who had a pistol beneath his jacket, refused.

Meanwhile, Yates was backing out of the store with his gun pointed at the owner. After being told to do so by Davis, Yates fired two shots. The first bullet caused flesh wounds in Wood; the second shot missed. Yates then jumped into the car and waited for Davis. When Davis did not appear, Yates drove off. Inside the store, although wounded, Wood pursued Davis. As the two struggled, Wood's mother came in and ran to help her son. During the struggle, Mrs. Wood was stabbed once in the chest and died at the scene. Wood then shot Davis five times, killing him.

After Yates was arrested and charged with murder, his primary defense was that Mrs. Wood's death was not the probable natural consequence of the robbery he had planned with Davis. He claimed that he had brought the weapon only to induce the owner to give him the cash and that neither he nor Davis intended to kill anyone during the robbery.

The prosecutor's case for murder hinged on the agreement between Yates and Davis to commit an armed robbery. He argued that they planned to kill any witness, thereby making homicide a probable or natural result of the robbery. The prosecutor concluded, "It makes no difference who actually struck the fatal blow, the hand of one is the hand of all."

In his instructions to the jury, the judge said,

> Malice is implied or presumed by the law from the willful, deliberate and intentional doing of an unlawful act without any just cause or excuse. In its general signification, malice means the doing of a wrongful act, intentionally, without justification or excuse.... I tell you, also, that malice is implied or presumed from the use of a deadly weapon.

The judge continued to instruct the jury on the theory of accomplice liability. The jury returned guilty verdicts on the murder charge and on all other counts in the indictment. Yates was sentenced to death.

Yates petitioned the South Carolina Supreme Court, asserting that the jury charge that "malice is implied or presumed from the use of a deadly weapon" was an unconstitutional burden-shifting instruction. The case was twice reviewed by the South Carolina Supreme Court, which agreed that the jury instructions were unconstitutional, but that allowing the jury to presume malice was a harmless error. The state found that the jury did not have to rely on presumptions of malice because Davis's "lunging" at Mrs. Wood and stabbing her were acts of malice.

The U.S. Supreme Court, in *Yates v. Evatt* (500 U.S. 391, 1991), reversed the decisions of the South Carolina Supreme Court and remanded the case (sent it back to the lower court for further proceedings). Justice David Souter, writing for the high court, ruled that the state supreme court failed to apply the proper harmless-error standard as stated in *Chapman*. "The issue under *Chapman* is whether the jury actually rested its verdict on evidence establishing the presumed fact beyond a reasonable doubt, independently of the presumption."

Justice Souter concluded by stating that there was clear evidence of Davis's attempt to kill Wood because he could have left the store with Yates but stayed to pursue Wood with a deadly weapon. The evidence that Davis intended to kill Mrs. Wood was not as clear. The record also showed that Yates heard a woman scream as he left the store but did not attempt to return and kill her.

The jury could have interpreted Yates's behavior to confirm his claim that he and Davis had not originally intended to kill anyone. Even the prosecutor, in summation, conceded that Mrs. Wood could have been killed inadvertently by Davis.

DUE PROCESS AND ADVANCE NOTICE OF IMPOSING THE DEATH PENALTY

Robert and Cheryl Bravence were beaten to death at their campsite near Santiam Creek, Idaho. Two brothers, Bryan and Mark Lankford, were charged with two counts of first-degree murder. At the arraignment (a summoning before a court to hear and answer charges), the trial judge advised Bryan Lankford that, if convicted of either of the two charges (he was charged with both murders), the maximum punishment he might receive was either life imprisonment or death.

After the arraignment Bryan Lankford's attorney made a deal with the prosecutor. Bryan Lankford entered a plea bargain in which he agreed to take two lie-detector tests in exchange for a lesser sentence. Although the results were somewhat unclear, they convinced the prosecutor that Lankford's older brother, Mark, was primarily responsible for the crimes and was the actual killer of both victims. Bryan Lankford's attorney and the prosecutor agreed on an indeterminate sentence with a 10-year minimum in exchange for a guilty plea, subject to commitment from the trial judge that he would impose that sentence. The judge refused to make such a commitment, and the case went to trial.

The judge refused to instruct the jury that a specific intent to kill was required to support a conviction of first-degree murder. The jury found Bryan Lankford guilty on both counts. The sentencing hearing was postponed until after Mark's trial. (He was also charged with both murders.)

Before the sentencing trial, at Bryan Lankford's request, the trial judge ordered the prosecutor to notify the court and Lankford whether it would seek the death penalty and, if so, to file a statement of the aggravating circumstance on which the death penalty would be based. The prosecutor notified the judge that the state would not recommend the death penalty. Several proceedings followed, including Lankford's request for a new attorney, a motion for a new trial, and a motion for continuance of the sentencing hearing. At none of the proceedings was there any mention that Lankford might receive the death penalty.

At the sentencing hearing the prosecutor recommended a life sentence, with a minimum ranging between 10 and 20 years. The trial judge indicated that he considered Lankford's testimony unbelievable and that the seriousness of the crime warranted more severe punishment than recommended by the state. He sentenced Lankford to death.

Lankford appealed, asserting that the trial judge violated the Constitution by failing to give notice that he intended to impose the death penalty in spite of the state's earlier notice that it would not seek the death penalty. The judge maintained that the Idaho Code provided Lankford with sufficient notice. The judge added that the fact the prosecutor said he would not seek the death penalty had "no bearing on the adequacy of notice to petitioner [Lankford] that the death penalty might be sought." The Idaho Supreme Court agreed with the judge's decision.

In *Lankford v. Idaho* (500 U.S. 110, 1991), the U.S. Supreme Court reversed the state supreme court ruling and remanded the case for a new trial. Writing for the majority, Justice Stevens stated that the due process clause of the Fourteenth Amendment was violated. Stevens noted,

> If the defense counsel had been notified that the trial judge was contemplating a death sentence based on five specific aggravating circumstances, presumably she would have advanced arguments that addressed these circumstances; however, she did not make these arguments because they were entirely inappropriate in a discussion about the length of the petitioner's possible incarceration.

Stevens further indicated that the trial judge's silence, in effect, hid from Lankford and his attorney, as well as from the prosecutor, the principal issues to be decided.

In a dissenting opinion, Justice Scalia wrote that Lankford's due process rights were not violated because he knew that he had been convicted of first-degree murder, and the Idaho Code clearly states that "every person guilty of murder of the first degree shall be punished by death or by imprisonment for life." At the arraignment the trial judge told Lankford that he could receive either punishment. Scalia further noted that, in Idaho, the death penalty statute places full responsibility for determining the sentence on the judge.

EVIDENCE AND APPEALS

Newly Discovered Evidence Does Not Stop Execution

On an evening in late September 1981 the body of Texas Department of Public Safety Officer David Rucker was found lying beside his patrol car. He had been shot in the head. At about the same time, police officer Enrique Carrisalez saw a vehicle speeding away from the area where Rucker's body had been found. Carrisalez and his partner chased the vehicle and pulled it over. Carrisalez walked to the car. The driver opened his door and exchanged a few words with the police officer before firing at least one shot into Carrisalez's chest. The officer died nine days later.

Leonel Torres Herrera was arrested a few days after the shootings and charged with capital murder. In January 1982 he was tried and found guilty of murdering Carrisalez. In July 1982 he pleaded guilty to Rucker's murder.

At the trial Officer Carrisalez's partner identified Herrera as the person who fired the gun. He also testified that there was only one person in the car. In a statement by Carrisalez before he died, he also identified Herrera. The speeding car belonged to Herrera's girlfriend, and Herrera had the car keys in his pocket when he was arrested. Splatters of blood on the car and on Herrera's clothes were the same type as Rucker's. Strands of hair found in the car also belonged to Rucker. Finally, a handwritten letter, which strongly implied that he had killed Rucker, was found on Herrera when he was arrested.

In 1992, 10 years after the initial trial, Herrera appealed to the federal courts, alleging that he was innocent of the murders of Rucker and Carrisalez and that his execution would violate the Eighth and Fourteenth Amendments. He presented affidavits (sworn statements) claiming that he had not killed the officers, but that his now dead brother had. The brother's attorney, one of Herrera's cellmates, and a school friend all swore that the brother had killed the police officers. The dead brother's son also said that he had witnessed his father killing the men.

The U.S. Supreme Court, in *Herrera v. Collins* (506 U.S. 390, 1993), ruled in a 7–3 decision that executing Herrera would not violate the Eighth and Fourteenth Amendments. The high court said that the trial and not the appeals process judges guilt or innocence. Appeals courts determine only the fairness of the proceedings.

Writing for the majority, Chief Justice Rehnquist stated,

> A person when first charged with a crime is entitled to a presumption of innocence and may insist that his guilt be established beyond a reasonable doubt.... Once a defendant has been afforded a fair trial and convicted of the offense for which he was charged, the presumption of innocence disappears.... Here, it is not disputed that the State met its burden of proving at trial that petitioner was guilty of the capital murder of Officer Carrisalez beyond a reasonable doubt. Thus, in the eyes of the law, petitioner does not come before the Court as one who is "innocent," but on the contrary as one who has been convicted by due process of two brutal murders.

> Based on affidavits here filed, petitioner claims that evidence never presented to the trial court proves him innocent....

> Claims of actual innocence based on newly discovered evidence have never been held to state a ground for [court] relief, absent an independent constitutional violation occurring in the underlying state criminal proceeding....

> This rule is grounded in the principle that ... [appeals] courts sit to ensure that individuals are not imprisoned in violation of the Constitution—not to correct errors of fact.

Rehnquist continued that states all allow the introduction of new evidence. Texas was one of 17 states that require a new trial motion based on new evidence within 60 days. Herrera's appeal came 10 years later. The chief justice, however, emphasized that Herrera still had options, saying,

> For under Texas law, petitioner may file a request for executive clemency. Executive clemency has provided the "fail safe" in our criminal justice system.... It is an unalterable fact that our judicial system, like the human beings who administer it, is fallible. But history is replete with examples of wrongfully convicted persons who have been pardoned in the wake of after-discovered evidence establishing their innocence.

The majority opinion found the information presented in the affidavits inconsistent with the other evidence. The justices questioned why the affidavits were produced at the very last minute. The justices also wondered why Herrera had pleaded guilty to Rucker's murder if he had been innocent. They did note that some of the information in the affidavits might have been important to the jury, "but coming 10 years after the ... trial, this showing of innocence falls far short of that which would have to be made in order to trigger the sort of constitutional claim [to decide for a retrial]."

Speaking for the minority, Justice Blackmun wrote,

> We really are being asked to decide whether the Constitution forbids the execution of a person who has been validly convicted and sentenced but who, nonetheless,

can prove his innocence with newly discovered evidence. Despite the State of Texas' astonishing protestation to the contrary ... I do not see how the answer can be anything but "yes."

> The Eighth Amendment prohibits "cruel and unusual punishments." This proscription [prohibition] is not static [fixed] but rather reflects evolving standards of decency. I think it is crystal clear that the execution of an innocent person is "at odds with contemporary standards of fairness and decency...." The protection of the Eighth Amendment does not end once a defendant has been validly convicted and sentenced.

Claim of Miscarriage of Justice

Lloyd Schlup, a Missouri prisoner, was convicted of participating in the murder of a fellow inmate and sentenced to death. He had filed one petition for *habeas corpus,* arguing that he had inadequate counsel. He filed a second petition, alleging that constitutional error at his trial deprived the jury of crucial evidence that would have established his innocence.

Using a previous U.S. Supreme Court ruling (*Sawyer v. Whitley,* 505 U.S. 333, 1992), the district court claimed that Schlup had not shown "by clear and convincing evidence that, but for a constitutional error, no reasonable juror would have found him guilty." Schlup's lawyers argued that the district court should have used another ruling (*Murray v. Carrier,* 477 U.S. 478, 1986), in which a petitioner need only to show that "a constitutional violation has probably resulted in the conviction of one who is actually innocent." The appellate court affirmed the district court's ruling, noting that Schlup's guilt, which had been proven at the trial, barred any consideration of his constitutional claim.

The U.S. Supreme Court, upon appeal, reviewed the case to determine whether the *Sawyer* standard provides enough protection from a miscarriage of justice that would result from the execution of an innocent person. In *Schlup v. Delo* (513 U.S. 298, 1995), the Court observed,

> If a petitioner such as Schlup presents evidence of innocence so strong that a court cannot have confidence in the outcome of the trial unless the court is also satisfied that the trial was free of non-harmless constitutional error, the petitioner should be allowed to ... argue the merits of his underlying claims.

The justices concluded that the *Carrier,* rather than *Sawyer,* standard focuses the investigation on the actual innocence, allowing the Court to review relevant evidence that might have been excluded or unavailable during the trial.

Suppressed Evidence Means a New Trial

Curtis Lee Kyles was convicted by a Louisiana jury of the first-degree murder of a woman in a grocery store parking lot in 1984. He was sentenced to death. It was revealed on review that the prosecutor had never disclosed certain evidence favorable to the defendant. Among the evidence were conflicting statements by an informant who, the defense believed, wanted to get rid of Kyles in order to get his girlfriend. The state supreme court, the federal district court, and the Fifth Circuit Court denied Kyles's appeals. The U.S. Supreme Court, in *Kyles v. Whitley* (514 U.S. 419, 1995), reversed the lower courts' decisions. The high court ruled,

> Favorable evidence is material, and constitutional error results from its suppression by the government, if there is a "reasonable probability" that, had the evidence been disclosed to the defense, the result of the proceeding would have been different.... [The] net effect of the state-suppressed evidence favoring Kyles raises a reasonable probability that disclosure would have produced a different result at trial.

The conviction was overturned. Four mistrials followed. On February 18, 1998, after his fifth and final trial ended with a hung jury, Curtis Lee Kyles was released from prison. He had spent 14 years on death row.

VICTIM IMPACT STATEMENTS

First, They Are Not Constitutional

John Booth and Willie Reid stole money from elderly neighbors to buy heroin. Booth, knowing his neighbors could identify him, tied up the elderly couple and then repeatedly stabbed them in the chest with a kitchen knife. The couple's son found their bodies two days later. Booth and Reid were found guilty.

The state of Maryland permitted a victim impact statement (VIS) to be read to the jury during the sentencing phase of the trial. The VIS prepared in this case explained the tremendous pain caused by the murder of the parents and grandparents to the family. It revealed that not only had the murdered victims suffered but that their family also suffered severely in many ways, including sleepless nights, lack of trust, depression, and disorientation. A 5–4 Supreme Court, in *Booth v. Maryland* (482 U.S. 496, 1987), while recognizing the agony caused to the victim's family, ruled that victim impact statements, as required by Maryland's statute, were unconstitutional and could not be used during the sentencing phase of a capital murder trial.

Writing for the majority, Justice Lewis Powell indicated that a jury must determine whether the defendant should be executed, based on the circumstances of the crime and the character of the offender. These factors had nothing to do with the victim. The high court noted that it is the crime and the criminal that were at issue. Had Booth and Reid viciously murdered a drunken bum, the crime would have been just as horrible.

Furthermore, some families could express the pain and disruption they suffered as a result of the murder bet-

ter than other families. Should a sentencing depend on how well a family could express its grief? In addition, if the character of the victim should play a role in determining the sentence, then the prisoner should have the right to attack that character to show it was not as flawless as presented. This could likely lead to attacks on the character of the victim and more pain for the victim's family.

...And Then They Are

Pervis Tyronne Payne spent the morning and early afternoon injecting cocaine and drinking beer. Later, he drove around the town with a friend, each of them taking turns reading a pornographic magazine. In midafternoon, Payne went to his girlfriend's apartment across the hall from the apartment of Charisse Christopher. He entered Christopher's apartment and made sexual advances toward Christopher, who resisted. Payne became violent.

The first police officer to arrive at the scene saw Payne leaving the building so covered with blood that he appeared to be "sweating blood." Inside the apartment the police saw Christopher and her children lying on the kitchen floor. Blood covered the walls and floor throughout the apartment.

Christopher had 42 direct knife wounds and 42 defensive wounds on her arms and hands. Her two-year-old daughter had suffered stab wounds to the chest, abdomen, back, and head. The murder weapon, a butcher knife, was found at her feet. Christopher's three-year-old son, despite several stab wounds that went completely through his body, was still alive. Payne was arrested, and a Tennessee jury convicted him of the first-degree murders of Christopher and her daughter and of the first-degree assault, with intent to murder, of Christopher's son, Nicholas.

During the sentencing phase of the trial, Payne called his parents, his girlfriend, and a clinical psychologist to testify about the mitigating aspects of his background and character. The prosecutor, however, called Nicholas's grandmother, who testified how much the child missed his mother and baby sister. In arguing for the death penalty, the prosecutor commented on the continuing effects the crime was having on Nicholas and his family. The jury sentenced Payne to death on each of the murder counts. The state supreme court agreed, rejecting Payne's claim that the admission of the grandmother's testimony and the state's closing argument violated his Eighth Amendment rights under *Booth v. Maryland.*

On hearing the appeal (*Payne v. Tennessee*, 501 U.S. 808, 1991), a 6–3 U.S. Supreme Court upheld the death penalty and overturned both *Booth v. Maryland* and *South Carolina v. Gathers* (490 U.S. 805, 1989; in *Gathers,* the Court reversed the defendant's death sentence because of the prosecutor's statement about the victim being a religious man and a registered voter). In *Payne,* the Court ruled that the Eighth Amendment does not prohibit a jury from considering, at the sentencing phase of a capital trial, victim impact evidence relating to a victim's personal characteristics and the emotional impact of the murder on the victim's family. The Eighth Amendment also does not bar a prosecutor from arguing such evidence at the sentencing phase.

The Court reasoned that the assessment of harm caused by a defendant as a result of a crime has long been an important concern of criminal law in determining both the elements of the offense and the appropriate punishment. Victim impact evidence is simply another form or method of informing the sentencing jury or judge about the specific harm caused by the crime in question.

The *Booth* case unfairly weighted the scales in a capital trial. No limits were placed on the mitigating evidence the defendant introduced relating to his own circumstances. The state, however, was barred from offering a glimpse of the life of the victim, which the defendant chose to extinguish, or from showing the loss to the victim's family or to society. *Booth* and *Gathers* were decided by narrow margins, the Court continued, and had been questioned by members of the Supreme Court as well as by the lower courts.

Chief Justice Rehnquist, delivering the opinion of the Court, stated,

The State has a legitimate interest in counteracting the mitigating evidence which the defendant is entitled to put in, by reminding the sentencer that just as the murderer should be considered as an individual, so too the victim is an individual whose death represents a unique loss to society and in particular to his family.

Justice Stevens, dissenting, stated,

[A victim impact statement] sheds no light on the defendant's guilt or moral culpability [blameworthiness] and thus serves no purpose other than to encourage jurors to decide in favor of death rather than life on the basis of their emotions rather than their reason.

Victim impact evidence, as used in this case, has two flaws. First, aspects of the character of the victim, unforeseeable to the defendant at the time of his crime, are irrelevant to the defendant's "personal responsibility and moral guilt" and therefore cannot justify a death sentence....

Second, the quantity and quality of victim impact evidence sufficient to turn a verdict of life in prison into a verdict of death is not defined until after the crime has been committed and therefore cannot possibly be applied consistently in different cases.

CHAPTER 4

LEGAL DECISIONS—YOUTH, INSANITY, MENTAL RETARDATION, RACE, METHODS OF EXECUTION, AND *HABEAS CORPUS* REVIEW UNDER THE ANTITERRORISM ACT

CAN A MINOR BE SENTENCED TO DEATH?

On April 4, 1977, 16-year-old Monty Lee Eddings and several friends were pulled over by a police officer as they traveled in a car. Eddings had several guns in the car, which he had taken from his father. When the police officer approached the car, Eddings shot and killed him. Eddings was tried as an adult even though he was 16 at the time of the murder. He was convicted of first-degree murder for killing a police officer and was sentenced to death.

At the sentencing hearing following the conviction, Eddings's lawyer presented substantial evidence of a turbulent family history, beatings by a harsh father, and serious emotional disturbance. The judge refused, as a matter of law, to consider the mitigating circumstances of Eddings's unhappy upbringing and emotional problems. He ruled that the only mitigating circumstance was the petitioner's youth, which was insufficient to outweigh the aggravating circumstances. (Mitigating circumstances may lessen responsibility for a crime, while aggravating circumstances may add to responsibility for a crime.)

In *Eddings v. Oklahoma* (455 U.S. 104, 1982), the Supreme Court, in a 5–4 opinion, ordered the case remanded (sent back to the lower courts for further proceedings). The justices based their ruling on *Lockett v. Ohio* (438 U.S. 586, 1978), which required the trial court to consider and weigh all of the mitigating evidence concerning the petitioner's family background and personal history.

By implication, since the majority did not reverse the case on the issue of age, the decision let stand Oklahoma's decision to try Eddings as an adult. Meanwhile, Chief Justice Warren Burger, who filed the dissenting opinion in which Justices Byron White, Harry A. Blackmun, and William H. Rehnquist joined, observed,

> The Constitution does not authorize us to determine whether sentences imposed by state courts are sentences we consider "appropriate"; our only authority is to decide whether they are constitutional under the Eighth Amendment. The Court stops far short of suggesting that there is any constitutional proscription [prohibition] against imposition of the death penalty on a person who was under age 18 when the murder was committed.

Hence, while the high court did not directly rule on the question of minors being sentenced to death, the sense of the Court would appear to be that it would uphold such a sentencing.

Not at 15 Years Old

With three adults, William Thompson brutally murdered a former brother-in-law. Thompson was 15 at the time of the murder, but the state determined that Thompson, who had a long history of violent assault, had "virtually no reasonable prospects for rehabilitation ... within the juvenile system and ... should be held accountable for his acts as if he were an adult and should be certified to stand trial as an adult." Thompson was tried as an adult and found guilty. As in *Eddings,* Thompson's age was considered a mitigating circumstance, but the jury still sentenced him to death.

Thompson appealed, and while the Court of Criminal Appeals of Oklahoma upheld the decision, the U.S. Supreme Court, in *Thompson v. Oklahoma* (487 U.S. 815, 1988), did not. In a 5–3 majority vote, with Justice Sandra Day O'Connor agreeing to vacate (annul) the sentence but not agreeing with the majority reasoning, the case was reversed. (Justice Anthony Kennedy took no part in the decision.)

Writing for the majority (Justices John Stevens, William J. Brennan, Thurgood Marshall, and Blackmun), Justice Stevens observed,

> Inexperience, less education, and less intelligence make the teenager less able to evaluate the consequences of his or her conduct, while at the same time he or she is much more apt to be motivated by mere emotion or peer pres-

sure than is an adult. The reasons why juveniles are not trusted with the privileges and responsibilities of an adult also explain why their irresponsible conduct is not as morally reprehensible [blameworthy] as that of an adult.

Justice Stevens noted that 18 states required the age of at least 16 years before the death penalty could be considered. Counting the 14 states prohibiting capital punishment, a total of 32 states did not execute people under 16.

Justice O'Connor agreed with the judgment of the Court that the appellate court's ruling should be reversed. O'Connor pointed out, however, that, although most 15-year-old criminals are generally less blameworthy than adults who commit the same crimes, some may fully understand the horrible deeds they have done. Individuals, after all, have different characteristics, including their capability to distinguish right from wrong.

Writing for the minority (Justices Antonin Scalia, Rehnquist, and White), Justice Scalia found no national consensus forbidding the execution of a person who was 16 at the commission of the murder. The justice could not understand the majority's calculations establishing a "contemporary standard" that forbade the execution of young minors. He reasoned that abolitionist states (states with no death penalty) should not be considered in the issue of executing minors since they did not have executions in the first place. Rather, the 18 states that prohibited the execution of offenders who were younger than 16 when they murdered should be compared to the 19 states that applied the death penalty to young offenders.

But It May Be Done at 16 or 17

A majority of the Court, with Justice O'Connor straddling the fence, found the death penalty unacceptable for an offender who was less than 16 when he or she committed murder. A majority of the Court, however, found the death sentence acceptable for a minor who was 16 or 17 during the commission of murder. The Supreme Court, in two jointly considered cases, *Stanford v. Kentucky* and *Wilkins v. Missouri* (492 U.S. 361, 1989), ruled that persons who committed their crimes at ages 16 or 17 could be executed for murder.

When he was 17 years old, Kevin Stanford and an accomplice raped Baerbel Poore, an attendant at a gas station they were robbing. They then took the woman to a secluded area near the station, where Stanford shot her in the face and in the back of her head. Stressing the seriousness of the offense and Stanford's long history of criminal behavior, the Court certified him as an adult. He was tried, found guilty, and sentenced to death.

When he was 16 years old, Heath Wilkins stabbed Nancy Allen to death while he was robbing the convenience store where she worked. Wilkins indicated he murdered Allen because "a dead person can't talk." Based on his long history of juvenile delinquency, the Court

ordered Wilkins tried as an adult. He was found guilty and sentenced to die.

Writing for the majority (Justices Scalia, Rehnquist, White, and Kennedy), Justice Scalia could find no national consensus that executing minors ages 16 and 17 constituted cruel and unusual punishment. Scalia observed that of the 37 states whose statutes allowed the death penalty, just 12 refused to impose it on 17-year-old offenders, and in addition to those 12, only 3 more states refused to impose it on 16-year-old offenders.

Further, Justice Scalia saw no connection between the defendant's argument that those under 18 were denied the right to drive, drink, or vote because they were not considered mature enough to do so responsibly and whether this standard of maturity should be applied to a minor's understanding that murder is terribly wrong. Scalia added,

> Even if the requisite degrees of maturity were comparable, the age statutes in question would still not be relevant. These laws set the appropriate ages for the operation of a system that makes its determinations in gross, and that does not conduct individualized maturity tests for each driver, drinker, or voter. The criminal justice system, however, does provide individualized testing. In the realm of capital punishment in particular, "individualized consideration [is] a constitutional requirement," and one of the individualized mitigating factors that sentencers must be permitted to consider is the defendant's age.

Justice O'Connor also concluded that no national consensus prohibited the imposition of the death penalty on Stanford and Wilkins. O'Connor, however, believed that the high court had the constitutional obligation to determine whether the punishment imposed was proportional to the defendants' blameworthiness.

Writing for the minority (Justices Brennan, Marshall, Blackmun, and Stevens), Justice Brennan found a national consensus among 30 states when he added the 12 states forbidding the execution of a person who was 16 years during the commission of the crime to those with no capital punishment, and the states that, in practice if not in law, did not execute minors. Justice Brennan, taking serious exception to the majority's observation that they had to find a national consensus in the laws passed by the state legislatures, stated,

> Our judgment about the constitutionality of a punishment under the Eighth Amendment is informed, though not determined ... by an examination of contemporary attitudes toward the punishment, as evidenced in the actions of legislatures and of juries. The views of organizations with expertise in relevant fields and the choices of governments elsewhere in the world also merit our attention as indicators whether a punishment is acceptable in a civilized society.

Supreme Court Rejects Stanford's Last Appeal

Kevin Stanford has appealed his case several times since the 1989 Supreme Court decision. As a last resort,

Stanford filed a *habeas corpus* petition to the high court, claiming it would be unconstitutional to execute him because he was under the age of 18 when he committed his crime. This petition required five votes to be heard. On October 21, 2002, a 5–4 majority rejected his appeal, announcing their decision without a written opinion.

Justice Stevens wrote a dissenting opinion, joined by Justices Breyer, Ginsburg, and Souter (*In re Stanford,* 123 S.Ct. 472). Justice Stevens believed that the reasons supporting the *Atkins v. Virginia* decision should apply to the execution of juvenile offenders. In *Atkins v. Virginia* (536 U.S. 304, 2002), the Court held that executing mentally retarded persons violates the Eighth Amendment's ban on cruel and unusual punishment. Justice Stevens repeated Justice Brennan's dissent in *Stanford v. Kentucky,* adding that

> [I]n the last 13 years, a national consensus has developed that juvenile offenders should not be executed. No state has lowered the age of eligibility to either 16 or 17 since our decision in 1989....
>
> ... The practice of executing [juvenile] offenders is a relic of the past and is inconsistent with evolving standards of decency in a civilized society. We should put an end to this shameful practice.

Youth—A Mitigating Circumstance

Dorsie Lee Johnson Jr., age 19, and an accomplice staked out a convenience store, with the intention of robbing it. They found out that only one employee worked during the predawn hours. Agreeing to leave no witnesses to the crime, Johnson shot and killed the clerk, Jack Huddleston. They then emptied the cash register and stole some cigarettes.

The following month Johnson was arrested and subsequently confessed to the murder and the robbery. During jury selection the defense attorneys asked potential jurors whether they believed that people were capable of change and whether they, the potential jurors, had ever done things in their youth that they would not now do.

The only witness the defense called was Johnson's father, who told of his son's drug use, grief over the death of his mother two years before the crime, and the murder of his sister the following year. He spoke of his son's youth and the fact that, at age 19, he did not evaluate things the way a person of 30 or 35 would.

Johnson was tried and convicted of capital murder. Under Texas law, the homicide qualified as a capital offense because Johnson intentionally or knowingly caused Huddleston's death. Moreover, the murder was carried out in the course of committing a robbery.

In the sentencing phase of the trial, the judge instructed the jury to answer two questions: (1) whether Johnson's actions were deliberate and intended to kill, and (2) whether there was a possibility that he would continue to commit violent crimes and be a threat to society. If the jury answered "yes" to both questions, Johnson would be sentenced to death. If the jury returned a "no" answer to either question, the defendant would be sentenced to life in prison. The jury was not to consider or discuss the possibility of parole.

Of equal importance was the instruction that the jury could consider all the evidence, both aggravating and mitigating, in either phase of the trial. The jury unanimously answered yes to both questions, and Johnson was sentenced to death.

Five days after the state appellate court denied Johnson's motions for a rehearing, the U.S. Supreme Court issued its opinion in another case, *Penry v. Lynaugh* (492 U.S. 302, 1989). Based on the *Penry* ruling, Dorsie Lee Johnson Jr. claimed that a separate instruction should have been given to the jurors that would have allowed them to consider his youth. (In *Penry,* the Court held that the jury should have been instructed that it could consider mental retardation as a mitigating factor during the penalty phase.) Again, the appellate court rejected Johnson's petition.

Affirming the Texas appellate court decision, Justice Kennedy delivered the opinion of the Supreme Court in *Johnson v. Texas* (509 U.S. 350, 1993). He was joined by Justices Rehnquist, White, Scalia, and Clarence Thomas. Kennedy noted that the Texas special-issues system (two questions asked of the jury and instruction to consider all evidence) allowed for adequate consideration of Johnson's youth. Justice Kennedy stated,

> Even on a cold record, one cannot be unmoved by the testimony of petitioner's father urging that his son's actions were due in large part to his youth. It strains credulity to suppose that the jury would have viewed the evidence of petitioner's youth as outside its effective reach in answering the second special issue. The relevance of youth as a mitigating factor derives from the fact that the signature qualities of youth are transient; as individuals mature, the impetuousness and recklessness that may dominate in younger years can subside.... As long as the mitigating evidence is within "the effective reach of the sentencer," the requirements of the Eighth Amendment are satisfied.

Justice O'Connor, in a dissenting opinion joined by Justices Blackmun, Stevens, and David Souter, stated that the jurors were not allowed to give "full effect to his strongest mitigating circumstance: his youth." Hearing of his less than exemplary youth, a jury might easily conclude, as Johnson's did, that he would continue to be a threat to society.

ROLE OF PSYCHIATRISTS

Validity of a Psychiatrist's Testimony

In 1978 Thomas Barefoot was convicted of murdering a police officer. During the sentencing phase of the trial, the prosecution put two psychiatrists on the stand. Neither psychiatrist had actually interviewed Barefoot, nor did either ask to do so. Both psychiatrists agreed that an individual with Barefoot's background and who had acted as Barefoot had in murdering the policeman represented a future threat to society. Partially based on their testimony, the jury sentenced Barefoot to death.

Barefoot's conviction and sentence were appealed numerous times, and in 1983 his case was argued before the U.S. Supreme Court. Among the issues debated was the validity of the testimony of psychiatrists. Barefoot's lawyers questioned whether it was necessary for the psychiatrists to have interviewed Barefoot or if it was enough for them to answer hypothetical questions that pertained to a hypothetical individual who acted like Barefoot.

Barefoot's attorneys claimed that psychiatrists could not reliably predict that a particular offender would commit other crimes in the future and be a threat to society. They further argued that psychiatrists should also not be allowed to testify about an offender's future dangerousness in response to hypothetical situations presented by the prosecutor and without having first examined the offender.

In *Barefoot v. Estelle* (463 U.S. 880, 1983), the Supreme Court ruled 6–3 that local juries were in the best position to decide guilt and impose a sentence. The Court referred to *Jurek v. Texas* (428 U.S. 262, 1976), an earlier case that, among other things, upheld the testimony of laypersons concerning a defendant's possible future actions. The Court, therefore, looked upon psychiatrists as just another group of people presenting testimony to the jury for consideration. Like all evidence presented to the jury, the Court claimed,

> [A psychiatric observation] should be admitted and its weight left to the fact finder, who would have the benefit of cross examination and contrary evidence by the opposing party. Psychiatric testimony predicting dangerousness may be countered not only as erroneous in a particular case but as generally so unreliable that it should be ignored. If the jury may make up its mind about future dangerousness unaided by psychiatric testimony, jurors should not be barred from hearing the views of the State's psychiatrists along with opposing views of the defendant's doctors.

The high court dismissed the *amicus curiae* brief (a friend-of-the-court brief prepared to enlighten the court) presented by the American Psychiatric Association (APA), indicating that psychiatric testimony was "almost entirely unreliable" in determining future actions. The Court countered that such testimony had been traditionally accepted. The Court also observed that arguments, such as the APA brief, were founded "on the premise that a jury will not be able to separate the wheat from the chaff," a sentiment with which the Court did not agree.

The high court also dismissed Barefoot's contention that the psychiatrists should have personally interviewed him. Such methods of observation and conclusion were quite normal in courtroom procedures, and the psychiatric observations had been based on established facts. Barefoot's appeal was denied.

Justice Blackmun strongly dissented from the majority decision. He declared,

> In the present state of psychiatric knowledge, this is too much for me. One may accept this in a routine lawsuit for money damages, but when a person's life is at stake—no matter how heinous his offense—a requirement of greater reliability should prevail. In a capital case, the specious [seemingly fair but not so] testimony of a psychiatrist, colored in the eyes of an impressionable jury by the inevitable untouchability of a medical specialist's words, equates with death itself.

A Prisoner Maintains Rights During Psychiatric Examination

During the commission of a robbery, Ernest Smith's accomplice fatally shot a grocery clerk (Smith had tried to shoot the clerk, but his weapon had jammed). The state of Texas sought the death penalty against Smith based on the Texas law governing premeditated murder.

Thereafter, the judge ordered a psychiatric examination of Smith by Dr. James Grigson to determine if Smith was competent to stand trial. Without permission from Smith's lawyer, Dr. Grigson interviewed Smith in jail for about 90 minutes and found him competent. Dr. Grigson then discussed his conclusions and diagnosis with the state attorney. Smith was found guilty. During the sentencing phase of the trial, over the protests of the defendant's lawyers, Dr. Grigson testified that Smith was a "very severe sociopath," who would continue his previous behavior, which would get worse. The jury sentenced Smith to death.

Smith appealed his sentence, claiming he was not informed of his rights. Both the federal district court and the appeals court agreed. So did a unanimous Supreme Court. In *Estelle v. Smith* (451 U.S. 454, 1981), the Court ruled that the trial court had the right to determine if Smith was capable of standing trial. It had no right, however, to use the information gathered without first advising him of his Fifth Amendment right against self-incrimination. According to the Court, the psychiatrist was "an agent of the state" about whom the defendant had not been warned, but who was reporting about the defendant. Noting *Miranda v. Arizona* (384 U.S. 436, 1966), the Court continued,

> The Fifth Amendment privilege is available outside of criminal court proceedings and serves to protect persons in all settings in which their freedom of action is curtailed in any significant way from being compelled to incriminate themselves.... The prosecution may not use statements, whether exculpatory [proving innocence] or inculpatory [incriminating], stemming from custodial

[while under arrest] interrogation of the defendant unless it demonstrates the use of procedural safeguards effective to secure the privilege against self-incrimination.

Needing a Psychiatrist to Prove Insanity

In 1979 Glen Burton Ake and Steven Hatch shot and killed the Reverend Richard and Marilyn Douglass and wounded their children, Brooks and Leslie. Before the trial, due to Ake's bizarre behavior, the trial judge ordered him examined by a psychiatrist to determine if he should be put under observation. The psychiatrist diagnosed Ake as a probable paranoid schizophrenic and reported that his client claimed "to be the 'sword of vengeance' of the Lord." The physician recommended a long-term psychiatric examination to determine Ake's competency to stand trial.

Ake's psychiatric evaluation confirmed his paranoid schizophrenia. Consequently, the court pronounced him incompetent to stand trial and ordered him committed to the state mental hospital.

Six weeks later the hospital psychiatrist informed the court that Ake had become competent to stand trial. Under daily treatment with an antipsychotic drug, he could stand trial. The state of Oklahoma resumed proceedings against the accused murderer.

Prior to the trial Ake's lawyer told the Court of his client's insanity defense. He also informed the court that in order for him to defend Ake adequately, he needed to have Ake examined by a psychiatrist to determine his mental condition at the time he committed murder. During his stay at the mental hospital, Ake was evaluated as to his "present sanity" to stand trial but not his mental state during the murder. Since Ake could not afford a psychiatrist, his counsel asked the court to provide a psychiatrist or the money to hire one. The trial judge refused his request, claiming the state is not obligated to provide a psychiatrist, even to poor defendants in capital cases.

Ake was tried for two counts of first-degree murder and for two counts of shooting with intent to kill. During the trial Ake's only defense was insanity; none of the psychiatrists at the state mental hospital, however, could testify to his mental state at the time of the crime.

The judge instructed the jurors that Ake could be found not guilty by reason of insanity if he could not distinguish right from wrong when he committed murder. The jurors were told they could presume Ake sane at the time of the crime unless he presented sufficient evidence to raise a reasonable doubt about his sanity during the crime. The jury found him guilty on all counts. The jury sentenced Ake to death based on the earlier testimony of the psychiatrist who concluded he was a threat to society. Upon appeal, the Oklahoma Court of Appeals agreed with the trial court that the state did not have the responsibility to provide an indigent (poor) defendant with a psychiatrist to help with his defense.

The U.S. Supreme Court disagreed. In an 8–1 ruling, the Court, in *Ake v. Oklahoma* (470 U.S. 68, 1985), reversed the lower court's ruling, finding that "there was no expert testimony for either side on Ake's sanity at the time of the offense." The high court further observed:

> This Court has long recognized that when a State brings its judicial power to bear on an indigent defendant in a criminal proceeding, it must take steps to assure that the defendant has a fair opportunity to present his defense. This elementary principle, grounded in significant part on the Fourteenth Amendment's due process guarantee of fundamental fairness, derives from the belief that justice cannot be equal where, simply as a result of his poverty, a defendant is denied the opportunity to participate meaningfully in a judicial proceeding in which his liberty is at stake.

CAN AN INSANE PERSON BE EXECUTED?

In 1974 Alvin Ford was convicted of murder and sentenced to death. There was no question that he was completely sane at the time of his crime, at the trial, and at the sentencing. Eight years later, Ford began to show signs of delusion—from thinking that people were conspiring to force him to commit suicide to believing that family members were being held hostage in prison.

Ford's lawyers had a psychiatrist examine their client. After 14 months of evaluation and investigation, the doctor concluded that Ford suffered from a severe mental disorder that would preclude him from assisting in the defense of his life. A second psychiatrist concluded that Ford did not understand why he was on death row.

Florida law required the governor to appoint a panel of three psychiatrists to determine whether Ford was mentally capable of understanding the death penalty and the reasons he was being sentenced to death. The three state-appointed doctors met with Ford once for about 30 minutes and then filed separate reports. Ford's lawyers were present but were ordered by the judge not to participate in the examination "in any adversarial manner."

The three psychiatrists submitted different diagnoses, but all agreed that Ford was sane enough to be executed. Ford's lawyers attempted to submit the reports of the first two psychiatrists along with other materials. The governor, refusing to inform the lawyers whether he would consider these reports, proceeded to sign Ford's death warrant.

Ford's appeals were denied in state and federal courts, but a 7–2 Supreme Court, in *Ford v. Wainwright* (477 U.S. 399, 1986), reversed the earlier judgments. Writing for the majority, Justice Marshall observed that, while the reasons appear unclear, English common law forbade the execution of the insane. The English jurist Sir William Blackstone (1723–80) had labeled such a practice "savage and inhuman." Likewise, the other noted English judicial resource, Sir Edward Coke (1552–1634), observed that, while the execution of a criminal was to serve as an example, the execution of a madman was considered "of extreme inhumanity and cruelty, and can be no example to others." Consequently, since the Eighth Amendment forbidding cruel and unusual punishment was prepared by men who accepted English common law, there could be no question that the Eighth Amendment prohibited the execution of the insane.

The issue then became the method the state used to determine Ford's insanity. The high court noted that Florida did not allow the submission of materials that might be relevant to the decision whether or not to execute the condemned man. In addition, Ford's lawyers were not given the chance to question the state-appointed psychiatrists about the basis for finding their client competent. Questions the defense could have asked included the possibility of personal bias on the doctors' part toward the death penalty, any history of error in their judgment, and their degree of certainty in reaching their conclusions. Finally, the justices pointed out that the greatest defect in Florida's practice is its entrusting the ultimate decision about the execution entirely to the executive branch. The high court observed,

> Under this procedure, the person who appoints the experts and ultimately decides whether the State will be able to carry out the sentence that it has long sought is the Governor, whose subordinates have been responsible for initiating every stage of the prosecution of the condemned from arrest through sentencing. The commander of the State's corps of prosecutors cannot be said to have the neutrality that is necessary for reliability in the fact-finding proceeding.

The high court further observed that, even though a prisoner has been sentenced to death, he is still protected by the Constitution. Therefore, ascertaining his sanity as a basis for a legal execution is as important as other proceedings in a capital case.

In dissent, Justice Rehnquist, joined by Chief Justice Burger, thought the Florida procedure consistent with English common law, which had left the decision to the executive branch. Rehnquist warned,

> A claim of insanity may be made at any time before sentence and, once rejected, may be raised again; a prisoner found sane two days before execution might claim to have lost his sanity the next day, thus necessitating another judicial determination of his sanity and presumably another stay of his execution.

CAN A MENTALLY RETARDED PERSON BE EXECUTED?

Penry I

In 1979 Pamela Carpenter was brutally raped, beaten, and stabbed with a pair of scissors. Before she died, she was able to describe her attacker, and as a result, Johnny Paul Penry was arrested for, and later confessed to, the crime. At the time of the crime, Penry was out on parole for another rape. He was found guilty for the murder of Carpenter and sentenced to die.

Among the issues considered in his appeal was whether the state of Texas could execute a mentally retarded person. At Penry's competency hearing a psychiatrist testified that the defendant had an intelligence quotient (IQ) of 54. (Penry had been tested in the past as having an IQ between 50 and 63, indicating mild to moderate retardation.) According to the psychiatrist, during the commission of the crime, 22-year-old Penry had the mental age of a child six and a half years old and the social maturity of someone who was 9 to 10 years old. Penry's attorneys argued,

> Because of their mental disabilities, mentally retarded people do not possess the level of moral culpability [blameworthiness] to justify imposing the death sentence.... [T]here is an emerging national consensus [majority view] against executing the retarded.

Writing for the five-person majority (Justices O'Connor, Rehnquist, White, Scalia, and Kennedy) regarding the execution of mentally retarded persons, Justice O'Connor, in *Penry v. Lynaugh* (492 U.S. 302, 1989), found no emerging national consensus against such execution. Furthermore, while, historically, idiots and profoundly retarded persons had not been executed for murder, Penry did not fall into this group.

Justice O'Connor noted that Penry was found competent to stand trial. He was able to consult rationally with his lawyer and understood the proceedings against him. Justice O'Connor thought that the defense was guilty of lumping all mentally retarded persons together, ascribing, among other things, a lack of moral capacity to be culpable for actions that call for the death punishment. Justice O'Connor wrote,

> Mentally retarded persons are individuals whose abilities and experiences can vary greatly. If the mentally retarded were not treated as individuals, but as an undifferentiated group, a mildly mentally retarded person could be denied the opportunity to enter into contracts or to marry by virtue of the fact that he had a "mental age" of a young child. In light of the diverse capacities and life experiences of mentally retarded persons, it cannot be said on the record before us today that all mentally retarded people, by definition, can never act with the level of culpability associated with the death penalty.

Further, the majority could find no national movement toward any type of consensus on this issue. While *Penry* produced several public opinion polls that indicated strong public opposition to executing the retarded, almost none of this public opinion was reflected in death penalty legislation. Only the federal Anti-Drug Abuse Act of 1988 (Public Law 100-690) and the states of Georgia and Maryland at the time banned the execution of retarded persons found guilty of a capital crime.

Justice Brennan disagreed. While he agreed that lumping mentally retarded people together might result in stereotyping and discrimination, he believed there are characteristics that fall under the clinical definition of mental retardation. Citing the *amicus curiae* brief prepared by the American Association on Mental Retardation, Justice Brennan noted,

> Every individual who has mental retardation—irrespective of his or her precise capacities or experiences—has a substantial disability in cognitive ability and adaptive behavior.... Though individuals, particularly those who are mildly retarded, may be quite capable of overcoming these limitations to the extent of being able to "maintain themselves independently or semi-independently in the community," nevertheless, the mentally retarded, by definition, "have a reduced ability to cope with and function in the everyday world."

Justice Brennan did not believe that executing a person not fully responsible for his or her actions would serve the "penal goals of retribution or deterrence." What is the point of executing someone who did not fully recognize the terrible evil that he or she had done? Furthermore, he argued, executing a mentally retarded person would not deter nonretarded people, those who would be aware of the possibility of an execution.

Although the Supreme Court held that executing persons with mental retardation was not a violation of the Eighth Amendment, it ruled that Penry's Eighth Amendment right was violated because the jury was not instructed that it could consider mental retardation as a mitigating factor during sentencing. The case was sent back to the lower court. In 1990 Texas retried Penry, and he was again found guilty of capital murder. During the sentencing phase the prosecution used a specific portion of a psychiatric report to point out the doctor's opinion that, if released from custody, Penry would be a threat to society. Penry appealed his case all the way to the Supreme Court. Ten years later, in November 2000, with Penry less than three hours from being put to death, the Supreme Court granted a stay of execution in order to hear Penry's claims.

Penry II

In his appeal to the Supreme Court, Penry argued that the use of a portion of a psychiatric report (unrelated to the Pamela Carpenter case) violated his Fifth Amendment right against self-incrimination. In 1977, during another rape case trial, the state of Texas provided Penry with a psychiatrist at the request of his lawyer. The psychiatrist was to determine the defendant's competency to stand trial. In 2000 Penry argued that the psychiatrist was an "agent of the state," and the prosecution's use of his report violated Penry's right against self-incrimination. Penry also claimed jury instructions were inadequate.

On June 4, 2001, the Supreme Court, in *Penry v. Johnson* (532 U.S. 782), ruled 6–3 that the admission of the psychiatrist's report did not violate Penry's Fifth Amendment right. The Court held that this case was different from *Estelle v. Smith,* discussed earlier, in which the justices found that the psychiatrist's testimony about the defendant's future dangerousness based on the defendant's statements without his lawyer present violated his Fifth Amendment right. The justices emphasized that *Estelle* was restricted to that particular case.

The justices, however, remanded (sent back) the case to the trial court for resentencing because, as in the original *Penry,* the state did not give the sentencing jury adequate instructions about how to weigh mental retardation as a mitigating factor.

The Court Revisits Mental Retardation

Daryl Renard Atkins was convicted and sentenced to death for a 1996 abduction, armed robbery, and capital murder. On appeal to the Virginia Supreme Court, Atkins argued that he could not be executed because he was mentally retarded. Relying on *Penry v. Lynaugh,* the court affirmed the conviction. The court ordered a sentencing retrial because the trial court had used the wrong verdict form. As with the first penalty trial, a psychologist testified that Atkins was "mildly mentally retarded," having an IQ of 59. The jury sentenced Atkins to death for a second time. Atkins again appealed to the Virginia Supreme Court, which upheld the trial court ruling.

The U.S. Supreme Court unanimously agreed to hear Atkins' case. Thirteen years after ruling that executing the mentally retarded does not violate the Constitution, the Supreme Court, in a 6–3 decision, reversed its 1989 *Penry* decision. On June 20, 2002, in *Atkins v. Virginia* (536 U.S. 304), the majority of the Court held that "executions of mentally retarded criminals are 'cruel and unusual punishments' prohibited by the Eighth Amendment."

Justice Stevens delivered the opinion of the Court. Justices O'Connor, Kennedy, Souter, Ginsburg, and Breyer joined the opinion. According to the Court, since *Penry,* many states have concluded that death is not a suitable punishment for mentally retarded offenders, reflecting society's sentiments that these individuals are less culpable than average offenders. The Court observed,

> Mentally retarded persons ... have diminished capacities to understand and process information, to communicate, to abstract from mistakes and learn from experience, to engage in logical reasoning, to control impulses, and to understand the reactions of others.... Their deficiencies do not warrant an exemption from criminal sanctions, but they do diminish their personal culpability.

The Justices also noted that, while the theory is that capital punishment would serve as deterrence to those contemplating murder, this theory does not apply to the mentally retarded because their diminished mental capacities prevent them from appreciating the possibility of execution as punishment. Moreover, the lesser culpability of mentally retarded criminals does not warrant the severe punishment of death.

Justice Scalia disagreed with the ruling that a person who is slightly mentally retarded does not possess the culpability to be sentenced to death. He claimed that the ruling finds "no support in the text or history of the Eighth Amendment." The justice also noted that current social attitudes do not support the majority decision. He pointed out that the state laws that the majority claimed reflect society's attitudes against executing the mentally retarded are still in their infancy and have not undergone the test of time.

On the relationship between a criminal's culpability and the deserved punishment, Justice Scalia stated,

> Surely culpability, and deservedness of the most severe retribution, depends not merely (if at all) upon the mental capacity of the criminal (above the level where he is able to distinguish right from wrong) but also upon the depravity of the crime—which is precisely why this sort of question has traditionally been thought answerable not by a categorical rule of the sort the Court today imposes upon all trials, but rather by the sentencer's weighing of the circumstances (both degree of retardation and depravity of crime) in the particular case. The fact that juries continue to sentence mentally retarded offenders to death for extreme crimes shows that society's moral outrage sometimes demands execution of retarded offenders. By what principle of law, science, or logic can the Court pronounce that this is wrong? There is none. Once the Court admits (as it does) that mental retardation does not render the offender morally *blameless* ... there is no basis for saying that the death penalty is *never* appropriate retribution, no matter *how* heinous the crime.

Penry Is Sentenced a Third Time

On July 3, 2002, about two weeks after the U.S. Supreme Court ruled that it is unconstitutional to execute a mentally retarded person, a Texas jury concluded that Penry is not mentally retarded. For the third time, Penry received the death penalty. As of late 2003, his case was being appealed.

COMPETENCY STANDARD

On August 2, 1984, Richard Allen Moran fatally shot a bartender and a patron four times each, and several days later, his former wife. Failing a suicide attempt, Moran confessed to his crimes. Later the defendant pleaded not guilty to three counts of first-degree murder. Two psychiatrists examined Moran and concluded that he was competent to stand trial. Approximately 10 weeks after the evaluations, the defendant decided to dismiss his attorneys and change his plea to guilty. After review of the psychiatric reports, the trial court accepted the waiver for counsel and the guilty plea. The defendant was later sentenced to death.

Seven months later Moran appealed his case, claiming that he had been "mentally incompetent to represent himself." The appellate court reversed the conviction, ruling that "competency to waive constitutional rights requires a higher level of mental functioning than that required to stand trial." A defendant is considered competent to stand trial if he can understand the proceedings and help in his defense. Yet, for a defendant to be considered competent to waive counsel or to plead guilty, he has to be capable of "'reasoned choice' among the alternatives available to him." The appellate court found Moran mentally incapable of the reasoned choice needed to be in a position to waive his constitutional rights.

In a 7–2 decision, the Supreme Court, in *Godinez v. Moran* (509 U.S. 389, 1993), reversed the judgment of the court of appeals, holding that the standard for measuring a criminal defendant's competency to plead guilty or to waive his right to counsel is not higher than the standard for standing trial. The high court then sent the case back to the lower courts for further proceedings.

RACE/ETHNICITY AS A CONSIDERATION

In 1978 Willie Lloyd Turner, a black man, robbed a jewelry store in Franklin, Virginia. Angered because the owner had set off a silent alarm, Turner first shot the owner in the head, wounding him, and then shot him twice in the chest, killing him for "snitching." Turner's lawyer included the following question for the jurors:

> The defendant, Willie Lloyd Turner, is a member of the Negro race. The victim, W. Jack Smith, Jr., was a white Caucasian. Will these facts prejudice you against Willie Lloyd Turner or affect your ability to render a fair and impartial verdict based solely on the evidence?

The judge refused to allow this question to be asked. A jury of eight whites and four blacks convicted Turner and then, in a separate sentencing hearing, recommended the death sentence, which the judge imposed.

Turner appealed his conviction, claiming that the judge's refusal to ask prospective jurors about their racial attitudes deprived him of his right to a fair trial. Although his argument failed to convince state and federal appeals courts, the U.S. Supreme Court heard his case. In *Turner v. Murray* (476 U.S. 28, 1986), the high court, in a 7–2 decision, overturned Turner's death sentence, but not his conviction.

Writing for the majority, Justice White noted that, in considering a death sentence, the jury makes a subjective decision that is uniquely his or her own regarding what punishment should be meted out to the offender. Justice White further stated,

> Because of the range of discretion entrusted to a jury in a capital sentencing hearing, there is a unique opportunity for racial prejudice to operate but remain undetected. On the facts of this case, a juror who believes that blacks are violence-prone or morally inferior might well be influenced by that belief in deciding whether peti-

tioner's crime involved the aggravating factors specified under Virginia law. Such a juror might also be less favorably inclined toward petitioner's evidence of mental disturbance as a mitigating circumstance. More subtle, less consciously held racial attitudes could also influence a juror's decision in this case. Fear of blacks, which could easily be stirred up by the violent facts of petitioner's crime, might incline a juror to favor the death penalty.

The high court recognized that the death sentence differs from all other punishments and, therefore, requires a more comprehensive examination of how it is imposed. The lower court judge, by not asking prospective jurors about their racial attitudes, had not exercised this thorough examination. Consequently, the Supreme Court reversed Turner's death sentence. Justice Lewis Powell, in his dissent, observed,

> [The Court ruling seemed to be] based on what amounts to a constitutional presumption that jurors in capital cases are racially biased. Such presumption unjustifiably suggests that criminal justice in our courts of law is meted out on racial grounds.

Limits to Consideration of Racial Attitudes

Warren McCleskey and three armed men robbed a furniture store in Fulton County, Georgia. A police officer, responding to a silent alarm, entered the store, was shot twice, and died. McCleskey was black; the officer was white. McCleskey admitted taking part in the robbery but denied shooting the policeman. The state proved that at least one shot came from the weapon McCleskey was carrying and produced two witnesses who had heard McCleskey admit to the shooting. A jury found him guilty and McCleskey, offering no mitigating circumstances during the sentencing phase, received the death penalty.

McCleskey eventually appealed his case all the way to the U.S. Supreme Court. Part of his appeal was based on two major statistical studies of more than 2,000 Georgia murder cases that occurred during the 1970s. Prepared by Professors David C. Baldus, George Woodworth, and Charles Pulanski, the statistical analyses were referred to as the Baldus study. (The two studies were "Comparative Review of Death Sentences: An Empirical Study of the Georgia Experience," *Journal of Criminal Law and Criminology,* volume 74, pages 661–753, 1983, and "Monitoring and Evaluating Contemporary Death Sentencing Systems: Lessons from Georgia," *University of California Davis Law Review,* volume 18, pages 1375–1407, 1985.)

The Baldus study found that defendants charged with killing white persons received the death penalty in 11 percent of cases, but defendants charged with killing blacks received the death penalty in only 1 percent of the cases. The study also found a reverse racial difference, based on the defendant's race—4 percent of the black defendants received the death penalty, as opposed to 7 percent of the white defendants.

Furthermore, the Baldus study reported on the cases based on the combination of the defendant's race and that of the victim. The death penalty was imposed in 22 percent of the cases involving black defendants and white victims, in 8 percent of the cases involving white defendants and white victims, in 3 percent of the cases involving white defendants and black victims, and in 1 percent of the cases involving black defendants and black victims.

The Baldus study also found that prosecutors sought the death penalty in 70 percent of the cases involving black defendants and white victims, in 32 percent of the cases involving white defendants and white victims, in 19 percent of the cases involving white defendants and black victims, and in 15 percent of the cases involving black defendants and black victims.

Finally, after taking account of variables that could have explained the differences on nonracial grounds, the study concluded that defendants charged with killing white victims were 4.3 times as likely to receive the death penalty as defendants charged with killing blacks. In addition, black defendants were 1.1 times as likely to get a death sentence as other defendants were. Therefore, McCleskey, who was black and killed a white victim, had the greatest likelihood of being sentenced to death.

In court testimony Dr. Baldus testified that, in really brutal cases where there is no question the death penalty should be imposed, racial discrimination on the part of the jurors tends to disappear. The racial factors usually come into play in midrange cases, such as McCleskey's, where the jurors were faced with choices.

While the federal district court did not accept the Baldus study, both the court of appeals and the U.S. Supreme Court accepted the study as valid. A 5–4 Supreme Court, however, in *McCleskey v. Kemp* (481 U.S. 279, 1987), rejected McCleskey's appeal. McCleskey had to show that the state of Georgia had acted in a discriminatory manner in his case, and the Baldus study was not enough to support the defendant's claim that any of the jurors had acted with discrimination.

Justice Powell noted that statistics, at most, may show that a certain factor might likely enter some decision-making processes. The Court recognized that a jury's decision could be influenced by racial prejudice, but the majority believed previous rulings had built in enough safeguards to guarantee equal protection for every defendant. The Court declared,

> At most, the Baldus study indicates a discrepancy that appears to correlate with race. Apparent disparities in sentencing are an inevitable part of our criminal justice system.... Where the discretion that is fundamental to

our criminal process is involved, we decline to assume that what is unexplained is invidious [unfairly discriminatory].... We hold that the Baldus study does not demonstrate a constitutionally significant risk of racial bias affecting the Georgia capital-sentencing process.

The Court expressed concern that if it ruled that Baldus's findings did represent a risk, the findings might well be applied to lesser cases. It further noted that it is the job of the legislative branch to consider these findings and incorporate them into the laws to guarantee equal protection in courts of law.

Justice Brennan, who, along with Justice Marshall, believed capital punishment constitutes cruel and unusual punishment and, therefore, is unconstitutional, thought the Baldus study powerfully demonstrated that it is impossible to eliminate arbitrariness in the imposition of the death penalty. Therefore, he argued, the death penalty must be abolished altogether because the Court cannot rely on legal safeguards to guarantee a black defendant a fair sentencing. While the Baldus study did not show that racism necessarily led to McCleskey's death sentence, it had surely shown that McCleskey faced a considerably greater likelihood of being sentenced to death because he was a black man convicted of killing a white man.

Also writing in dissent, Justice Blackmun thought the Court majority had concentrated too much on the potential racial attitudes of the jury. As important, he thought, were the racial attitudes of the prosecutor's office, which the Baldus study found to be much more likely to seek the death penalty for a black person who had killed a white person than for other categories.

The district attorney for Fulton County had testified that no county policy existed on how to prosecute capital cases. Decisions to seek the death penalty were left to the judgment of the assistant district attorneys who handled the cases. Blackmun thought that such a system was certainly open to abuse. Without guidelines, the prosecutors could let their racial prejudices influence their decisions.

Blackmun also noted that the Court majority had totally dismissed Georgia's history of racial prejudice as past history. While it should not be the overriding factor, this bias should be considered in any case presented to the high court, he thought. Justice Blackmun found most disturbing the Court's concern that, if the Baldus findings were upheld, they might be applied to other cases, leading to constitutional challenges. Blackmun thought that a closer scrutiny of the effects of racial discrimination would benefit the criminal justice system and, ultimately, society.

Prosecutor's Racially Based Use of Peremptory Challenges in Jury Selection

James A. Ford, a black man, was charged with the kidnapping, rape, and murder of a white woman. The state of Georgia informed Ford that it planned to seek the death penalty. Before the trial, Ford filed a "Motion to Restrict Racial Use of Peremptory Challenges," claiming that the prosecutor had consistently excluded black persons from juries where the victims were white.

At a hearing on the defendant's motion, Ford's lawyer noted that it had been his experience that the district attorney and his assistants had used their peremptory challenges (the right to reject a juror without giving a reason) to excuse potential black jurors. Ford's lawyer asked the trial judge to prevent this from happening by ordering the district attorney to justify on the record his reasons for excusing potential black jurors.

The prosecutor denied any discrimination on his part. He referred to the U.S. Supreme Court decision in *Swain v. Alabama* (380 U.S. 202, 1965), which said, in part, "It would be an unreasonable burden to require an attorney for either side to justify his use of peremptory challenges." The judge denied Ford's attorney's motion because he had previously seen the district attorney passing over prospective white jurors in favor of potential black jurors.

During jury selection the prosecutor used 9 of his 10 peremptory challenges to dismiss prospective black jurors, leaving only one black member seated on the jury. In closed sessions, the judge allowed Ford's attorney's observation, for the record, that 9 of the 10 black prospective members had been dismissed on peremptory challenges by the prosecutor. The judge, however, told the prosecutor that he did not have to offer any reasons for his peremptory actions.

Ford was convicted on all counts and was sentenced to death. His attorney called for a new trial and claimed that Ford's "right to an impartial jury as guaranteed by the Sixth Amendment [calling for a fair cross-section of the community] of the United States Constitution was violated by the prosecutor's exercise of his peremptory challenges on a racial basis." On appeal, the Supreme Court of Georgia affirmed the conviction.

Ford appealed to the U.S. Supreme Court. In *Ford v. Georgia* (498 U.S. 411, 1991), the high court reversed the decision of the Georgia Supreme Court. The Court vacated (annulled) Ford's conviction and ruled that its decision on *Batson v. Kentucky* (476 U.S. 79, 1986) could be applied retroactively to Ford's case. In 1986 the high court had ruled in *Batson,* which dropped the *Swain* requirement of proof of prior discrimination, that a black defendant could make a case claiming the denial of equal protection of the laws. The defendant could do so solely on evidence that the prosecutor had used peremptory challenges to exclude members of the defendant's race from the jury.

Delivering the opinion for a unanimous Court, Justice Souter held that the Georgia Supreme Court had erred when it ruled that Ford had failed to present a proper equal protection claim. Although Ford's pretrial motion did not mention the Equal Protection Clause (of the Fourteenth Amendment), and his new trial motion had cited the Sixth Amendment rather than the Fourteenth, the motion referring to a pattern of excluding black members "over a long period of time asserts an equal protection claim."

Using Race/Ethnicity to Obtain a Death Sentence

On June 5, 2000, the Supreme Court, in a summary disposition, ordered the Texas Court of Criminal Appeals to hold a new sentencing hearing for Victor Saldano, an Argentine national on death row. (In a summary disposition, the Court decides a case in a simple proceeding without the aid of a jury.) In *Saldano v. Texas* (99-8119), the Court cited the confession of error by Texas Attorney General John Cornyn regarding the use of race as a factor in sentencing the defendant.

Texas death penalty statutes require that the jury consider a defendant's future dangerousness to determine whether or not to impose the death penalty. At the sentencing hearing court-appointed psychologist Dr. Walter Quijano testified that Saldano was "a continuing threat to society" because he is Hispanic. Dr. Quijano told the jury that because Hispanics are "over-represented" in prisons they are more likely to be dangerous. Since then the attorney general announced that the psychiatrist had given similar testimony in six other cases of death row inmates sentenced to death.

METHODS OF EXECUTION

Lethal Injection May Be Used for Executions

The injection of a deadly combination of drugs has become the method of execution in most states permitting capital punishment. Condemned prisoners from Texas and Oklahoma, two of the first states to introduce this method, brought suit claiming that, while the drugs used had been approved by the U.S. Food and Drug Administration (FDA) for medical purposes, they had never been approved for use in nor tested for human executions.

The petitioners further claimed that, since the drugs would likely be administered by untrained personnel, they might not cause the quick and painless death intended. They alleged these drugs had been "misbranded," a violation of 21 U.S.C. para. 352 (f), which states, "A drug or device shall be deemed to be misbranded ... unless its labeling bears (1) adequate directions for use." In addition, since the drugs were being put to a new use, they had to be reapproved by the FDA to determine if they were "safe and effective" for human execution.

The FDA commissioner refused to act, claiming serious questions as to whether the agency had jurisdiction in the area. He further noted,

Generally, enforcement proceedings in this area are initiated only when there is a serious danger to the public health or a blatant scheme to defraud. We cannot conclude that those dangers are present under State lethal injections laws, which are duly authorized statutory enactments in furtherance of proper State [goals].

The U.S. District Court for the District of Columbia disagreed with the condemned prisoners that the FDA had a responsibility to determine if the lethal mixture used during execution was safe and effective. The court noted that decisions by a federal agency not to take action were not reviewable in court.

A divided Court of Appeals for the District of Columbia reversed the lower court ruling, noting that the FDA's own policy required the FDA to investigate the unapproved use of an approved drug when such use became "widespread" or "endanger[ed] the public health." Therefore, the prisoners who risked a "cruel and protracted" death were entitled to a more thorough investigation of the drugs used in their execution.

A generally irritated U.S. Supreme Court agreed to hear the case "to review the implausible result that the FDA is required to exercise its enforcement power to ensure that States use only drugs that are 'safe and effective' for human execution."

In *Heckler v. Chaney* (470 U.S. 821, 1985), the unanimous Court agreed that, in this case, the FDA did not have jurisdiction, although Justices Brennan and Marshall indicated that the limitation on court jurisdiction should not apply to all agency decisions not to intervene. The remaining justices, however, thought the courts had no right to question an agency's decision not to take action.

Writing for all but Justices Marshall and Brennan, Justice Rehnquist explained why the majority of justices concluded that the FDA decision not to investigate the prisoners' request was simply not the high court's business:

First, an agency decision not to enforce often involves a complicated balancing of a number of factors which are peculiarly within its expertise. Thus, the agency must not only assess where a violation has occurred, but whether agency resources are best spent on this violation or another, whether the agency is likely to succeed if it acts, whether the particular enforcement action requested best fits the agency's overall policies, and indeed, whether the agency has enough resources to undertake the action at all. An agency generally cannot act against each technical violation of the statute it is charged with enforcing. The agency is better equipped than the courts to deal with the many variables involved in the proper ordering of its priorities.

Is Execution by Hanging Constitutional?

Washington state law imposes capital punishment either by "hanging by the neck" or, if the condemned chooses, by lethal injection. Charles Rodham Campbell was convicted of three counts of murder in 1982 and sentenced to death. Campbell, in challenging the constitutionality of hanging under the Washington statute, claimed that execution by hanging violated his Eighth Amendment right because it was cruel and unusual punishment. Furthermore, the direction that he be hanged unless he chose lethal injection was cruel and unusual punishment. He claimed that such instruction further violated his First Amendment right by forcing him to participate in his own execution to avoid hanging.

In *Campbell v. Wood* (18 F.3d. 662, 9th Cir. 1994), the U.S. Court of Appeals for the Ninth Circuit noted,

> We do not consider hanging to be cruel and unusual simply because it causes death, or because there may be some pain associated with death.... As used in the Constitution, "cruel" implies "something inhuman and barbarous, something more than the mere extinguishment of life." ... Campbell is entitled to an execution free only of "the unnecessary and wanton infliction of pain."

According to the Court, just because the defendant was given a choice of a method of execution did not mean that he was being subjected to cruel and unusual punishment:

> We believe that benefits to prisoners who may choose to exercise the option and who may feel relieved that they can elect lethal injection outweigh the emotional costs to those who find the mere existence of an option objectionable.

Campbell argued that the state was infringing on his First Amendment right of free exercise of his religion. He claimed that it was against his religion to participate in his own execution by being allowed to elect lethal injection over hanging.

The Court contended that Campbell did not have to choose an execution method or participate in his own execution. "He may remain absolutely silent and refuse to participate in any election." The death penalty statute does not require him to choose the method of execution; it simply offers a choice. Upon appeal (*Campbell v. Wood*, 511 U.S. 1119, 1994), the U.S. Supreme Court decided not to hear the case.

Is Execution by Lethal Gas Constitutional?

On April 17, 1992, three California death row inmates (David Fierro, Alejandro Gilbert Ruiz, and Robert Alton Harris) filed a suit on behalf of themselves and all others under sentence of execution by lethal gas. In *Fierro v. Gomez* (790 F. Supp. 966 [N.D. Cal. 1992], also referred to as *Fierro I*), the inmates alleged that California's method of execution by lethal gas violated the Eighth and Fourteenth Amendments. Harris was scheduled to be executed four days later, on April 21, 1992.

The district court prohibited James Gomez, director of the California Department of Corrections, and Arthur Calderon, warden of San Quentin Prison, from executing any inmate until a hearing was held. On appeal from Gomez and Calderon, the U.S. Court of Appeals for the Ninth Circuit vacated the district court's ruling. On his execution day Harris had filed a *habeas corpus* petition with the California Supreme Court, challenging the constitutionality of the gas chamber. The court declined to review the case, and Harris was put to death that day. In the aftermath of Harris's execution, the California legislature, in 1993, amended its death penalty statute, providing that, if lethal gas "is held invalid, the punishment of death shall be imposed by the alternative means," lethal injection.

In October 1994 a federal district judge, Marilyn Hall Patel, ruled that execution by lethal gas "is inhumane and has no place in civilized society" (865 F. Supp. at 1415; also referred to as *Fierro II*). She then ordered California's gas chamber closed and that lethal injection be used instead. This was the first time a federal judge had ruled that any method of execution violated the Eighth and Fourteenth Amendments. While the state of California maintained that cyanide gas caused almost instant unconsciousness, the judge referred to doctors' reports and witnesses' accounts of gas chamber executions, which indicated that the dying inmates stayed conscious for 15 seconds to a minute or longer and suffered "intense physical pain."

Gomez and Calderon appealed Judge Patel's ruling on the unconstitutionality of the gas chamber before the U.S. Court of Appeals for the Ninth Circuit. They also appealed the permanent injunction against the use of lethal gas as a method of execution. In February 1996, in *Fierro v. Gomez* (77 F.3d. 301, 9th Cir.), the appellate court affirmed Judge Patel's ruling.

Gomez and Calderon appealed the case to the U.S. Supreme Court. In October 1996 the 7–2 Supreme Court, in *Gomez v. Fierro* (519 U.S. 918), vacated the appellate court's ruling and returned the case to the appellate court for additional proceedings, citing the death penalty statute amended in 1993 (lethal injection as an alternative to lethal gas).

Does Electrocution Constitute a Cruel and Unusual Punishment?

In the 1990s, although Florida had three botched executions using the electric chair, the state supreme court ruled each time that electrocution does not constitute cruel or unusual punishment. In 1990 and 1997 flames shot out from the headpiece worn by the condemned man. On July 8, 1999, Allen Lee Davis developed a nosebleed during his execution in the electric chair.

Thomas Provenzano, scheduled to be electrocuted after Davis, challenged the use of the electric chair as Florida's sole method of execution. In *Provenzano v. Moore* (No. 95,973, September 24, 1999), the Florida

Supreme Court, in a 4–3 decision, ruled that the electric chair was not cruel and unusual punishment. The court further reported that Davis's nosebleed occurred prior to the execution and did not result from the electrocution.

Subsequently, the court, as it routinely does with all its rulings, posted the *Provenzano* decision on the Internet. Three photographs of Davis, covered with blood, were posted as part of Justice Leander Shaw's dissenting opinion. The photographs brought public outcry worldwide. Justice Shaw claimed that Davis was "brutally tortured to death."

In October 1999, for the first time, the U.S. Supreme Court agreed to consider the constitutionality of electrocution. Death row inmate Anthony Braden Bryan asked the U.S. Supreme Court to review his case, based on the unreliability of the electric chair. Before the high court could hear the case, however, the Florida legislature, in a special session, voted to replace electrocution with lethal injection as the primary method of execution, but allowing a condemned person to choose the electric chair as an alternative.

On January 24, 2000, the Supreme Court dismissed *Bryan v. Moore* (No. 99-6723) as moot, or irrelevant, based on Florida's new legislation. Governor Jeb Bush agreed to sign the bill in conjunction with a second bill that limits, in most cases, death row inmates to two appeals in state courts, with the second appeal to be filed within six months of the first. This provision cut in half the time limit for the second appeal.

In 2001 the Georgia Supreme Court became the first appellate court to rule a method of execution unconstitutional. On October 5 the court held that electrocution was cruel and unusual punishment in violation of the state constitution. Voting 4–3 in two consolidated cases (*Dawson v. State,* S01A1041, and *Moore v. State,* S01A1210), the majority stated,

> The United States Supreme Court has recognized that punishment is cruel and unusual when it unnecessarily involves "something more than the mere extinguishment of life." *In re Kemmler,* 136 U.S. 436, 446 (1890).... [W]e conclude that death by electrocution ... "inflicts purposeless physical violence and needless mutilation that makes no measurable contribution to accepted goals of punishment." *Fleming v. Zant,* supra, 259 Ga. at 689 (3).

Justice Hugh P. Thompson, joined by Justices George H. Carley and P. Harris Hines, dissented. The justices observed that courts are supposed to interpret the laws, not make them, which was what the majority did when it decided that lethal injection will be the method of execution for the state of Georgia. The justices added,

> However tempted, however much they may dislike a law, courts should not use judicial powers to transform their preferences into constitutional mandates. Because today's decision reflects not the evolving standards of decency of the people of Georgia, but the evolving opinions of the majority members of this Court, I dissent.

In 2000 the Georgia legislature had passed a law making lethal injection the sole method of execution. Prior to the state supreme court ruling in October 2001, that law applied only to those sentenced after May 1, 2000. As of November 30, 2003, Nebraska was the only state left that authorized electrocution as the sole means of execution. On July 1, 2002, Alabama, which used electrocution as the primary method of execution, replaced it with lethal injection. However, an inmate in that state may request electrocution.

CHALLENGING THE ANTITERRORISM ACT OF 1996

The Antiterrorism and Effective Death Penalty Act (AEDPA; Public Law 104-132) became law on April 24, 1996, around the first anniversary of the Oklahoma City bombing. AEDPA aims in part to "deter terrorism, provide justice for victims, and provide for an effective death penalty." After passage of the law the lower courts differed in their interpretations of certain core provisions. For the first time, on October 18, 2000, the U.S. Supreme Court addressed these problems. Note that the defendants in the two cases share the same last name.

Federal *Habeas Corpus* Relief and the AEDPA

The AEDPA restricts the power of federal courts to grant *habeas corpus* relief to state inmates. Through the writ of *habeas corpus,* an inmate could have a federal court review his or her conviction or sentencing. The AEDPA bars a federal court from granting an application for a writ of *habeas corpus* unless the state court's decision "was contrary to, or involved an unreasonable application of, clearly established federal law, as determined by the Supreme Court of the United States."

In 1986 Terry Williams, while incarcerated in a Danville, Virginia, city jail, wrote to police that he had killed two people and that he was sorry for his acts. He also confessed to stealing money from one of the victims. He was subsequently convicted of robbery and capital murder.

During the sentencing hearing the prosecutor presented numerous crimes Williams had committed in addition to the murder for which he was convicted. Two state witnesses also testified to the defendant's future dangerousness.

Williams's lawyer, however, called on his mother to testify to his being a nonviolent person. The defense also played a taped portion of a psychiatrist's statement, saying that Williams told the psychiatrist he had removed bullets from a gun used during robbery so as not to harm anyone. During his closing statement, however, the lawyer noted that the jury would probably find it hard to give his client mercy because he did not show mercy to his victims. The jury sentenced Williams to death, and the trial judge imposed the sentence.

Williams appealed to the Virginia Supreme Court, claiming that the trial judge did not consider the mitigating factor that he had turned himself in. The court refused to review the case, affirming the conviction and sentence.

In 1988 Williams filed a state *habeas corpus* petition. The Danville Circuit Court found Williams's conviction valid. The court found, however, that the defense lawyer's failure to present several mitigating factors at the sentencing phase violated Williams's right to effective assistance of counsel as prescribed by *Strickland v. Washington* (466 U.S. 668, 1984). The mitigating circumstances included early childhood abuse and borderline mental retardation. The *habeas corpus* hearing further revealed that the state expert witnesses had testified that if Williams were kept in a "structured environment," he would not be a threat to society. The circuit court recommended a new sentencing hearing.

While Williams's petition was pending, a new state law gave the Virginia Supreme Court the exclusive power to grant *habeas corpus* review. In 1997 the state supreme court rejected the district court's recommendation for a new sentencing hearing, concluding that the omitted evidence would not have affected the sentence.

Next, Williams filed a federal *habeas corpus* petition. The federal trial judge ruled not only that the death sentence was "constitutionally infirm" but that defense counsel was ineffective. The Fourth Circuit Court of Appeals, however, reversed the federal trial judge's decision, holding that the AEDPA prohibits a federal court from granting *habeas corpus* relief unless the state courts "decided the question by interpreting or applying the relevant precedent in a manner that reasonable jurists would all agree is unreasonable."

On April 18, 2000, the U.S. Supreme Court, in *(Terry) Williams v. Taylor* (529 U.S. 362, 2000), reversed the Fourth Circuit Court's ruling by a 6–3 decision. The Court concluded that the Virginia Supreme Court's decision rejecting Williams's claim of ineffective assistance was contrary to a Supreme Court established precedent (*Strickland v. Washington*), as well as an unreasonable application of that precedent. This was the first time the Supreme Court had granted relief on such a claim.

On November 14, 2000, during a court hearing Terry Williams accepted a plea agreement of a life sentence without parole after prosecutors agreed not to seek the death penalty again.

Federal Evidentiary Hearings for Constitutional Claims

Under an AEDPA provision, if the petitioner has failed to develop the facts of his or her challenges of a constitutional claim in state court proceedings, the federal court shall not hold an evidentiary hearing on the claim unless the facts involve an exception listed by the AEDPA.

In 1993, after robbing the home of Morris Keller Jr. and his wife, Mary Elizabeth, Michael Wayne Williams and his friend Jeffrey Alan Cruse raped the woman and then killed the couple. In exchange for the state's promise not to seek capital punishment, Cruse described details of the crimes. Williams received the death sentence for the capital murders. The prosecution told the jury about the plea agreement with Cruse. The state later revoked the plea agreement after discovering that Cruse had also raped the wife and failed to disclose it. After Cruse's court testimony against Williams, however, the state gave Cruse a life sentence, which Williams alleged amounted to a second, informal plea agreement.

Williams filed a *habeas* petition in state court, claiming he was not told of the second plea agreement between the state and his codefendant. The Virginia Supreme Court dismissed the petition (1994), and the U.S. Supreme Court refused to review the case (1995).

In 1996, upon appeal, a federal district court agreed to an evidentiary hearing of Williams's claims of the undisclosed second plea agreement. The defendant had also claimed that a psychiatric report about Cruse, which was not revealed by prosecution, could have shown that Cruse was not credible. Moreover, a certain juror might have had possible bias, which the prosecution failed to disclose. Before the hearing could be held, the state concluded that the AEDPA prohibited such a hearing. Consequently, the federal district court dismissed Williams's petition.

When the case was brought before the U.S. Court of Appeals for the Fourth Circuit, the court, interpreting the AEDPA, concluded that the defendant had failed to develop the facts of his claims. On April 18, 2000, in *(Michael) Williams v. Taylor* (529 U.S. 420), a unanimous U.S. Supreme Court did not address Williams's claim of the undisclosed plea agreement between Cruse and the state. Instead, the high court held that the defendant was entitled to a federal district court evidentiary hearing regarding his other claims. According to the Court,

> Under the [AEDPA], a failure to develop the factual basis of a claim is not established unless there is lack of diligence, or some greater fault, attributable to the prisoner or the prisoner's counsel. We conclude petitioner has met the burden of showing he was diligent in efforts to develop the facts supporting his juror bias and prosecutorial misconduct claims in collateral proceedings before the Virginia Supreme Court.

High Court Upholds Restriction on Federal Appeals

Although the Supreme Court ruled in favor of new resentencing hearings for Terry Williams and Michael Williams, it stressed that the AEDPA places a new restriction on federal courts with respect to granting *habeas* relief to state inmates. The court noted,

> ... Under [the AEDPA], the writ may issue only if one of the following two conditions is satisfied—the state-court adjudication resulted in a decision that (1) "was contrary to ... clearly established Federal law, as determined by the Supreme Court of the United States," or (2) "involved an unreasonable application of ... clearly established Federal law, as determined by the Supreme Court of the United States." Under the "contrary to" clause, a federal *habeas* court may grant the writ if the state court arrives at a conclusion opposite to that reached by this Court on a question of law or if the state court decides a case differently than this Court has on a set of materially indistinguishable facts. Under the "unreasonable application" clause, a federal *habeas* court may grant the writ if the state court identifies the correct governing legal principle from this Court's decisions but unreasonably applies that principle to the facts of the prisoner's case.

CHAPTER 5
DEATH PENALTY STATUTES AND METHODS

CAPITAL OFFENSES

Most death penalty statutes in force prior to the *Furman v. Georgia* (408 U.S. 238) decision of June 29, 1972, provided for the imposition of the death penalty for capital murder and, in some states, for other crimes. In *Furman,* however, the U.S. Supreme Court found that the death penalty, as then being administered, was cruel and unusual punishment in violation of the Eighth Amendment to the U.S. Constitution. Many states revised their laws to conform to standards set by the *Furman* decision. Since *Furman,* review of individual state statutes has continued as appeals of capital sentences reach state courts or the U.S. Supreme Court.

Under revised state laws, different types of capital murder have been specifically defined. Although varying somewhat from one jurisdiction to another, the types of homicide most commonly specified are murder carried out during the commission of a felony (serious offense such as rape, robbery, or arson); murder of a peace officer, corrections employee, or firefighter engaged in the performance of official duties; murder by an inmate serving a life sentence; and murder for hire (contract murder). Different statutory terminology may be used by different states to designate basically identical crimes. In some states, such terms as "capital murder," "first-degree murder," "capital felony," or "murder Class 1 felony" may indicate the same capital offense. At year-end 2002 the death penalty was authorized for certain cases of homicide by the statutes of 38 states (See Table 5.1.) and by the federal government (See Table 5.2.).

While other offenses (most notably, treason and air piracy, or hijacking) also carry the death penalty, most have not yet had their constitutionality tested. The U.S. Supreme Court has held, in *Coker v. Georgia* (433 U.S. 584, 1977) and *Eberheart v. Georgia* (433 U.S. 917, 1977), that rape and kidnapping, as horrible as they are, do not result in death and, therefore, do not warrant the death penalty. Nonetheless, in 1995 the Louisiana legislature

amended statute La. R.S. 14:42(C) to allow for the death penalty when the victim of rape is less than 12 years old.

STATUTORY CHANGES

As of November 30, 2003, no state enacted new legislation authorizing capital punishment. As in the past, states continued to revise their statutory provisions relating to the death penalty.

In the aftermath of the September 11, 2001, attacks on the World Trade Center and the Pentagon, several states, both death penalty and non-death penalty states, expanded their laws. Among states that impose the death penalty, in 2001, New York, Florida, and North Carolina amended their death penalty statutes, making murder committed in furtherance of a terrorist act a capital crime. In 2002, 10 more states—Georgia, Idaho, New Jersey, Ohio, Oklahoma, South Carolina, South Dakota, Tennessee, Utah, and Virginia—added murder committed in the perpetration of terrorism punishable by death.

Some of the statutory changes in 2001 involved the addition of aggravating circumstances that made an offender death-eligible. Arkansas added to its aggravating circumstances the murder of a child age 12 or under. Connecticut added murder committed to avoid arrest or prosecution as an aggravating factor. Wyoming added as an aggravating circumstance the fact that the murder is that of an officer of the law or of an officer of the court, including "a judicial officer, former judicial officer, district attorney, former district attorney, defending attorney, peace officer, juror or witness, during or because of the exercise of his official duty or because of the victim's former or present official status."

In 2002 South Carolina added to its aggravating circumstances for death penalty eligibility the murder of a current or former law enforcement officer, peace officer, corrections officer, or fireman during or because of the

TABLE 5.1

Capital offenses, by state, 2002

Alabama. Intentional murder with 18 aggravating factors (Ala. Stat. Ann. 13A-5-40(a)(1)-(18)).
Arizona*. First-degree murder accompanied by at least 1 of 10 aggravating factors (A.R.S 13-703(F)).
Arkansas*. Capital murder (Ark. Code Ann. 5-10-101) with a finding of at least 1 of 10 aggravating circumstances; treason.
California. First-degree murder with special circumstances; train wrecking; treason; perjury causing execution.
Colorado*. First-degree murder with at least 1 of 15 aggravating factors; treason.
Connecticut*. Capital felony with 8 forms of aggravated homicide (C.G.S. 53a-54b).
Delaware*. First-degree murder with aggravating circumstances.
Florida*. First-degree murder; felony murder; capital drug trafficking; capital sexual battery.
Georgia*. Murder; kidnaping with bodily injury or ransom when the victim dies; aircraft hijacking; treason.
Idaho. First-degree murder with aggravating factors; aggravated kidnaping.
Illinois. First-degree murder with 1 of 15 aggravating circumstances.
Indiana*. Murder with 16 aggravating circumstances (IC 35-50-2-9).
Kansas*. Capital murder with 8 aggravating circumstances (KSA 21-3439).
Kentucky*. Murder with aggravating factors; kidnaping with aggravating factors (KRS 532.025).
Louisiana. First-degree murder; aggravated rape of victim under age 12; treason (La. R.S. 14:30, 14:42, and 14:113).
Maryland*. First-degree murder, either premeditated or during the commission of a felony, provided that certain death eligibility requirements are satisfied.
Mississippi. Capital murder (97-3-19(2) MCA); aircraft piracy (97-25-55(1) MCA).
Missouri*. First-degree murder (565.020 RSMO 1994).
Montana. Capital murder with 1 of 9 aggravating circumstances (46-18-303 MCA); capital sexual assault (45-5-503 MCA).
Nebraska*. First-degree murder with a finding of at least 1 statutorily-defined aggravating circumstance.
Nevada. First-degree murder with at least 1 of 14 aggravating circumstances (NRS 200.030, 200.033, 200.035).
New Hampshire. Six categories of capital murder (RSA 630:1, RSA 630:5).
New Jersey. Knowing/purposeful murder by one's own conduct; contract murder; solicitation by command or threat in furtherance of a narcotics conspiracy (NJSA 2C:11-3C).
New Mexico*. First-degree murder with at least 1 of 7 statutorily-defined aggravating circumstances (Section 30-2-1 A, NMSA).
New York*. First-degree murder with 1 of 12 aggravating factors (NY Penal Law §125.27).
North Carolina*. First-degree murder (NCGS §14-17).
Ohio. Aggravated murder with at least 1 of 9 aggravating circumstances (O.R.C. secs. 2903.01, 2929.02, and 2929.04).
Oklahoma. First-degree murder in conjunction with a finding of at least 1 of 8 statutorily defined aggravating circumstances.
Oregon. Aggravated murder (ORS 163.095).
Pennsylvania. First-degree murder with 18 aggravating circumstances.
South Carolina*. Murder with 1 of 10 aggravating circumstances (§ 16-3-20(C)(a)).
South Dakota*. First-degree murder with 1of 10 aggravating circumstances; aggravated kidnaping.
Tennessee*. First-degree murder with 1 of 15 aggravating circumstances (Tenn. Code Ann. § 39-13-204).
Texas. Criminal homicide with 1 of 8 aggravating circumstances (TX Penal Code 19.03).
Utah*. Aggravated murder (76-5-202, Utah Code Annotated).
Virginia. First-degree murder with 1 of 13 aggravating circumstances (VA Code § 18.2-31).
Washington*. Aggravated first-degree murder.
Wyoming. First-degree murder.

*Nineteen states excluded mentally retarded persons from capital sentencing as of December 31, 2002: Arizona, Arkansas, Colorado, Connecticut, Delaware, Florida, Georgia, Indiana, Kansas, Kentucky, Maryland, Missouri, Nebraska, New Mexico, New York, North Carolina, South Dakota, Tennessee, and Washington. Mental retardation is a mitigating factor in South Carolina and Utah.

SOURCE: Thomas P. Bonczar and Tracy L. Snell, "Table 1. Capital offenses, by State, 2002," in *Capital Punishment, 2002*, U.S. Department of Justice, Bureau of Justice Statistics, Washington, DC, November 2003

performance of his official duties. Indiana passed legislation banning the execution of inmates who were under age 18 at the time of the crime.

In 2001 just two states—Alabama and Nebraska—authorized electrocution as the sole method of execution. In 2002 Alabama amended its capital statute, authorizing lethal injection as the primary means of execution, although an inmate may request electrocution.

In light of the U.S. Supreme Court ruling in *Ring v. Arizona* (536 U.S. 584) in 2002, seven states—Arizona, Colorado, Delaware, Idaho, Indiana, Montana, and Nebraska—revised their capital statute to allow for jury determination of a death sentence. In March 2002 Indiana revised its capital statute, raising the minimum age for death penalty eligibility from 16 to 18 years.

CHALLENGES TO STATE DEATH PENALTY LAWS

Louisiana

In August 1995 Louisiana became the first state to allow the death penalty for rape when the victims are under age 12. In December 1995 Anthony Wilson was charged by a grand jury with the aggravated rape of a five-year-old girl. (A grand jury differs from a regular jury in that the former, typically consisting of up to 23 jurors determines whether the criminal complaint brought by the prosecutor warrants an indictment, and eventually a trial.) Patrick Dwayne Bethley was charged with raping three girls, one of whom was his daughter. At the time of the rape, the girls were five, seven, and nine years old. The two defendants moved to quash their indictments. They claimed that the death penalty, when imposed for rape, constitutes "cruel and unusual punishment" and, therefore, is unconstitutional under the Eighth Amendment and Article I, Section 20, of the Louisiana Constitution. On December 13, 1996, the Louisiana Supreme Court, in *State v. Wilson* (685 So.2d 1063), held by a 5–2 vote that the state death penalty statute was constitutional. The Louisiana Supreme Court concluded,

Given the appalling nature of the crime, the severity of the harm inflicted upon the victim, and the harm imposed on society, the death penalty is not an

TABLE 5.2

Federal laws providing for the death penalty, 2002

8 U.S.C. 1342 — Murder related to the smuggling of aliens.
18 U.S.C. 32-34 — Destruction of aircraft, motor vehicles, or related facilities resulting in death.
18 U.S.C. 36 — Murder committed during a drug-related drive-by shooting.
18 U.S.C. 37 — Murder committed at an airport serving international civil aviation.
18 U.S.C. 115(b)(3) [by cross-reference to 18 U.S.C. 1111] — Retaliatory murder of a member of the immediate family of law enforcement officials.
18 U.S.C. 241, 242, 245, 247 — Civil rights offenses resulting in death.
18 U.S.C. 351 [by cross-reference to 18 U.S.C. 1111] — Murder of a member of Congress, an important executive official, or a Supreme Court Justice.
18 U.S.C. 794 — Espionage.
18 U.S.C. 844(d), (f), (i) — Death resulting from offenses involving transportation of explosives, destruction of government property, or destruction of property related to foreign or interstate commerce.
18 U.S.C. 924(i) — Murder committed by the use of a firearm during a crime of violence or a drug-trafficking crime.
18 U.S.C. 930 — Murder committed in a federal government facility.
18 U.S.C. 1091 — Genocide.
18 U.S.C. 1111 — First-degree murder.
18 U.S.C. 1114 — Murder of a federal judge or law enforcement official.
18 U.S.C. 1116 — Murder of a foreign official.
18 U.S.C. 1118 — Murder by a federal prisoner.
18 U.S.C. 1119 — Murder of a U.S. national in a foreign country.
18 U.S.C. 1120 — Murder by an escaped federal prisoner already sentenced to life imprisonment.
18 U.S.C. 1121 — Murder of a state or local law enforcement official or other person aiding in a federal investigation; murder of a state correctional officer.
18 U.S.C. 1201 — Murder during a kidnaping.
18 U.S.C. 1203 — Murder during a hostage taking.
18 U.S.C. 1503 — Murder of a court officer or juror.
18 U.S.C. 1512 — Murder with the intent of preventing testimony by a witness, victim, or informant.
18 U.S.C. 1513 — Retaliatory murder of a witness, victim, or informant.
18 U.S.C. 1716 — Mailing of injurious articles with intent to kill or resulting in death.
18 U.S.C. 1751 [by cross-reference to 18 U.S.C. 1111] — Assassination or kidnaping resulting in the death of the president or vice president.
18 U.S.C. 1958 — Murder for hire.
18 U.S.C. 1959 — Murder involved in a racketeering offense.
18 U.S.C. 1992 — Willful wrecking of a train resulting in death.
18 U.S.C. 2113 — Bank-robbery-related murder or kidnaping.
18 U.S.C. 2119 — Murder related to a carjacking.
18 U.S.C. 2245 — Murder related to rape or child molestation.
18 U.S.C. 2251 — Murder related to sexual exploitation of children.
18 U.S.C. 2280 — Murder committed during an offense against maritime navigation.
18 U.S.C. 2281 — Murder committed during an offense against a maritime fixed platform.
18 U.S.C. 2332 — Terrorist murder of a U.S. national in another country.
18 U.S.C. 2332a — Murder by the use of a weapon of mass destruction.
18 U.S.C. 2340 — Murder involving torture.
18 U.S.C. 2381 — Treason.
21 U.S.C. 848(e) — Murder related to a continuing criminal enterprise or related murder of a federal, state, or local law enforcement officer.
49 U.S.C. 1472-1473 — Death resulting from aircraft hijacking.

Note: Items above include references to the United States Code (U.S.C.).

SOURCE: Thomas P. Bonczar and Tracy L. Snell, "Appendix table 1. Federal laws providing for the death penalty, 2002," in *Capital Punishment, 2002,* U.S. Department of Justice, Bureau of Justice Statistics, Washington, DC, November 2003

excessive penalty for the crime of rape when the victim is a child under the age of twelve years old.

In 1998 Bethley entered into a plea agreement with prosecutors in which he received a life sentence for rape. In turn, the state of Louisiana did not seek the death penalty against him. In 1999, upon appeal, Wilson was found mentally retarded and, therefore, unable to assist in his defense.

In August 2002, for the first time in Louisiana, a jury imposed the death penalty for the rape of a child. Patrick O. Kennedy had been convicted of repeatedly raping his eight-year-old stepdaughter in 1998. Some experts believe Kennedy's case might be heard by the U.S. Supreme Court because the Court's decision in *Coker v. Georgia* (433 U.S. 584, 1977) addressed only the rape of an adult woman. Others observe that, partly in light of the growing number of Catholic priests found guilty of abusing children, states might pursue such cases more vehemently.

New York

Until 1998 New York's death penalty statute prohibited the imposition of a death sentence when a defendant entered a guilty plea. However, a defendant who pleaded not guilty would have to stand trial and face the possibility of a death sentence. The maximum penalty in the first case would be life imprisonment without parole. In other words, the law provided two levels of penalty for the same offense, imposing the death penalty only on those who claimed innocence.

Defendants in two capital cases challenged the plea provisions of New York's death penalty statute, claiming these provisions violated their Fifth Amendment right against self-incrimination and Sixth Amendment right to a jury trial. This was the first major constitutional challenge to New York's death penalty law. On December 22, 1998, the New York Court of Appeals, in *Hynes v. Tomei* (including *Relin v.*

Mateo, 92 N.Y. 2d. 613, 706 N.E. 2d. 1201, 684 N.Y.S. 2d. 177), unanimously agreed, striking down these plea-bargaining provisions as unconstitutional. The court, relying on the U.S. Supreme Court decision in *United States v. Jackson* (390 U.S. 570, 1968), observed that "the Supreme Court in *Jackson* prohibited statutes that 'needlessly' encourage guilty pleas, which are not constitutionally protected, by impermissibly burdening constitutional rights."

MINIMUM AGE FOR EXECUTION

Under state laws, the term *juvenile* refers to persons below the age of 18. Literature on the death penalty typically considers "juvenile offenders" as persons younger than 18 at the time of their crimes. Professor Victor L. Streib traced the first execution of a juvenile, Thomas Graunger, to Plymouth Colony, Massachusetts, in 1642 (*The Juvenile Death Penalty Today: Death Sentences and Executions for Juvenile Crimes, January 1, 1973–September 30, 2003,* Ohio Northern University, Claude W. Pettit College of Law, Ada, OH, October 6, 2003). Professor Streib reported that the United States has since executed an estimated 366 persons (as of September 30, 2003) who were juveniles during the commission of the crime. Inmates spent from 6 years to more than 20 years on death row prior to execution.

According to Professor Streib, in the modern death penalty era (1973–2003), 22 inmates who were juveniles at the time of their crimes had been executed. Texas implemented the death penalty of 13 juvenile offenders, followed by Virginia (3) and Oklahoma (2). Georgia, Louisiana, Missouri, and South Carolina each executed one juvenile offender.

In February 1999, for the first time in 40 years, the United States executed an offender who was 16 when he committed his crime. Sean Sellers of Oklahoma was 29 years old at the time of execution. He was convicted for the murders of his mother, stepfather, and a convenience-store clerk. His supporters claimed Sellers suffered from multiple personality disorder, which was diagnosed after his conviction. The last execution of a person who was 16 at the time of his crime occurred on April 10, 1959, when Maryland executed Leonard Shockley.

As of September 30, 2003, 17 states and the federal government (including the military courts) required that a person had to be at least 18 years old to receive the death sentence. Five states specified 17 as the minimum age for the death penalty, while 16 states designated a minimum age of 16. Of these 16 states, 5 states had the minimum age requirement in their statutes, and the remaining 11 states followed court decisions. (See Table 5.3.)

EXECUTING MENTALLY RETARDED PERSONS

In 1989 the U.S. Supreme Court held, in *Penry v. Lynaugh* (492 U.S. 302), that it was not unconstitutional

TABLE 5.3

Minimum death penalty ages, by jurisdiction, as of September 30, 2003

Age eighteen		Age seventeen	Age sixteen	
California[1]	New Jersey[1]	Florida[2]	Alabama[1]	Nevada[1]
Colorado[1]	New Mexico[1]	Georgia[1]	Arizona[2]	Oklahoma[2]
Connecticut[1]	New York[1]	New Hampshire[1]	Arkansas[2]	Pennsylvania[2]
Illinois[1]	Ohio[1]	North Carolina[1]	Delaware[2]	South Carolina[2]
Indiana[1]	Oregon[1]	Texas[1]	Idaho[2]	South Dakota[2]
Kansas[1]	Tennessee[1]		Kentucky[1]	Utah[2]
Maryland[1]	Washington[1]	5 states	Louisiana[2]	Virginia[1]
Missouri[2]	Federal civilian[1]		Mississippi[2]	Wyoming[1]
Montana[1]	Federal military[1]			
Nebraska[1]			16 states	

17 states and 2 federal jurisdictions

[1]Express minimum age in statute
[2]Minimum age required state or federal court decision.

SOURCE: Victor L. Streib, "Table 3: Minimum Death Penalty Ages by Jurisdiction as of September 30, 2003," in *The Juvenile Death Penalty Today: Death Sentences and Executions for Juvenile Crimes, January 1, 1973–September 30, 2003,* Ohio Northern University, The Claude W. Pettit College of Law, Ada, OH, October 6, 2003 [Online] http://www.law.onu.edu/faculty/streib/JuvDeathSept2003.pdf [accessed October 17, 2003]. Reproduced with permission.

to execute a mentally retarded person found guilty of a capital crime. According to the Court, there was no emerging national consensus against such execution. Just two death-penalty states—Georgia and Maryland—banned putting mentally retarded persons to death. In 1988 Georgia became the first state to prohibit the execution of murderers found "guilty but mentally retarded." The legislation resulted from the 1986 execution of Jerome Bowden, who had an IQ (intelligence quotient) of 65. It is generally accepted that an IQ below 70 is evidence of mental retardation. (Normal IQ is considered 90 and above). In 1988 Maryland passed similar legislation, which took effect in July 1989.

Between 1989 and 2001, 18 states outlawed the execution of offenders with mental retardation. The federal government also forbids the execution of mentally retarded inmates. In the Anti-Drug Abuse Act of 1988 (Public Law 100-690), the government permits the death penalty for any person working "in furtherance of a continuing criminal enterprise or any person engaging in a drug-related felony offense, who intentionally kills or counsels, commands, or causes the intentional killing of an individual," but forbids the imposition of the death penalty against anyone who is mentally retarded who commits such a crime. In 1994, when Congress enacted the Federal Death Penalty Act (Public Law 103-322), adding more than 50 crimes punishable by death, it also exempted persons with mental retardation from the death sentence.

In March 2001 the U.S. Supreme Court agreed to review the case of North Carolina death row inmate Ernest McCarver to consider whether it is cruel and

The Oklahoma statute puts no limit on the number of immediate family members who may view the execution. Each family member has to be 18 years or older and may be "the spouse, a child by birth or adoption, a stepchild, a parent, a grandparent, or a sibling of the deceased victim." The family views the execution in an area separate from the other witnesses. If a separate room for direct viewing is not available, a closed-circuit television is provided. However, in Delaware and Louisiana, only a single family member or representative is allowed to attend the execution.

Six other states—Florida, Illinois, Montana, Texas, Utah, and Virginia—allow victims' families to be present at executions by policy. Only one state, New Jersey, prohibits "any person who is related by either blood or marriage to the sentenced person or to the victim to be present at the execution."

Televising Executions

Timothy McVeigh was sentenced to die in 2001 for the bombing of the federal building in Oklahoma City that killed 168 people in 1995. In April 2001 the Gallup Organization polled the American public, asking if they thought the execution of Timothy McVeigh (initially set for May 16, 2001) should be televised. Of those polled, 43 percent indicated that they thought it should not be televised at all, and 39 percent thought it should be televised only on closed-circuit television for the victims' families to watch. Very few people indicated that they thought the execution should be televised for the general public—only 17 percent.

The poll also asked if Americans would watch McVeigh's execution if it were nationally televised. Three-quarters (76 percent) of the respondents said they would not watch, while nearly one-quarter (23 percent) indicated they would watch. When asked, however, if they would watch if a family member had been a victim of the bombing, an additional 21 percent (for a total of 44 percent) said they would watch. Over half (52 percent) of the people indicated they would not watch the televised execution under any circumstance. Of those polled, more men (52 percent) than women (37 percent) said they would watch the execution.

McVeigh's death sentence raised the question of how the prison facility would accommodate the hundreds of victims' relatives who would wish to witness the execution. The Justice Department reported that 232 survivors and family members would view the execution. On June 11, 2001, the day of the execution, 10 survivors of the bombing and members of victims' families chosen by lottery watched McVeigh die in Terre Haute, Indiana, behind tinted glass, unseen by the condemned. In addition, 10 journalists, four people selected by McVeigh, and several government officials witnessed the execution. Survivors and family members of the victims not chosen by lottery

were allowed to witness the execution on closed-circuit television in a federal prison in Oklahoma City.

Does Witnessing an Execution Bring Closure?

Some family members of murder victims feel that witnessing the death of their loved ones' murderers has helped bring closure to their tragedy. In August 1996 State Senator Brooks Douglass (R-OK) witnessed the execution of Steven Hatch, one of the men who killed his parents, raped his sister, and shot him in the back in 1979. Douglass wrote the state law allowing family members of victims to be present at executions. After Hatch's execution, Senator Douglass stated, "It wasn't revenge; it wasn't retribution. But for the first time since I was 16, I felt some closure. I felt like I had finally put the past behind me. I know it was the right thing." The second person (Glen Ake) convicted for Douglass's parents' murder is serving a life sentence. The Supreme Court, in *Ake v. Oklahoma* (470 U.S. 68, 1985), overturned the man's conviction. He received two life sentences on retrial.

Witnessing the execution of the condemned, however, does not necessarily bring closure. The mother of Baylee Almon, the one-year-old infant who, pictured dead in the arms of a firefighter, became a symbol of the Oklahoma City tragedy, admitted she did not believe McVeigh's execution would ever bring closure.

Some victims' families would like to experience a measure of closure. In 2002 the U.S. Supreme Court ruled in *Ring v. Arizona* (536 U.S. 5842) that a jury, not a judge, should determine whether a defendant lives or dies. This decision potentially affected the fate of death row inmates in nine states. Some experts noted that resentencing of many cases might occur. Victims' families claimed they had waited too long for closure and now the justice system had taken that away from them.

In November 2003 a Virginia jury imposed the death sentence on John Allen Muhammad, one of the D.C.-area snipers, for the shooting death of Dean Harold Meyers while the victim was refueling at a gas station more than a year ago. After the verdict, Bob Meyers, Dean's brother, told reporters: "Certainly, this is a huge step in the pursuit of closure, but I would really doubt that full closure ever comes because there's always an open wound that remains."

Media Witnesses

Up until 1936, when California used hanging as a method of execution, witnesses could watch the execution from the moment the inmate ascended the gallows to the time the trapdoor fell. When lethal gas replaced hanging in 1937, witnesses viewed the execution from the time the inmate was escorted into the gas chamber until death was pronounced.

On February 23, 1996, William Bonin became the first person in California to be executed by lethal

---

TABLE 5.4

Death penalty states that have enacted laws banning the execution of mentally retarded offenders, 2002

Year of enactment	States
1988	Georgia, Maryland
1990	Kentucky, Tennessee
1991	New Mexico
1993	Arkansas, Colorado, Washington
1994	Indiana, Kansas
1995	New York
1998	Nebraska
2000	South Dakota
2001	Arizona, Connecticut, Florida, Missouri, North Carolina
2002	Delaware, Idaho, Louisiana, Nevada, Utah, Virginia

SOURCE: Table constructed by Gale Group staff from information in U.S. Supreme Court case *Atkins v. Virginia* (536 U.S. 304, 2002) and state death penalty statutes

unusual, and therefore, unconstitutional, to execute inmates with mental retardation. The passage of a bill banning the execution of inmates with mental retardation, however, had rendered that case moot.

On June 20, 2002, the U.S. Supreme Court finally ruled on a case involving the execution of mentally retarded persons. In *Atkins v. Virginia* (536 U.S. 304), the Court ruled 6–3 that executing the mentally retarded violates the Eighth Amendment ban against cruel and unusual punishment. Since the *Atkins* ruling, six more states—Delaware, Idaho, Louisiana, Nevada, Utah, and Virginia—passed legislation banning such execution. (See Table 5.4.) The Supreme Court did not say what mental retardation consists of and left it to the states to set their own definitions.

DEATH PENALTY METHODS

The Eighth Amendment of the U.S. Bill of Rights, using the language of the English Bill of Rights of 1689, prohibits the use of "cruel and unusual punishment" in carrying out an execution. Although one person was pressed to death (made to lie down, facing up, and have heavy weights put on the chest until the person died) during the Salem witchcraft trials, and some rebellious blacks were burned at the stake during the early 1700s, these were exceptional cases.

For the most part, neither the colonies nor the United States ever used excessively brutal methods of execution, such as drawing and quartering, burying alive, boiling in oil, sawing in half, or crucifixion. Throughout most of the 19th century civilians sentenced to death were hanged, while the military usually shot spies, traitors, and deserters.

The federal government currently authorizes the method of execution under two different laws. Crimes prosecuted under 28 Code of Federal Regulations (CFR), Part 26, call for execution by lethal injection, while offenses covered by the Violent Crime Control and Law

---

TABLE 5.5

Method of execution, by state, 2002

Lethal injection		Electrocution	Lethal gas
Alabama	Nevada	Alabama[1]	Arizona[1,2]
Arizona[2]	New Hampshire[1]	Arkansas[1,3]	California[1]
Arkansas[1,3]	New Jersey	Florida[1]	Missouri[1]
California[1]	New Mexico	Kentucky[1,4]	Wyoming[1,5]
Colorado	New York	Nebraska	
Connecticut	North Carolina	Oklahoma[6]	
Delaware[1,7]	Ohio	South Carolina[1]	
Florida[1]	Oklahoma[1]	Tennessee[1,8]	
Georgia	Oregon	Virginia[1]	
Idaho[1]	Pennsylvania		
Illinois	South Carolina[1]		
Indiana	South Dakota	**Hanging**	**Firing squad**
Kansas	Tennessee[1,8]	Delaware[1,7]	Idaho[1]
Kentucky[1,4]	Texas	New Hampshire[1,9]	Oklahoma[6]
Louisiana	Utah[1]	Washington[1]	Utah[1]
Maryland	Virginia[1]		
Mississippi	Washington[1]		
Missouri[1]	Wyoming[1]		
Montana			

[1]Authorizes 2 methods of execution.
[2]Authorizes lethal injection for persons sentenced after 11/15/92; for those sentenced before that date, the condemned may select lethal injection or lethal gas.
[3]Authorizes lethal injection for those whose captial offense occurred on or after 7/4/83; for those whose offense occurred before that date may select lethal injection or electrocution.
[4]Authorizes lethal injection for persons sentenced on or after 3/31/98; for those sentenced before that date, the condemned may select lethal injection or electrocution.
[5]Authorizes lethal gas if lethal injection is ever held to be unconstitutional.
[6]Authorizes electrocution if lethal injection is ever held to be unconstitutional, and firing squad if both lethal injection and and electrocution are held unconstitutional.
[7]Authorizes lethal injection for those whose capital offense occurred after 6/13/86; for those before that date, the condemned may select lethal injection or hanging.
[8]Authorizes lethal injection for those whose capital offense occurred after 12/31/98; those before that date may select electrocution.
[9]Authorizes hanging only if lethal injection cannot be given.

SOURCE: Thomas P. Bonczar and Tracy L. Snell, "Table 2. Method of execution, by State, 2002," in *Capital Punishment, 2002*, U.S. Department of Justice, Bureau of Justice Statistics, Washington, DC, November 2003

Enforcement Act of 1994 (Public Law 103-322, also known as the Federal Death Penalty Act of 1994) are referred to the state where the conviction occurred.

In 2002, 37 states used lethal injection as the primary method of execution. Of these states, 20 used lethal injection as the sole means of execution. Seventeen states authorized more than one method of execution—lethal injection and an alternative method—generally letting the condemned prisoner choose the method. Of these 17 states, Arizona, Arkansas, Delaware, Kentucky, and Tennessee specified which method must be used, depending on the date of sentencing. (See Table 5.5.)

Idaho, Oklahoma, and Utah authorized the firing squad method. While Utah let inmates choose between lethal injection and the firing squad, Idaho authorized the firing squad only if lethal injection is "impractical." For example, an inmate might have collapsed veins from using drugs and, therefore, could not be given lethal injection. Like Idaho, Oklahoma kept the firing squad method only as a backup. It authorized electrocution if lethal

---

injection is ever held to be unconstitutional and the firing squad if both lethal injection and electrocution are held unconstitutional. So far, Utah has been the only state that has used the firing squad. In 1977 Gary Gilmore asked the state of Utah to carry out his execution using the firing squad. Nineteen years later, in January 1996, John Albert Taylor was executed by firing squad. Both inmates chose that method of execution.

Lethal Injection

In 1993, 25 of 36 states with capital punishment used lethal injection as the primary method of execution. Since then, more and more states have adopted lethal injection as a more humane alternative to other methods of execution—from 27 of 37 states in 1994, to 32 of 38 states in 1995, to 37 of 38 states in 2002. On February 18, 1993, the federal government adopted lethal injection as its sole means of execution. In 1977 Oklahoma became the first state to authorize lethal injection. It was not until 1982, however, that lethal injection was first used, when Texas executed Charlie Brooks. Following several legal challenges, the Supreme Court, in *Heckler v. Chaney* (470 U.S. 821, 1985), upheld the use of lethal injection as a method of execution.

Electrocution

At the end of the 19th century, alternating current (AC) electricity became one of the dominant symbols of progress. Many people thought this modern convenience would provide a more humane method of execution. In 1888 New York built the first electric chair and in 1890 executed William Kemmler with the crude mechanism.

In 2000 Alabama and Nebraska used electrocution as the only means of execution. Georgia authorized lethal injection for those whose capital crimes occurred on or after May 1, 2000. Prisoners whose crimes occurred before that date were subject to electrocution. In October 2001 the Georgia Supreme Court ruled that electrocution was cruel and unusual punishment, ordering the use of lethal injection in its place. This was the first time a state supreme court had ever changed a method of execution. As of July 1, 2002, Alabama authorized lethal injection as the predominant form of execution, although an inmate may request electrocution. As of December 2002, nine states authorized electrocution as the method of execution. Except for Nebraska, which used electrocution as the sole method of execution, the other eight states gave the inmate the choice of lethal injection. (See Table 5.5.) The last electrocution occurred in July 2000 in Virginia (as of November 30, 2003).

Lethal Gas

In 1921 Nevada became the first state to authorize the use of lethal gas for capital punishment. In 1924 Nevada executed Jon Gee using cyanide gas. This was the first time lethal gas was used for execution in the United States. The Nevada statute called for the condemned man to be executed in his cell, without warning, while asleep. Prison officials, unable to figure out a practical way to carry out the execution, ended up constructing a gas chamber. In 1994 a U.S. district judge in California ruled that lethal gas was an inhumane method of execution, a decision upheld by the U.S. Ninth Circuit Court of Appeals in 1995. The U.S. Supreme Court declined to rule on the case and remanded it back to the circuit court in 1996. In 2002 four states still authorized the use of lethal gas. (See Table 5.5.) The last execution using lethal gas was carried out in Arizona in 1999 (as of November 30, 2003).

Hanging

As of year-end 2002 Delaware, New Hampshire, and Washington authorized hanging as a method of execution. The state of Washington gave the condemned person the choice of death by lethal injection, while New Hampshire authorized hanging only if, for some reason, lethal injection could not be administered. (See Table 5.5.) On July 8, 2003, Delaware dismantled its gallows because it no longer had an inmate eligible for the option to choose hanging. Since the dismantling of the gallows, lethal injection, authorized as the official method of execution in 1986 in Delaware, is the sole method of putting inmates to death.

Washington last hanged two inmates in 1993 and 1994, while Delaware hanged its last death row inmate in 1996. It was Delaware's first hanging in 50 years. New Hampshire's last hanging occurred in 1939.

PUBLIC AND PRIVATE EXECUTIONS

Early arguments for capital punishment centered around the issue of deterrence—that the thought of the death penalty might dissuade a person from committing a crime. Executions used to be held in public as a warning to others. Many executions were conducted in a circus atmosphere, leading to opposition to such public displays. Large crowds would flock around the gallows waiting for the hanging. People would eat and drink while visiting with neighbors. Many spectators often got drunk, turning unruly and sometimes even violent. In 1828 the state of New York passed a law allowing county sheriffs to hold executions in private. The law, however, was not mandatory, and no sheriff took advantage of it. In 1830 Connecticut became the first state to pass a law prohibiting all public executions. The Pennsylvania legislature followed suit in 1834.

In 1835 the New York legislature passed a law requiring that all public executions be held within the prison walls. The law further required that 12 respectable citizens be chosen to witness the hanging and report on the execution through the state newspaper.

David G. Chardavoyne recounted the last public execution (1830) in the Territory of Michigan in a small village called Detroit in his book, *A Hanging in Detroit: Stephen Gifford Simmons and the Last Execution under Michigan Law* (Wayne State University Press, Detroit, MI, 2003). Chardavoyne observed that "[h]istorically, public executions owed much of their continuing legitimacy to the use of ritual." The ritual lasted for hours while the participants performed their parts. Public officials would announce the condemned prisoner's crime and sentence. The prisoner, dressed in white, might be made to ride through the crowd with his coffin by his side and a noose around his neck. Religious leaders delivered sermons. The condemned had even been known to deliver his own speech of repentance.

Chardavoyne wrote that at Simmons's execution, the authorities dispensed with "most of the humiliating and demeaning rituals." His research of that event revealed that the officials did not seem very eager to promote the expected rituals. In fact, those who could do so missed the hanging. Simmons, sentenced to death for killing his wife while in a drunken rage, was not subjected to prolonged public display. He walked to the gallows in his own clothes, and no religious preachings occurred. The author noted that no other execution took place in Michigan during the 16 years before the death penalty was outlawed.

The idea of private executions did not catch on quickly. Even when executions were confined to jail courtyards, it was often not difficult to find a perch from which to watch the hanging. By the end of the 1800s, private executions had become the norm, although many public executions still took place. In 1936 Rainey Bethea, an African American, was hanged before a crowd of about 20,000 in Owensboro, Kentucky. Bethea was convicted for the rape and murder of a 70-year-old woman. Many people found the holiday atmosphere, recorded on wire-service photographs, so abhorrent that the Kentucky legislature banned public executions two years later. The last public hanging occurred on May 21, 1937, in Galena, Missouri, when Roscoe "Red" Jackson was executed before about 1,500 spectators. Historians disagree about which of the two should be considered the last public hanging. Although tickets to Jackson's hanging were sold to the public, some people from out of state, the execution was conducted within a fenced-in area. The hanging in Owensboro could be viewed by anyone. In 1938 Missouri banned public hangings and required executions to be conducted in a gas chamber by prison officials at a state penitentiary.

Today some opponents of capital punishment support the idea of public executions. They feel that private executions hide the acts from the public, making them more acceptable. Others have recommended televised executions. However, some proponents of the death penalty support public executions in the hope that they might act as deterrents to future murderers.

Sister Helen Prejean, honorary chairperson of [?]um Campaign and author of the book *Dead Ma[?]* (Random House, New York, 1993), supported the v[?] televised broadcast of convicted Oklahoma City[?] Timothy McVeigh's execution. She believes that A[?] are so far removed from actual executions that they[?] the consequences of our actions—that we are re[?] against evil deeds by performing evil deeds firsthan[?]

WITNESSES TO EXECUTIONS

Death penalty states have statutes or policies[?] that specify which witnesses may be present at a[?] tion. Witnesses usually include prison officials[?] cians, the condemned person's relatives, the[?] relatives, spiritual advisers, selected state citize[?] reporters. In celebrated cases, however, such as th[?] Rosenbergs, who were the convicted spies (19[?] notorious California killer Caryl Chessman (19[?] convicted Oklahoma City bomber Timothy M[?] (2001), the witnesses made up a larger group.

Robert Jay Lifton and Greg Mitchell, in *Wh[?] Death? Capital Punishment, the American Conscie[?] the End of Executions* (William Morrow, New York[?] reported that the number of witnesses allowed at an[?] tion varies from state to state. For example, Penns[?] and North Carolina allow 6 official witnesses, New[?] shire allows 12, and other states have different r[?] numbers. The authors observe, however, that as the[?] of executions rises, some prison authorities have res[?] going on the Internet to recruit witnesses. Others tel[?] the public to invite them to witness executions.

Victims' Families as Witnesses

As of November 2003 the laws of 21 states—A[?] ma, Arizona, Arkansas, California, Colorado, Dela[?] Georgia, Kentucky, Louisiana, Maryland, Missis[?] Missouri, Nevada, Ohio, Oklahoma, North Carolina[?] gon (also specified by policy), Pennsylvania, South[?] olina, Tennessee, and Washington—allowed vic[?] families to be present at executions. The federal go[?] ment also allows victims' families to witness an exec[?]

According to the National Center for Victim[?] Crime (*FYI: Rights of Survivors of Homicide*, Was[?] ton, D.C., 1999), the statutes of the different states va[?] their procedural requirements, which victims' rela[?] have to follow in order to request notification an[?] attendance. For example, the Nevada statute de[?] immediate family as those "who are related by bl[?] adoption or marriage, within the second degree of con[?] guinity (blood relationship) or affinity (relationshi[?] marriage or adoption rather than by blood)." The vict[?] relatives may write the director of the prison departme[?] they wish notification of the execution. Requests to v[?] the execution also have to be submitted in writing.

injection. Based on the state's new public witness procedure (Procedure 770), officials at San Quentin Prison opened the curtain to the observation room only after the condemned had been strapped to the gurney and the intravenous (IV) solution had been inserted and was running. The reporters did not see the condemned being escorted to the death chamber, his demeanor, his being secured to the gurney, and the insertion of the IV tubes. After the curtain was opened, the execution order was given (without telling the witnesses) and lethal chemicals were administered. Five minutes later, the witnesses were told the inmate was dead.

In April 1996 the Society of Professional Journalists' Northern California Chapter and the California First Amendment Coalition filed a lawsuit claiming that Procedure 770 violated their First Amendment right to view the entire execution procedure. The journalists argued that because they were not allowed to see the part in which Bonin was initially secured to a gurney, they could not inform the public of the whole process of execution. Therefore, the public had to rely on reports from prison officials about what went on during the state execution.

San Quentin Prison officials maintained that, with executions by lethal injection, it could take the execution team as long as 20 minutes to prepare the condemned, compared to about a one-minute preparation during lethal gas executions. They were concerned that the prolonged "exposure to witnesses will increase the likelihood of an identification of execution team members." This would in turn subject the staff and their families to possible repercussions that might affect their safety and job performance, as well as affect prison security.

On May 1, 1996, the U.S. District Court issued an injunction forbidding prison officials from limiting media access to the entire execution. On May 3, 1996, reporters were able to witness Keith Daniel Williams's execution in its entirety. In February 1997 the U.S. District Court for the Northern District of California, in *California First Amendment Coalition v. Calderon* (956 F. Supp. 883 [N.D. Cal. 1997]), ruled that "the First Amendment requires prison officials to allow the public and the media to witness lethal injection from the time just before the prisoner is strapped down to a gurney until after death." The court found that a long history of access to executions has helped inform the public "on whether the state's 'awesome' power to commit executions was properly exercised."

Prison officials appealed their case to the U.S. Court of Appeals for the Ninth Circuit in July 1998. In *California*

First Amendment Coalition v. Calderon (150 F.3d 976, 983, 9th Cir 1998), the court ruled that Procedure 770 does not violate the First Amendment rights of the press or the public by not allowing the viewing of executions in their entirety. The case was remanded to the district court so it could determine "whether the Coalition has presented 'substantial evidence' that Procedure 770 represents an exaggerated response to Calderon's security and safety concerns."

On July 26, 2000, in *California First Amendment Coalition v. Woodford* (No. C-96-1291-VRW), U.S. District Judge Vaughn Walker concluded that the prison officials' practice of restricting witness observation was "an exaggerated response to [their own] safety concerns." The judge ruled that media witnesses could view the execution procedure from the time the condemned is brought into the execution room to the time he or she is pronounced dead.

In March 2001, prior to Robert Lee Massie's execution, the state filed an emergency motion before the Ninth Circuit and, subsequently, before the U.S. Supreme Court to overturn the rulings that allowed the media full access to the execution proceedings. On March 26, 2001, both the appellate and high courts denied the motion. The next day witnesses saw Massie's entire execution. On August 2, 2002, in the latest court ruling on California's Procedure 770, the U.S. Court of Appeals for the Ninth Circuit upheld Judge Walker's ruling. In *California First Amendment Coalition v. Woodford* (No.00-16752), the court stated,

> We hold that Procedure 770 is an exaggerated, unreasonable response to prison officials' legitimate concerns about the safety of prison staff and thereby unconstitutionally restricts the public's First Amendment right to view executions from the moment the condemned is escorted into the execution chamber.
>
> An informed public debate is the main purpose for granting a right of access to governmental proceedings. Prison officials simply do not have the same incentives to describe fully the potential shortcomings of lethal injection executions. As Warden Calderon's memo demonstrates, a prison official's perception of the execution process may be vastly different—and markedly less critical—than that of the public.
>
> [T]here exists a ready, low-cost alternative that would fully accommodate the public's First Amendment right of access and adequately address defendants' security concerns as well. [T]he district court found that "[t]he use of surgical garb is a practical alternative to restricting access to witness lethal injection executions in order to conceal the identity of such execution staff should security concerns warrant such concealment."

CHAPTER 6
EXECUTIONS—HISTORICAL STATISTICS

NUMBER OF EXECUTIONS

Until 1930 the U.S. government did not keep any record of the number of people executed under the death penalty. According to the Bureau of Justice Statistics (BJS) of the U.S. Department of Justice, from 1930 through 2002 a total of 4,679 executions were conducted under civil authority in the United States. Military authorities carried out an additional 160 executions between 1930 and 1961, the date of the last military execution.

From 1930 to 1939 a total of 1,667 inmates were executed, the highest number of persons put to death in any decade. The number of executions generally declined between the 1930s and the 1960s. In 1930, 155 executions took place, reaching a high of 199 in 1935. By 1950 executions were down to 82, further dropping to 49 each in 1958 and 1959, and then rising slightly to 56 in 1960. (See Table 6.1.) In 1967 a 10-year moratorium (temporary suspension) of the death penalty began as states waited for the U.S. Supreme Court to determine a constitutionally acceptable procedure for carrying out the death penalty.

The moratorium ended in 1976, but no executions occurred that year. The first execution following the moratorium occurred in Utah in 1977. In 1999, 98 inmates were put to death, the most in one year since the death penalty was reinstated. In 2000 the number of executions (85) declined 13 percent from the previous year, further dropping 22 percent to 66 executions in 2001. In 2002 the number of executions rose slightly to 71. Between 1976 and 2002, 820 persons were put to death. (See Table 6.1.)

LOCATIONS OF EXECUTIONS

The Death Penalty Information Center (DPIC, Washington, D.C.), which provides up-to-date information on capital punishment, reported that from 1976 to October 3, 2003, approximately four out of every five executions (721

out of 877 civil executions) took place in the South. Thirty-two states carried out executions. The federal government executed three men. The largest single number (310) of executions occurred in Texas, followed by Virginia (89), Oklahoma (69), Missouri (60), and Florida (56). Together, these five states carried out more than 66 percent of all executions during this 27-year period. (See Table 6.2.)

In 2000 Texas accounted for the largest number of executions (40), the most in a single year in any state in the nation's history, according to the DPIC. That same year Tennessee executed its first inmate since 1960, while Arkansas put to death a female inmate, the first woman ever executed in that state.

Oklahoma led the nation in executions (18) in 2001, followed by Texas (17). In 2002 Texas resumed its lead, executing 33 inmates, almost five times as many as the next leading state, Oklahoma (7 inmates). (See Table 6.2.) The DPIC reported that between 1993 and October 1, 2003, the number of executions in Texas (256) comprised 38 percent of the total number during that 10-year period, with the rest of the states accounting for 62 percent (432 executions). (See Figure 6.1.)

GENDER

The NAACP Legal Defense and Educational Fund, Inc. (LDF, New York), publishes the quarterly *Death Row USA*, which not only reports the number of death row inmates but also the number of inmates executed since January 1, 1976. The latest LDF report showed that between 1976 and October 1, 2003, 866 men and 10 women had been executed. (See Table 6.3.)

Professor Victor L. Streib of the Claude W. Pettit College of Law of Ohio Northern University (Ada, Ohio) has been compiling information on female offenders and the death penalty since 1984. In *Death Penalty for Female Offenders: January 1, 1973, through December 31, 2003*

TABLE 6.1

Number of persons executed, 1930–2002

Year	Executions
1930	155
1931	153
1932	140
1933	160
1934	168
1935	199
1936	195
1937	147
1938	190
1939	160
1940	124
1941	123
1942	147
1943	131
1944	120
1945	117
1946	131
1947	153
1948	119
1949	119
1950	82
1951	105
1952	83
1953	62
1954	81
1955	76
1956	65
1957	65
1958	49
1959	49
1960	56
1961	42
1962	47
1963	21
1964	15
1965	7
1966	1
1967	2
1968	0
1969	0
1970	0
1971	0
1972	0
1973	0
1974	0
1975	0
1976	0
1977	1
1978	0
1979	2
1980	0
1981	1
1982	2
1983	5
1984	21
1985	18
1986	18
1987	25
1988	11
1989	16
1990	23
1991	14
1992	31
1993	38
1994	31
1995	56
1996	45
1997	74
1998	68
1999	98
2000	85
2001	66
2002	71

SOURCE: Tracy L. Snell and Laura M. Maruschak, "Number of persons executed in the United States, 1930–2002," in *Capital Punishment, 2001,* U.S. Department of Justice, Bureau of Justice Statistics, Washington, DC, January 8, 2003 [Online] http://www.ojp.usdoj.gov/bjs/glance/exe.htm [accessed October 13, 2003]

TABLE 6.2

Number of executions by state, 1976–October 3, 2003

State	Total	2002	2003	State	Total	2002	2003
Texas	310	33	21	Nevada	9		
Virginia	89	4	2	Ohio	8	3	3
Oklahoma	69	7	14	Mississippi	6	2	
Missouri	60	6	1	Utah	6		
Florida	56	3	2	Washington	4		
Georgia	33	4	2	Maryland	3		
Alabama	28	2	3	Nebraska	3		
South Carolina	28	3		Pennsylvania	3		
Louisiana	27	1		Kentucky	2		
North Carolina	27	2	4	Montana	2		
Arkansas	25		1	Oregon	2		
Arizona	22			Colorado	1		
Delaware	13			Idaho	1		
Illinois	12			New Mexico	1		
Indiana	11		2	Tennessee	1		
California	10	1		Wyoming	1		
				Federal	3		1
				Total	**876**	**71**	**56**

Note: Latest exectuion included took place October 3, 2003, in North Carolina.

SOURCE: "Number of Executions by State Since 1976," in *Number of Executions by State and Region Since 1976,* Death Penalty Information Center, Washington, DC, October 3, 2003 [Online] http://www.deathpenaltyinfo.org/article.php?scid=8&did=186 [accessed October 19, 2003]. Reproduced with permission.

FIGURE 6.1

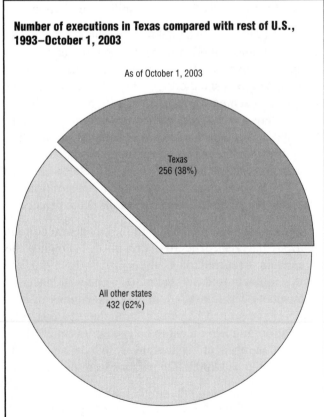

Number of executions in Texas compared with rest of U.S., 1993–October 1, 2003

As of October 1, 2003

Texas
256 (38%)

All other states
432 (62%)

SOURCE: "Executions in the United States from 1993 to 2003 (As of October 1, 2003)," in *Executions in the United States,* Death Penalty Information Center, Washington, DC, 2003 [Online] http://www.deathpenaltyinfo.org/article.php?did=414&scid=8 [accessed October 19, 2003]. Reproduced with permission.

TABLE 6.3

Total number of executions, by demographic characteristics, 1976–October 1, 2003

Total number of executions since the 1976 reinstatement of capital punishment: 876

77	78	79	80	81	82	83	84	85	86	87	88	89	90	91	92	93	94	95	96	97	98	99	00	01	02	03
1	0	2	0	1	2	5	21	18	18	25	11	16	23	14	31	38	31	56	45	74	68	98	85	66	71	56

Gender of defendants executed
total number 876

Female	10	(1.14%)
Male	866	(98.86%)

Gender of victims
total number 1327

Female	646	(48.68%)
Male	681	(51.32%)

Race of defendants executed

White	500	(57.08%)
Black	299	(34.13%)
Latino/a	57	(6.51%)
Native American	14	(1.60%)
Asian	6	(.68%)

Race of victims

White	1064	(80.18%)
Black	183	(13.79%)
Latino/a	53	(3.99%)
Native American	5	(.38%)
Asian	22	(1.66%)

Defendant-victim racial combinations

	White victim		Black victim		Latino/a victim		Asian victim		Native American victim	
White defendant	470	(53.65%)	12	(1.37%)	6	(.68%)	3	(.34%)	0	(0%)
Black defendant	184	(21.00%)	93	(10.62%)	11	(1.26%)	7	(.80%)	0	(0%)
Latino/a defendant	28	(3.20%)	2	(.23%)	23	(2.63%)	1	(.11%)	0	(0%)
Asian defendant	2	(.23%)	0	(0%)	0	(0%)	4	(.46%)	0	(0%)
Native American defendant	12	(1.37%)	0	(0%)	0	(0%)	0	(0%)	2	(.23%)
Total	**696**	**(79.45%)**	**107**	**(12.21%)**	**40**	**(4.57%)**	**15**	**(1.71%)**	**2**	**(.23%)**

Note: In addition, there were 16 defendants executed for the murders of multiple victims of different races. Of those, 9 defendants were white, 4 black and 3 Latino. (1.83%)

SOURCE: "Execution Update (As of October 1, 2003)," in *Death Row USA, Fall 2003,* NAACP Legal Defense and Educational Fund, Inc., New York, NY, 2003. Reproduced with permission.

(December 2003), Professor Streib reported that between 1632 and December 31, 2000, 566 documented executions of women had been reported. Of this number, 49 women were put to death between 1900 and 2003. (See Table 6.4.)

In 1984 Margie Velma Barfield was executed in North Carolina for poisoning her boyfriend. Karla Faye Tucker of Texas was convicted of beating two people to death with a pickax. In February 1998 Tucker became the first woman to be executed in Texas since the Civil War. (In 1863 Chipita Rodriguez, the last woman to be executed in Texas, was put to death by hanging. Her crime—she was convicted of the axe murder of a horse trader.) In Florida Judias Buenoano was convicted of poisoning her husband with arsenic. She was also convicted of drowning her paraplegic son and of trying to kill her boyfriend. In March 1998 Buenoano became the first woman to be executed in Florida since 1848, when a freed slave named Celia was hanged for killing her former owner. (See Table 6.5.)

In February 2000 Betty Lou Beets was executed in Texas for killing her fifth husband. (See Table 6.5.) Christina Marie Riggs, convicted of killing her two children, was executed in Arkansas in May 2000. The last woman put to death in Arkansas prior to Riggs—Lavinia Burnett—was hanged in 1845 for being an accessory to murder.

In 2001 Oklahoma executed three female inmates. In January 2001 Wanda Jean Allen became the first woman to

be executed in Oklahoma since 1903. She was also the first black woman to be put to death in the United States since 1954. Allen was convicted of murdering her gay lover in 1988. In May 2001 Marilyn Kay Plantz was executed for the 1988 murder of her husband. Plantz had hired two men to kill her husband. One of the men, William Bryson, was executed in June 2000 for the murder, and the other, Clinton McKimble, received a life sentence in exchange for his testimony against Plantz and Bryson. Lois Nadean Smith, executed in December 2001, was convicted of killing her son's girlfriend in 1982. (See Table 6.5.)

Lynda Lyon Block and her husband, George Sibley, Jr., murdered a police officer in 1993. In May 2002 Alabama executed Block, making her the first woman to be executed in the state in 45 years. As of November 30, 2003, Sibley remained on death row. Aileen Carol Wuornos, convicted of killing six men in Florida, was put to death by lethal injection in October 2002. (See Table 6.5.)

RACE AND ETHNICITY

According to the Bureau of Justice Statistics' latest data on race, more than half of those executed between 1930 and 1997 were black (52 percent), 47 percent were white, and 1 percent was categorized as "other" race. (See Table 6.6.) Data compiled by the LDF show

TABLE 6.4

Executions of female offenders by state, January 1, 1900 through December 31, 2003

State	Date of execution	Name	Race	Age at crime
Alabama	01-24-1930	Gilmore, Selena	Black	[adult]
	09-04-1953	Dennison, Earle	White	54
	10-11-1957	Martin, Rhonda Belle	White	48
	05-10-2002	Block, Linda Lyon	White	45
Arizona	02-21-1930	Dugan, Eva	White	49
Arkansas	05-02-2000	Riggs, Christina Marie	White	26
California	11-21-1941	Spinelli, Eithel Leta Juanita	White	52
	04-11-1947	Peete, Louise	White	58
	06-03-1955	Graham, Barbara	White	32
	08-08-1962	Duncan, Elizabeth Ann	White	58
Delaware	06-07-1935	Carey, May H.	White	52
Florida	03-30-1998	Buenoano, Judias	White	28
	10-09-2002	Wuornos, Aileen	White	33
Georgia	03-05-1945	Baker, Lena	Black	44
Illinois	01-28-1938	Porter, Marie	White	38
Louisiana	02-01-1929	LeBoeuf, Ada	White	38
	02-08-1935	Moore, Julia (aka Powers; aka Williams)	?	[adult]
	11-28-1942	Henri, Toni Jo (aka Annie)	White	26
Mississippi	01-13-1922	Perdue, Pattie	Black	[adult]
	10-13-1922	Knight, Ann	Black	[adult]
	04-29-1937	Holmes, Mary	Black	32
	05-19-1944	Johnson, Mildred Louise (aka James)	Black	34
Missouri (federal)	12-18-1953	Heady, Bonnie Brown	White	41
New York	03-29-1909	Farmer, Mary	White	29
	01-12-1928	Snyder, Ruth Brown	White	33
	08-09-1934	Antonio, Anna	White	27
	06-27-1935	Coo, Eva	White	40
	07-16-1936	Creighton, Mary Francis	White	36
	11-16-1944	Fowler, Helen	Black	37
	03-08-1951	Beck, Martha	White	29
(federal)	06-19-1953	Rosenberg, Ethel[1]	White	32
North Carolina	01-01-1943	Phillips, Rosana Lightner	Black	25
	12-29-1944	Williams, Bessie May	Black	19
	11-02-1984	Barfield, Velma	White	52
Ohio	12-07-1938	Hahn, Anna Marie	White	32
	01-15-1954	Dean, Dovie Smarr	White	55
	06-12-1954	Butler, Betty	Black	25
Oklahoma	07-17-1903	Wright, Dora	Black	[adult]
	01-11-2001	Allen, Wanda Jean	Black	29
	05-01-2001	Plantz, Marilyn Kay	White	27
	12-04-2001	Smith, Lois Nadeen	White	41
Pennsylvania	02-23-1931	Schroeder, Irene	White	22
	10-14-1946	Sykes, Corrine	Black	22
South Carolina	01-15-1943	Logue, Sue Stidham	White	43
	01-17-1947	Stinette, Rose Marie	Black	49
Texas	02-03-1998	Tucker, Karla Faye	White	38
	02-24-2000	Beets, Betty Lou	White	46
Vermont	12-08-1905	Rogers, Mary Mabel	White	21
Virginia	08-16-1912	Christian, Virginia	Black	17

[1]Ethel Rosenberg's capital crime was espionage, the only one of these 20th and 21st century executions of female offenders which involved a crime other than murder.

SOURCE: Victor L. Streib, "Table 1. Executions of Female Offenders by State, January 1, 1900 through December 31, 2003," in *Death Penalty for Female Offenders, January 1, 1973 through December 31, 2003*, Ohio Northern University, The Claude W. Pettit College of Law, Ada, OH, December 2003 [Online] http://www.law.onu.edu/faculty/streib/FemDeathDec2003.pdf [accessed February 11, 2004]. Reproduced with permission.

TABLE 6.5

Executions of female offenders, by state, January 1, 1973–June 30, 2003

Date of execution	Date of crime	State	Name	Race	Age at crime	Age at execution
11-02-1984	02-01-1978	No. Carolina	Barfield, Velma	White	52	58
02-03-1998	06-13-1983	Texas	Tucker, Karla Faye	White	23	38
03-30-1998	09-16-1971	Florida	Buenoano, Judias	White	28	54
02-24-2000	08-06-1983	Texas	Beets, Betty Lou	White	46	62
05-02-2000	11-04-1997	Arkansas	Riggs, Christina	White	26	29
01-11-2001	12-01-1988	Oklahoma	Allen, Wanda Jean	Black	29	41
05-01-2001	08-26-1988	Oklahoma	Plantz, Marilyn Kay	White	27	40
12-04-2001	07-04-1982	Oklahoma	Smith, Lois Nadean	White	41	60
05-10-2002	10-04-1993	Alabama	Block, Linda Lyon	White	45	54
10-09-2002	1989-1990	Florida	Wuornos, Aileen	White	33	46

SOURCE: Victor L. Streib, "Table 2: Executions of Female Offenders by States During Current Era, January 1, 1973, through June 30, 2003," in *Death Penalty for Female Offenders, January 1, 1973, through June 30, 2003*, Ohio Northern University, The Claude W. Pettit College of Law, Ada, OH, July 1, 2003 [Online] http://www.law.onu.edu/faculty/streib/femdeath.pdf [accessed January 6, 2004]. Reproduced with permission.

that of the 876 prisoners executed from 1976 to October 1, 2003, 57 percent were white (500), 34.13 percent were black (299), 6.51 percent were Hispanic (who may be of any race; 57), 1.6 percent were Native American (14), and less than 1 percent were Asian (6). (See Table 6.3.)

LDF maintains statistics not only on the race of the executed prisoners, but also on their victims. These types of statistics have been used in court cases to decide the constitutionality of the death penalty. The courts have to consider whether whites who murdered blacks got lighter sentences than blacks who murdered whites and whether those sentences violated the equal protection rights of the Constitution.

From 1976 through October 1, 2003, 53.65 percent of those executed were whites who had murdered other whites, while 1.37 percent were whites who had murdered blacks. Twenty-one percent of those executed were blacks who had murdered whites, and 10.62 percent were blacks who had murdered other blacks. (See Table 6.3.)

CRIMES WARRANTING THE DEATH PENALTY

The vast majority of executions from 1930 through 1997 were for murder (85.4 percent), followed by rape (10.6 percent). The remaining 1 percent of executions included 25 cases for armed robbery, 20 for kidnapping, 11 for burglary, 6 for sabotage, 6 for aggravated assault, and 2 for espionage. Since 1965 all those executed have been convicted on murder charges. (See Table 6.6.)

The last executions for rape occurred in 1964. Six executions for rape occurred in three states that year—Arkansas (1), Missouri (2), and Texas (3). In 1977 in *Coker v. Georgia* (433 U.S. 584), the Supreme Court ruled that rape did not warrant the death penalty. The case concerned the rape of an adult woman. The court did not address the rape of a child. In December 1996, however, the Louisiana Supreme Court ruled that death is a just and

TABLE 6.6

Prisoners executed under civil authority, by race and offense, 1930–97

(- represents zero)

	Total				White				Black				Other			
	Total	Murder	Rape	Other offenses[a]	Total	Murder	Rape	Other offenses	Total	Murder	Rape	Other offenses	Total	Murder	Rape	Other offenses
1930-97	4,291	3,666	455	70	2,016	1,929	48	39	2,228	1,792	405	31	47	45	2	-
1997	74	74	-	-	45	45	-	-	27	27	-	-	2	2	-	-
1996	45	45	-	-	31	31	-	-	14	14	-	-	-	-	-	-
1995	56	56	-	-	33	33	-	-	22	22	-	-	1	1	-	-
1994	31	31	-	-	20	20	-	-	11	11	-	-	-	-	-	-
1993	38	38	-	-	23	23	-	-	14	14	-	-	1	1	-	-
1992	31	31	-	-	19	19	-	-	11	11	-	-	1	1	-	-
1991	14	14	-	-	7	7	-	-	7	7	-	-	-	-	-	-
1990	23	23	-	-	16	16	-	-	7	7	-	-	-	-	-	-
1989	16	16	-	-	8	8	-	-	8	8	-	-	-	-	-	-
1988	11	11	-	-	6	6	-	-	5	5	-	-	-	-	-	-
1987	25	25	-	-	13	13	-	-	12	12	-	-	-	-	-	-
1986	18	18	-	-	11	11	-	-	7	7	-	-	-	-	-	-
1985	18	18	-	-	11	11	-	-	7	7	-	-	-	-	-	-
1984	21	21	-	-	13	13	-	-	8	8	-	-	-	-	-	-
1983	5	5	-	-	4	4	-	-	1	1	-	-	-	-	-	-
1982	2	2	-	-	1	1	-	-	1	1	-	-	-	-	-	-
1981	1	1	-	-	1	1	-	-	-	-	-	-	-	-	-	-
1980	-	-	-	-	-	-	-	-	-	-	-	-	-	-	-	-
1979	2	2	-	-	2	2	-	-	-	-	-	-	-	-	-	-
1978	-	-	-	-	-	-	-	-	-	-	-	-	-	-	-	-
1977[b]	1	1	-	-	1	1	-	-	-	-	-	-	-	-	-	-
1967	2	2	-	-	1	1	-	-	1	1	-	-	-	-	-	-
1966	1	1	-	-	1	1	-	-	-	-	-	-	-	-	-	-
1965	7	7	-	-	6	6	-	-	1	1	-	-	-	-	-	-
1964	15	9	6	-	8	5	3	-	7	4	3	-	-	-	-	-
1963	21	18	2	1	13	12	-	1	8	6	2	-	-	-	-	-
1962	47	41	4	2	28	26	2	-	19	15	2	2	-	-	-	-
1961	42	33	8	1	20	18	1	1	22	15	7	-	-	-	-	-
1960	56	44	8	4	21	18	-	3	35	26	8	1	-	-	-	-
1959	49	41	8	-	16	15	1	-	33	26	7	-	-	-	-	-
1958	49	41	7	1	20	20	-	-	28	20	7	1	1	1	-	-
1957	65	54	10	1	34	32	2	-	31	22	8	1	-	-	-	-
1956	65	52	12	1	21	20	-	1	43	31	12	-	1	1	-	-
1955	76	65	7	4	44	41	1	2	32	24	6	2	-	-	-	-
1954	81	71	9	1	38	37	1	-	42	33	8	1	1	1	-	-
1953	62	51	7	4	30	25	1	4	31	25	6	-	1	1	-	-
1952	83	71	12	-	36	35	1	-	47	36	11	-	-	-	-	-
1951	105	87	17	1	57	55	2	-	47	31	15	1	1	1	-	-
1950	82	68	13	1	40	36	4	-	42	32	9	1	-	-	-	-
1949	119	107	10	2	50	49	-	1	67	56	10	1	2	2	-	-
1948	119	95	22	2	35	32	1	2	82	61	21	-	2	2	-	-
1947	153	129	23	1	42	40	2	-	111	89	21	1	-	-	-	-
1946	131	107	22	2	46	45	-	1	84	61	22	1	1	1	-	-
1945	117	90	26	1	41	37	4	-	75	52	22	1	1	1	-	-
1944	120	96	24	-	47	45	2	-	70	48	22	-	3	3	-	-
1943	131	118	13	-	54	54	-	-	74	63	11	-	3	1	2	-
1942	147	115	25	7	67	57	4	6	80	58	21	1	-	-	-	-
1941	123	102	20	1	59	55	4	-	63	46	16	1	1	1	-	-
1940	124	105	15	4	49	44	2	3	75	61	13	1	-	-	-	-
1939	160	145	12	3	80	79	-	1	77	63	12	2	3	3	-	-
1938	190	154	25	11	96	89	1	6	92	63	24	5	2	2	-	-
1937	147	133	13	1	69	67	2	-	74	62	11	1	4	4	-	-
1936	195	181	10	4	92	86	2	4	101	93	8	-	2	2	-	-
1935	199	184	13	2	119	115	2	2	77	66	11	-	3	3	-	-
1934	168	154	14	-	65	64	1	-	102	89	13	-	1	1	-	-
1933	160	151	7	2	77	75	1	1	81	74	6	1	2	2	-	-
1932	140	128	10	2	62	62	-	-	75	63	10	2	3	3	-	-
1931	153	137	15	1	77	76	1	-	72	57	14	1	4	4	-	-
1930	155	147	6	2	90	90	-	-	65	57	6	2	-	-	-	-

[a] Includes 25 executed for armed robbery, 20 for kidnaping, 11 for burglary, 6 for sabotage, 6 for aggravated assault, and 2 for espionage.
[b] There were no executions from 1968 through 1976.

SOURCE: Kathleen Maguire and Ann L. Pastore, eds., "Table 6.82: Prisoners executed under civil authority," in *Sourcebook of Criminal Justice Statistics 2001*, U.S. Department of Justice, Bureau of Justice Statistics, Washington, DC, 2002

TABLE 6.7

Executions, by state and method, 1977–2002

State	Number executed	Lethal injection	Electrocution	Lethal gas	Hanging	Firing squad
Total	**820**	**654**	**150**	**11**	**3**	**2**
Federal system	2	2	0	0	0	0
Alabama	25	1	24	0	0	0
Arizona	22	20	0	2	0	0
Arkansas	24	23	1	0	0	0
California	10	8	0	2	0	0
Colorado	1	1	0	0	0	0
Delaware	13	12	0	0	1	0
Florida	54	10	44	0	0	0
Georgia	31	8	23	0	0	0
Idaho	1	1	0	0	0	0
Illinois	12	12	0	0	0	0
Indiana	9	6	3	0	0	0
Kentucky	2	1	1	0	0	0
Louisiana	27	7	20	0	0	0
Maryland	3	3	0	0	0	0
Mississippi	6	2	0	4	0	0
Missouri	59	59	0	0	0	0
Montana	2	2	0	0	0	0
Nebraska	3	0	3	0	0	0
Nevada	9	8	0	1	0	0
New Mexico	1	1	0	0	0	0
North Carolina	23	21	0	2	0	0
Ohio	5	5	0	0	0	0
Oklahoma	55	55	0	0	0	0
Oregon	2	2	0	0	0	0
Pennsylvania	3	3	0	0	0	0
South Carolina	28	23	5	0	0	0
Tennessee	1	1	0	0	0	0
Texas	289	289	0	0	0	0
Utah	6	4	0	0	0	2
Virginia	87	61	26	0	0	0
Washington	4	2	0	0	2	0
Wyoming	1	1	0	0	0	0

SOURCE: Thomas P. Bonczar and Tracy L. Snell, "Appendix table 5. Executions, by State and method, 1977–2002," in *Capital Punishment, 2002,* U.S. Department of Justice, Bureau of Justice Statistics, Washington, DC, November 2003

constitutional punishment for the rape of a child under 12 years of age. As of November 30, 2003, no one had been executed under Louisiana's statute.

METHOD OF EXECUTION

Among the 820 prisoners executed between 1977 and 2002, nearly 80 percent (654) received lethal injection, fol-lowed by electrocution (18 percent, or 150). Eleven executions were carried out by lethal gas, 3 by hanging, and 2 by firing squad. Texas, the state with the largest number of prisoners executed, used lethal injection in all 289 cases. Virginia executed 61 inmates by lethal injection and 26 inmates by electrocution. Florida put to death 44 prisoners by electrocution and 10 prisoners by lethal injection. (See Table 6.7.)

CHAPTER 7
UNDER SENTENCE OF DEATH

The Bureau of Justice Statistics (BJS) of the U.S. Department of Justice reported that, at year-end 2002, a total of 3,557 prisoners were held under sentence of death in federal and state prisons. That was 20 fewer inmates than on December 31, 2001 (3,577). Between 1976, when the U.S. Supreme Court reinstated the death penalty, and the year 2000, the number of prisoners on death row increased each year. The year 2001 was the first time since 1976 that the number of death row inmates declined. (See Figure 7.1.)

Between January 1 and December 31, 2002, 27 state prisons received 154 persons under sentence of death. The federal Bureau of Prisons received five inmates. According to the BJS, 2002 was the fourth straight year that the number of death row admissions declined. In 1998 state and federal prisons received 304 inmates. The number entering death row dropped to 282 in 1999, 232 in 2000, and 163 in 2001. The 2002 admission of 159 inmates was the lowest number since 1973, when 44 persons entered death row.

Just a small number of prisoners are removed from death row for reasons other than execution—resentencing, retrial, commutation (replacement of the death sentence with a lesser sentence), or death while awaiting execution (natural death, murder, or suicide). For example, between 1973 and 2002 a total of 7,254 persons received the death sentence. Of these, 820 were executed, 268 died while awaiting execution, 2,403 had their sentences or convictions overturned, and 176 had their sentences commuted. As of December 31, 2002, about half (3,557 inmates) were still on death row awaiting execution. (See Table 7.1.)

In 2002 all 159 prisoners admitted to death row had been convicted of murder. Eighty-three prisoners from 26 states and the federal Bureau of Prisons had their death sentences overturned or removed. Florida and North Carolina each had 12 capital sentences vacated (annulled), more than any other state. In previous years Florida

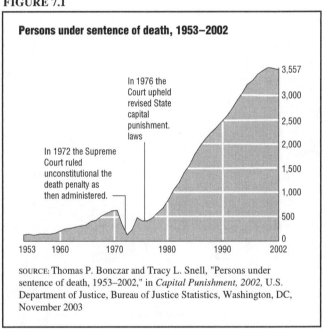

FIGURE 7.1

Persons under sentence of death, 1953–2002

In 1972 the Supreme Court ruled unconstitutional the death penalty as then administered.

In 1976 the Court upheld revised State capital punishment. laws

SOURCE: Thomas P. Bonczar and Tracy L. Snell, "Persons under sentence of death, 1953–2002," in *Capital Punishment, 2002*, U.S. Department of Justice, Bureau of Justice Statistics, Washington, DC, November 2003

reported the highest number of vacated capital sentences—11 in 2001, 9 in 2000, and 22 in 1999.

The NAACP Legal Defense and Educational Fund, Inc. (LDF), is a major source of death row statistics. While the BJS annual report counts only those on death row awaiting execution, the LDF statistics include persons who have been sentenced to death and are awaiting transfer to prison. As of October 1, 2003, the LDF report, *Death Row USA, Fall 2003* (New York, 2003) showed 3,511 prisoners under sentence of death. Seven prisoners were sentenced to death in more than one state. The actual number of prisoners under sentence of death was 3,504. (See Table 7.2.)

GEOGRAPHIC DISTRIBUTION

The LDF reported that, as of October 1, 2003, more than half (55 percent) of the state prisoners awaiting

TABLE 7.1

Number sentenced to death and number of removals, by jurisdiction and reason for removal, 1973–2002

State	Total sentenced to death, 1973-2002	Number of removals, 1973-2002					Under sentence of death, 12/31/02
		Executed	Died	Sentence or conviction overturned	Sentence commuted	Other removals	
U.S. total	7,254	820	268	2,403	176	30	3,557
Federal	32	2	0	5	1	0	24
Alabama	342	25	17	107	2	0	191
Arizona	239	22	11	79	6	1	120
Arkansas	99	24	2	31	2	0	40
California	795	10	37	119	15	0	614
Colorado	19	1	2	10	1	0	5
Connecticut	8	0	0	1	0	0	7
Delaware	48	13	0	21	0	0	14
Florida	872	54	35	397	18	2	366
Georgia	299	31	9	139	7	1	112
Idaho	40	1	1	15	3	0	20
Illinois	294	12	14	98	3	8	159
Indiana	97	9	2	46	2	2	36
Kansas	6	0	0	1	0	0	5
Kentucky	75	2	3	33	1	0	36
Louisiana	214	27	4	90	6	1	86
Maryland	52	3	2	28	4	0	15
Massachusetts	4	0	0	2	2	0	0
Mississippi	173	6	3	95	0	3	66
Missouri	167	59	9	31	2	0	66
Montana	15	2	0	6	1	0	6
Nebraska	27	3	3	12	2	0	7
Nevada	135	9	11	28	4	0	83
New Jersey	51	0	3	26	0	8	14
New Mexico	28	1	1	19	5	0	2
New York	9	0	0	4	0	0	5
North Carolina	504	23	13	254	8	0	206
Ohio	367	5	11	136	10	0	205
Oklahoma	313	55	10	135	1	0	112
Oregon	51	2	1	22	0	0	26
Pennsylvania	352	3	15	88	5	0	241
Rhode Island	2	0	0	2	0	0	0
South Carolina	179	28	4	72	3	0	72
South Dakota	5	0	0	0	0	0	5
Tennessee	204	1	10	93	3	2	95
Texas	925	289	28	108	49	1	450
Utah	26	6	0	8	1	0	11
Virginia	137	87	5	12	9	1	23
Washington	38	4	1	23	0	0	10
Wyoming	11	1	1	7	0	0	2
Percent	100%	11.3%	3.7%	33.1%	2.4%	0.4%	49.0%

Note: For those persons sentenced to death more than once, the numbers are based on the most recent death sentence.

SOURCE: Thomas P. Bonczar and Tracy L. Snell, "Appendix table 4. Number sentenced to death and number of removals, by jurisdiction and reason for removal, 1973–2002," in *Capital Punishment, 2002,* U.S. Department of Justice, Bureau of Justice Statistics, Washington, DC, November 2003

execution were in the South (15 states). An additional 26.6 percent were in the 11 western states, and 9.7 percent were in the 7 midwestern states. The northeastern states of Connecticut, New Jersey, New York, and Pennsylvania accounted for 7.7 percent. Nearly 42 percent of the condemned were awaiting execution in three states—California (632), Texas (451), and Florida (381). Of the 38 jurisdictions with statutes authorizing the death penalty, only New Hampshire had no one under a capital sentence, while Colorado, Montana, New Mexico, New York, South Dakota, and Wyoming had six or fewer. (See Table 7.2.)

RACE

As of October 1, 2003, 46 percent of all death row inmates were white, and 42 percent were black. Hispanic prisoners (who may be of any race) whose ethnicity was known accounted for 10 percent of those under a death sentence. Native Americans and Asians represented 1 percent each of death row inmates. Nearly 9 in 10 (88.6 percent) of the Hispanics on death row were imprisoned in five states—California, Texas, Florida, Arizona, and Pennsylvania. (See Table 7.2.)

GENDER

Death Row USA, Fall 2003 reported that as of October 1, 2003, 98.6 percent (3,455) of all prisoners under sentence of death were males. Forty-nine females were awaiting execution. Of the male inmates, 82 were juveniles.

In *Death Penalty for Female Offenders: January 1, 1973, through June 30, 2003* (July 1, 2003), Professor Victor

TABLE 7.2

Number of prisoners on death row, by state and race, October 1, 2003

State	Total	Black		White		Latino/a		Native American		Asian		Unknown	
Alabama	194	91	47%	100	52%	2	1%	0	–	1	.5%	0	–
Arizona	126	14	11%	89	71%	19	15%	3	2%	1	.8%	0	–
Arkansas	40	23	58%	16	40%	1	3%	0	–	0	–	0	–
California	632	226	36%	249	39%	124	20%	14	2%	19	3%	0	–
Colorado	6	2	33%	1	17%	2	33%	0	–	1	17%	0	–
Connecticut	7	3	43%	3	43%	1	14%	0	–	0	–	0	–
Delaware	21	8	38%	10	48%	3	14%	0	–	0	–	0	–
Florida	381	131	34%	214	56%	34	9%	1	.3%	1	.3%	0	–
Georgia	116	56	48%	57	49%	2	2%	0	–	1	.9%	0	–
Idaho	21	0	–	21	100%	0	–	0	–	0	–	0	–
Illinois	8	3	38%	5	63%	0	–	0	–	0	–	0	–
Indiana	39	13	33%	26	67%	0	–	0	–	0	–	0	–
Kansas	7	2	29%	5	71%	0	–	0	–	0	–	0	–
Kentucky	38	9	24%	28	74%	1	3%	0	–	0	–	0	–
Louisiana	92	63	68%	26	28%	2	2%	0	–	1	1%	0	–
Maryland	14	9	64%	5	36%	0	–	0	–	0	–	0	–
Mississippi	69	36	52%	32	46%	0	–	0	–	1	1%	0	–
Missouri	67	30	45%	37	55%	0	–	0	–	0	–	0	–
Montana	5	0	–	5	100%	0	–	0	–	0	–	0	–
Nebraska	7	1	14%	5	71%	1	14%	0	–	0	–	0	–
Nevada	89	36	40%	43	48%	9	10%	0	–	1	1%	0	–
New Jersey	15	6	40%	9	60%	0	–	0	–	0	–	0	–
New Mexico	2	0	–	2	100%	0	–	0	–	0	–	0	–
New York	6	2	33%	3	50%	1	17%	0	–	0	–	0	–
North Carolina	207	118	57%	75	36%	4	2%	8	4%	2	1%	0	–
Ohio	209	104	50%	99	47%	2	1%	2	1%	2	1%	0	–
Oklahoma	105	38	36%	55	52%	4	4%	7	7%	1	1%	0	–
Oregon	31	1	3%	26	84%	2	6%	1	3%	0	–	1	3%
Pennsylvania	241	148	61%	72	30%	19	8%	0	–	2	.8%	0	–
South Carolina	74	33	45%	41	55%	0	–	0	–	0	–	0	–
South Dakota	4	0	–	4	100%	0	–	0	–	0	–	0	–
Tennessee	104	41	39%	58	56%	1	1%	2	2%	2	2%	0	–
Texas	451	187	41%	143	32%	116	26%	0	–	5	1%	0	–
Utah	11	2	18%	6	55%	2	18%	1	9%	0	–	0	–
Virginia	27	12	44%	15	56%	0	–	0	–	0	–	0	–
Washington	11	5	45%	6	55%	0	–	0	–	0	–	0	–
Wyoming	1	0	–	1	–	0	100%	0	–	0	–	0	–
US Government	26	19	73%	6	23%	0	–	1	4%	0	–	0	–
Military	7	5	71%	1	14%	0	–	0	–	1	14%	0	–
Total	**3511**	**1477**	**42%**	**1599**	**46%**	**352**	**10%**	**40**	**1%**	**42**	**1%**	**1**	**.03%**

Note: 7 prisoners were sentenced to death in more than one state. They are included in the chart above for each state in which they were sentenced to death. The total number of prisoners under sentence of death is 3,504.

SOURCE: "Summary of State Lists of Prisoners on Death Row," in *Death Row USA, Fall 2003*, NAACP Legal Defense and Educational Fund, Inc., New York, NY, 2003. Reproduced with permission.

L. Streib of the Claude W. Pettit College of Law of Ohio Northern University (Ada, OH) reported on female offenders on death row. Between 1973 and June 30, 2003, 145 females had been sentenced to death in the United States. Nearly two-thirds (64 percent; 93 inmates) were white, and more than one-fourth (27 percent; 39 inmates) were black. Nine women were Hispanic, and four were American Indian. Of the 23 states with women on death row, California, North Carolina, Florida, Texas, and Ohio accounted for almost half (49.7 percent; 72 inmates). (See Table 7.3.)

CHARACTERISTICS OF PRISONERS

The BJS collects additional information on death row inmates. In 2002 the median age of those under sentence of death was 39 years (this means that half of the inmates were younger than 39 and half were older than that age).

Two-thirds (66.7 percent) were ages 25 to 44. Of these inmates, one-third (34.4 percent) were between 30 and 39 years old. Four inmates were under age 20, and 99 inmates were 60 and older. The youngest inmate was 18 years old and was sentenced to death in August 2002. The oldest was 87, having been sentenced in June 1983 at the age of 68. Almost half (49.7 percent) of all inmates under sentence of death were ages 20 to 29 when they were arrested for their capital offense. (See Table 7.4.)

Among those for whom information about education was available as of December 31, 2002, more than half (51.8 percent) had not graduated from high school, and only 1 in 10 had any college education. The median level of education was the 11th grade. Most had never married (54.3 percent), and about one-fourth (23.6 percent) were separated, divorced, or widowed. (See Table 7.5.)

TABLE 7.3

Number of female offenders sentenced to death, by state and race, January 1, 1973–June 30, 2003

Rank	Sentencing state	Race of offender				Total female sentences
		White	Black	Latin	American Indian	
1	California	9	3	5	0	16
	North Carolina	10	4	0	2	16
3	Florida	11	3	1	0	15
	Texas	10	5	0	0	15
5	Ohio	4	6	0	0	10
6	Alabama	6	3	0	0	9
7	Illinois	1	4	2	0	7
	Mississippi	5	2	0	0	7
	Oklahoma	6	1	0	0	7
10	Georgia	5	1	0	0	6
	Pennsylvania	3	3	0	0	6
12	Missouri	4	0	1	0	5
13	Indiana	2	2	0	0	4
14	Kentucky	3	0	0	0	3
	Maryland	1	0	0	2	3
16	New Jersey	3	0	0	0	3
17	Arizona	2	0	0	0	2
	Arkansas	2	0	0	0	2
	Idaho	2	0	0	0	2
	Louisiana	1	1	0	0	2
	Nevada	1	1	0	0	2
	Tennessee	2	0	0	0	2
23	South Carolina	1	0	0	0	1
	Totals	**93**	**39**	**9**	**4**	**145**

SOURCE: Victor L. Streib, "Table 4: State-by-State Breakdown of Death Sentences for Female Offenders, January 1, 1973, through June 30, 2003," in *Death Penalty for Female Offenders, January 1, 1973, through June 30, 2003,* Ohio Northern University, The Claude W. Pettit College of Law, Ada, OH, July 1, 2003 [Online] http://www.law.onu.edu/faculty/streib/femdeath.pdf [accessed January 6, 2004]. Reproduced with permission.

TABLE 7.4

Age at time of arrest for capital offense and age of prisoners under sentence of death, December 31, 2002

Age	Prisoners under sentence of death			
	At time of arrest		On December 31, 2002	
	Number*	Percent	Number	Percent
Total number under sentence of death on 12/31/02	3,299	100.0%	3,557	100.0%
17 or younger	74	2.2	0	
18-19	355	10.8	4	0.1
20-24	894	27.1	153	4.3
25-29	745	22.6	452	12.7
30-34	540	16.4	606	17.0
35-39	355	10.8	619	17.4
40-44	178	5.4	696	19.6
45-49	99	3.0	450	12.7
50-54	40	1.2	304	8.5
55-59	14	0.4	174	4.9
60-64	2	—	59	1.7
65 or older	3	0.1	40	1.1
Mean age	28 yrs.		39 yrs.	
Median age	27 yrs.		39 yrs.	

Note: The youngest person under sentence of death was a white male in Texas, born in April 1984 and sentenced to death in August 2002. The oldest person under sentence of death was a white male in Arizona, born in September 1915 and sentenced to death in June 1983.
—Less than 0.05%.
*Excludes 258 inmates for whom the date of arrest for capital offense was not available.

SOURCE: Thomas P. Bonczar and Tracy L. Snell, "Table 7. Age at time of arrest for capital offense and age of prisoners under sentence of death at yearend 2002," in *Capital Punishment, 2002,* U.S. Department of Justice, Bureau of Justice Statistics, Washington, DC, November 2003

CRIMINAL HISTORY OF DEATH ROW INMATES

The BJS reported that, as of December 31, 2002, among prisoners on death row, nearly two-thirds (64.3 percent) had prior felony convictions. Almost 1 in 12 (8 percent) had been previously convicted of murder or manslaughter. About two of five (40.2 percent) had an active criminal justice record at the time of the murder for which they were condemned. Almost half of those with an active criminal record were out on parole when they committed their crime, and one-fourth were on probation. The others had charges pending, were in prison, had escaped from prison, or had some other criminal justice status. (See Table 7.6.)

Criminal history patterns varied slightly by race and Hispanic origin. Blacks (69 percent) had somewhat more prior felony convictions than whites (61.5 percent) and Hispanics (58.5 percent). Blacks (8.1 percent) and whites (8.2 percent) had a higher proportion of prior homicide convictions than Hispanics (6.7 percent). Hispanics (23 percent) and blacks (18.5 percent) were more likely than whites (14.9 percent) to be on parole when arrested for their capital crime. (See Table 7.6.)

Since 1988 the BJS has been collecting information on the number of death sentences imposed on the offenders entering the prison system. Among the 4,005 individu-

als admitted under sentence of death between 1988 to 2002, nearly 1 in 7 (14 percent) was admitted with two or more death sentences.

A LONG WAIT

It can be a long wait on death row. Between 1977 and 2002 a total of 6,912 offenders had been under a death sentence for varying periods. Of these, 820 (11.9 percent) were actually executed. Another 2,535 (36.7 percent) were removed from under a death sentence because of appellate court decisions and reviews or commutations, or they had died while awaiting execution.

For those executed from 1977 to 2002, the average time between the imposition of the most recent death sentence and the execution was about 10 years and 3 months. White prisoners had waited an average of 9 years and 11 months, and black prisoners, 10 years and 10 months, before their execution. In 2002 the 71 inmates executed were under sentence of death for an average of 10 years and 7 months. (See Table 7.7.)

GETTING OFF DEATH ROW

Prisoners can get off death row by different means. The Bureau of Justice Statistics breaks down the outcome

TABLE 7.5

Demographic characteristics of prisoners under sentence of death, 2002

Characteristic	Prisoners under sentence of death, 2002		
	Yearend	Admissions	Removals
Total number under sentence of death	3,557	159	179
Gender			
Male	98.6%	96.9%	97.2%
Female	1.4	3.1	2.8
Race			
White	54.3%	52.2%	67.0%
Black	43.7	45.9	31.8
All other races*	2.0	1.9	1.2
Hispanic origin			
Hispanic	11.5%	14.9%	9.5%
Non-Hispanic	88.5	85.1	90.5
Education			
8th grade or less	14.7%	21.4%	14.5%
9th–11th grade	37.1	34.9	36.2
High school graduate/GED	38.5	37.3	36.2
Any college	9.7	6.3	13.1
Median	11th	11th	11th
Marital status			
Married	22.1%	25.8%	23.9%
Divorced/separated	20.8	16.7	22.0
Widowed	2.8	6.8	3.1
Never married	54.3	50.7	50.9

Note: Calculations are based on those cases for which data were reported. Missing data by category were as follows:

	Yearend	Admissions	Removals
Hispanic origin	399	38	21
Education	511	33	27
Marital status	342	27	20

*At yearend 2001, other races consisted of 27 American Indians, 32 Asians, and 12 self-identified Hispanics. During 2002, 2 Asians and 1 American Indian were admitted; and 1 Asian and 1 American Indian were removed.

SOURCE: Thomas P. Bonczar and Tracy L. Snell, "Table 5. Demographic characteristics of prisoners under sentence of death, 2002," in *Capital Punishment, 2002,* U.S. Department of Justice, Bureau of Justice Statistics, Washington, DC, November 2003

of the sentences for the 7,254 inmates condemned to death for the period 1973 through 2002. During this period, 820 (11.3 percent) were executed. One-third (2,403 inmates) of those who left death row were sentenced in states where the death penalty statute was later overturned or had their sentences or convictions overturned by an appellate or higher court. Some (176) had their sentences commuted, while another 268 died while awaiting execution. (See Table 7.8.)

Using a single year as an example, of the 318 persons sentenced to death in 1995, 26 were executed, 12 died while in confinement, and 41 had their convictions or sentences overturned. (Conviction and sentencing are two separate trials under the two-part system required in death penalty cases.) Of those prisoners sentenced to death in 1995, 238 remained on death row as of December 31, 2002. (See Table 7.8.)

THE APPEALS PROCESS IN CAPITAL CASES

The appeals process in capital cases varies slightly from state to state but generally consists of similar procedures. The first step is the direct appeal in which the death sentence is automatically appealed from the trial court to the highest court of the state with criminal jurisdiction. The highest court of the state may be either the state supreme court or the highest court of criminal appeals. The state high court evaluates the trial court records for constitutional or legal errors. If the high court upholds the conviction and sentence, the defendant seeks *certiorari* in the U.S. Supreme Court. The *writ of certiorari* is a petition to the Supreme Court to review the issues brought up in the direct appeal. If the Supreme Court denies *certiorari,* the trial court's ruling stands.

If the direct appeal is denied, the inmate may then seek state *habeas corpus* appeals, starting from the trial judge and going all the way to the state's highest court. This appeal differs from the direct appeal in that the condemned may raise issues that were not and could not have been raised during the direct appeal. These issues include the incompetence of the defense lawyer, jury bias, or the suppression of evidence by police or prosecution. If the state review is denied, the condemned can appeal to the U.S. Supreme Court.

A death row inmate who has exhausted all state appeals can file a petition for a federal *habeas corpus* review on grounds of violation of his or her constitutional rights. The right may involve a violation of the Eighth Amendment to the Constitution (the ban against cruel and unusual punishment), the Fourteenth Amendment (the right to due process), and the Sixth Amendment (the right to have the assistance of counsel for defense). The inmate files the appeal with the U.S. District Court in the state in which he or she was convicted. If the district court denies the appeal, the inmate can proceed to the U.S. Circuit Court of Appeals. Finally, if the circuit court denies the appeal, the condemned can ask the U.S. Supreme Court for a *certiorari* review.

Automatic Review of Death Sentences

At year-end 2002, among the 38 states with capital punishment statutes, 37 states provided for automatic review of all death sentences, regardless of the defendant's wishes. The remaining state, South Carolina, allowed the defendant to dispense with the sentence review if the court found him competent to decide for himself (per the Supreme Court decision in *State v. Torrence,* 473 S.E.2d. 703 [S.C. 1996]). The federal death penalty procedures, however, did not provide for automatic review after a death sentence was imposed.

Although most of the 37 states authorized an automatic review of both conviction and sentence, Idaho, Indiana, Kentucky, Oklahoma, and Tennessee required review

TABLE 7.6

Criminal history profile of prisoners under sentence of death, by race and Hispanic origin, 2002

	Number of prisoners under sentence of death				Percent of prisoners under sentence of death[1]			
	All[2]	White[3]	Black[3]	Hispanic	All[2]	White[3]	Black[3]	Hispanic
U.S. total	3,557	1,597	1,539	364	100%	100%	100%	100%
Prior felony convictions								
Yes	2,119	914	976	199	64.3%	61.5%	69.0%	58.5%
No	1,177	572	439	141	35.7	38.5	31.0	41.5
Not reported	261							
Prior homicide convictions								
Yes	280	129	122	24	8.0%	8.2%	8.1%	6.7%
No	3,203	1,438	1,379	335	92.0	91.8	91.9	93.3
Not reported	74							
Legal status at time of capital offense								
Charges pending	241	121	104	16	7.5%	8.3%	7.5%	4.8%
Probation	336	134	157	39	10.5	9.2	11.4	11.8
Parole	556	217	255	76	17.3	14.9	18.5	23.0
Prison escapee	38	21	11	5	1.2	1.4	0.8	1.5
Incarcerated	103	52	41	8	3.2	3.6	3.0	2.4
Other status	17	7	8	1	0.5	0.5	0.6	0.3
None	1,924	900	803	185	59.8	62.0	58.2	56.1
Not reported	342							

[1]Percentages are based on those offenders for whom data were reported. Detail may not add to total because of rounding.
[2]Includes American Indians, Asians, and persons of unknown race.
[3]White and black categories exclude Hispanics.

SOURCE: Thomas P. Bonczar and Tracy L. Snell, "Table 8. Criminal history profile of prisoners under sentence of death, by race and Hispanic origin, 2002," in *Capital Punishment, 2002,* U.S. Department of Justice, Bureau of Justice Statistics, Washington, DC, November 2003

TABLE 7.7

Time under sentence of death and execution, by race, 1977–2002

Year of execution	Number executed			Average elapsed time from sentence to execution for:		
	All races[1]	White[2]	Black[2]	All races[1]	White[2]	Black[2]
Total	820	524	283	123 mo	119 mo	130 mo
1977-83	11	9	2	51 mo	49 mo	58 mo
1984	21	13	8	74	76	71
1985	18	11	7	71	65	80
1986	18	11	7	87	78	102
1987	25	13	12	86	78	96
1988	11	6	5	80	72	89
1989	16	8	8	95	78	112
1990	23	16	7	95	97	91
1991	14	7	7	116	124	107
1992	31	19	11	114	104	135
1993	38	23	14	113	112	121
1994	31	20	11	122	117	132
1995	56	33	22	134	128	144
1996	45	31	14	125	112	153
1997	74	45	27	133	126	147
1998	68	48	18	130	128	132
1999	98	61	33	143	143	141
2000	85	49	35	137	134	142
2001	66	48	17	142	134	166
2002	71	53	18	127	130	120

Note: Average time was calculated from the most recent sentencing date.
[1]Includes American Indians and Asians.
[2]Includes Hispanics.

SOURCE: Thomas P. Bonczar and Tracy L. Snell, "Table 11. Time under sentence of death and execution, by race, 1977–2002," in *Capital Punishment, 2002,* U.S. Department of Justice, Bureau of Justice Statistics, Washington, DC, November 2003

TABLE 7.8

Prisoners sentenced to death and outcome of the sentence, by year of sentencing, 1973–2002

Year of sentence	Number sentenced to death	Execution	Other death	Appeals or higher courts overturned— Death penalty statute	Conviction	Sentence	Sentence commuted	Other or unknown reasons	Under sentence of death 12/31/2002
1973	42	2	0	14	9	8	9	0	0
1974	149	10	4	65	15	30	22	1	2
1975	298	6	4	171	24	67	21	2	3
1976	233	14	5	136	17	43	15	0	3
1977	137	19	3	40	26	32	7	0	10
1978	185	36	6	21	36	65	8	0	13
1979	151	28	13	2	28	59	5	1	15
1980	173	45	13	3	30	50	7	0	25
1981	224	54	13	0	42	74	6	1	34
1982	265	58	17	0	38	71	8	1	72
1983	252	60	17	1	27	62	8	2	75
1984	285	58	14	2	44	65	7	8	87
1985	266	39	7	1	42	72	5	3	97
1986	300	59	20	0	45	54	7	5	110
1987	289	44	19	5	39	61	2	6	113
1988	290	45	12	1	32	58	4	0	138
1989	259	35	10	0	31	50	6	0	127
1990	252	33	9	0	35	40	2	0	133
1991	267	29	10	0	32	34	5	0	157
1992	287	29	10	0	24	39	7	0	178
1993	289	30	13	0	17	25	6	0	198
1994	315	28	10	0	23	30	3	0	221
1995	318	26	12	0	15	26	1	0	238
1996	320	15	8	0	20	33	2	0	242
1997	276	5	4	0	20	18	1	0	228
1998	300	8	6	1	14	15	1	0	255
1999	279	2	5	0	13	7	1	0	251
2000	231	3	2	0	3	6	0	0	217
2001	163	0	1	0	3	2	0	0	157
2002	159	0	1	0	0	0	0	0	158
Total, 1973-2002	7,254	820	268	463	744	1,196	176	30	3,557

Note: For those persons sentenced to death more than once, the numbers are based on the most recent death sentence.

SOURCE: Thomas P. Bonczar and Tracy L. Snell, "Appendix table 2. Prisoners sentenced to death and outcome of the sentence, by year of sentencing, 1973–2002," in *Capital Punishment, 2002,* U.S. Department of Justice, Bureau of Justice Statistics, Washington, DC, November 2003

of the sentence only. In Idaho inmates who wanted their convictions reviewed had to file an appeal or lose the right to do so. In Indiana and Kentucky defendants were allowed to waive review of their convictions.

Generally, the state's highest court of appeals conducts the review whether or not the defendant requests it. If the appellate court vacates (annuls) the conviction or the sentence, the case could be returned to the trial court for additional proceedings or for retrial. Subsequent to the resentencing or retrial, the death sentence could be reinstated.

RIGHT TO COUNSEL

The Sixth Amendment to the U.S. Constitution guarantees the "assistance of counsel for defense" in federal criminal prosecution. In 1963 the U.S. Supreme Court extended the right to counsel to state criminal prosecution of indigent (poor) persons charged with felonies (*Gideon v. Wainwright,* 372 U.S. 335). In 1972 the high court held that poor persons charged with any crime that carries a sentence of imprisonment have the right to counsel (*Argersinger v. Hamlin,* 407 U.S. 25).

Ineffective Counsel

The release near the end of the 20th century of several inmates who were said to be innocent after serving time on death row called attention to the ineffective representation of defendants unable to afford private counsel. Death penalty experts claimed that some lawyers who defend capital cases are inexperienced and ill trained. They cited the well-publicized cases of inmates exonerated as a result of college students finding evidence that defense lawyers had failed to uncover. In their November 1999 five-part series, "The Failure of the Death Penalty in Illinois" (*Chicago Tribune,* Chicago, IL), Ken Armstrong and Steve Mills examined all 285 death penalty cases since Illinois reinstated the death penalty in 1977. The journalists reported that at least 33 defendants sentenced to death in Illinois had lawyers who were later suspended or disbarred, "sanctions reserved for conduct so incompetent, unethical, or even criminal the lawyer's license [was] taken away."

Observers note that, in an increasing number of death penalty cases, the nation's indigent defense system has not delivered effective counsel to the accused. States vary in fulfilling *Gideon*. Some states have undertaken the establishment and funding of an indigent defense system; others have passed the responsibility on to individual counties. Across the United States, different jurisdictions use one or a combination of three systems to provide counsel to poor defendants. The first system used by some jurisdictions has public defenders who are usually government employees. Under the second system, the court-assigned counsel system, a judge appoints private lawyers to represent the poor. A third system involves contract lawyers who bid for the job of providing indigent defense.

Court-assigned lawyers belong to a list of private lawyers who accept clients on a case-by-case basis. In jurisdictions that employ these lawyers, judges appoint lawyers from a list of private bar members and determine their pay. In most cases the pay is very low. Beth A. Wilkinson, co-chair of the Constitution Project's Death Penalty Initiative, testified before the U.S. Senate Judiciary Committee hearing (June 27, 2001) that many jurisdictions paid their court-appointed lawyers very low hourly rates for capital defense. For example, Alabama paid $20 to $40 an hour, with a limit of $2,000. This means that a lawyer spending 600 hours preparing for a capital case earned a little over $3 dollars an hour. (According to the American Civil Liberties Union [ACLU], defending a capital case at the trial level takes about 700 to 1,000 hours.) Wilkinson added that while Tennessee paid $20 to $30 an hour, Mississippi had a $1,000 limit. Moreover, courts often refuse to authorize the needed funds for investigating the case and using expert testimony. In contrast, the prosecution usually has unlimited funds at its disposal.

Some states, such as Colorado and New York, have both public defender offices and capital defender offices that specialize in death penalty cases. When New York brought back capital punishment in 1995, the death penalty statute required the establishment of a capital defender office with a $15 million allotment to train trial lawyers and investigators. But other states, such as Alabama, Georgia, Mississippi, and Virginia, have no statewide public defender system. Until 2001, of Texas's 254 counties, only 3 had a public defender program, but in June 2001 legislation was passed for the first time requiring state funding for indigent defense. In 1998 Mississippi passed a law providing for a statewide public defender system, but it was never funded. In 2000 the legislature repealed the law because of the shortage of funds. As of November 30, 2003, the state funded indigent defense in capital cases only.

Postconviction Review

While death row inmates have the right to seek review of their conviction and sentence, they do not have the right to counsel for postconviction proceedings (*Murray v. Giarratano,* 492 U.S. 1, 1989). Since most of those awaiting execution are poor, they must find lawyers willing to handle appeals for free. In 1995 Congress discontinued federal funding of private organizations (called resource centers) that represented death row inmates in postconviction proceedings. As a result, private organizations and law firms, both proponents and opponents of the death penalty, concerned with the increasing problems in capital cases, now volunteer their services. Some hold training seminars on the complex process of appellate review, while others provide research and investigation.

Some private organizations, however, cannot keep up with the large numbers of death row inmates. For example, the Equal Justice Initiative of Alabama (EJI; Montgomery), comprising five lawyers, has been representing a majority of Alabama inmates seeking appeals. As of November 2003, the EJI counted 190 death row inmates in the state, with 300 more facing trials involving capital murder. Under state law, lawyers appointed to represent indigent inmates could not be paid more than $1,000 per case.

ARE INNOCENT PERSONS BEING EXECUTED?

In 1993 the Subcommittee on Civil and Constitutional Rights of the U.S. House Judiciary Committee used data on death row exonerations provided by the Death Penalty Information Center (DPIC; Washington, D.C.) for its hearing on "Innocence and the Death Penalty: Assessing the Danger of Mistaken Executions." Since then, the DPIC has periodically updated its List of Inmates Released [from Death Row].

According to the DPIC, from 1973 to July 28, 2003, 111 death row inmates in 25 states were exonerated and freed from death row. Between 1973 and 1993 a total of 55 inmates were released, an average of 2.75 inmates each year. In 1996 that number increased to six inmates, rising to eight inmates each in 1999 and 2000. Between January 1 and July 28, 2003, nine inmates were freed from death row. (See Figure 7.2.)

Between 1973 and July 28, 2003, Florida accounted for the greatest number of exonerations (23), followed by Illinois (17), Oklahoma (7), and Texas (7). Georgia, Arizona, and Louisiana each released six inmates from death row. (See Figure 7.3.) Of the inmates released, 52 were black and 45 were white. Twelve were Hispanic, 1 was a Native American, and 1 was of "other" race. The inmates had spent an average of 8.91 years on death row.

According to the DPIC:

The definition of innocence that DPIC uses in placing defendants on the list is that they had been convicted

FIGURE 7.2

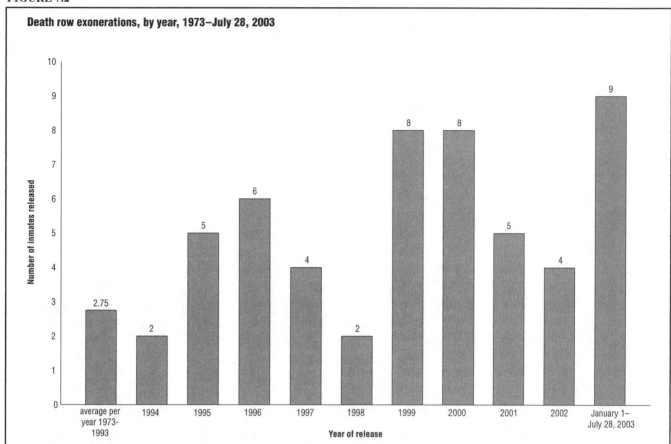

Death row exonerations, by year, 1973–July 28, 2003

SOURCE: Figure constructed by Gale Group staff from the graphic "Death Row Exonerations by Year (Total through 2001: 98)" and additional Death Penalty Information Center text data, in *Innocence and the Death Penalty,* Death Penalty Information Center, Washington, DC, 2003 [Online] http://www.deathpenaltyinfo.org/article.php?did=412&scid=6 [accessed October 19, 2003]. Reproduced with permission.

and sentenced to death, and subsequently either a) their conviction was overturned and they were acquitted at a retrial, or all charges were dropped; or b) they were given an absolute pardon by the governor based on new evidence of innocence.

Those who are concerned with the administration of the death penalty often refer to the increasing number of death row exonerations on the DPIC list. However, some death penalty supporters and researchers have challenged what they call the "death penalty innocents." In 2002 Ward A. Campbell, California Supervising Deputy Attorney General, investigated the 102 cases of exonerated death row inmates on the DPIC list. In his report, *Critique of DPIC List "Innocence: Freed from Death Row,"* Campbell concluded that at least 68 of the 102 inmates on the list should not have been included. Campbell found that "many defendants on the List were not 'actually innocent' [meaning prosecution found the defendant innocent of the crime]." Some have pled to lesser charges and had their sentences commuted. Campbell noted that "an acquittal because the prosecution has not proven guilt beyond a reasonable doubt does not mean that the defendant did not actually commit the crime."

On October 16, 2002, Senator Orrin Hatch (R-UT) confirmed Campbell's findings on the DPIC list of exonerees during the U.S. Senate Committee on the Judiciary's hearing on the Innocence Protection Act of 2002 (S. 486). Senator Hatch mentioned the example of 23 Florida inmates released from death row included on the list. On June 20, 2002, the Florida Commission on Capital Cases released the results of its investigation into these cases (*Case Histories: A Review of 23 Individuals Released from Death Row*). The commission concluded,

> Of these 23 inmates, none were found "innocent" even when acquitted, because no such verdict exists. A defendant is found guilty or not guilty, never innocent. The guilt of only four defendants, however, was ever truly doubted.... An analysis of the remaining 19 inmates can be divided into three categories that account for their releases: (1) six cases were remanded due to evidence issues, (2) an additional seven were remanded in light of witness issues, and (3) the remaining six were remanded as a result of issues involving court officials.

A Case of Innocence

Anthony Porter of Illinois was convicted of two 1982 murders and sentenced to death in 1983. He was convicted

FIGURE 7.3

Death row exonerations by state, 1973–July 28, 2003

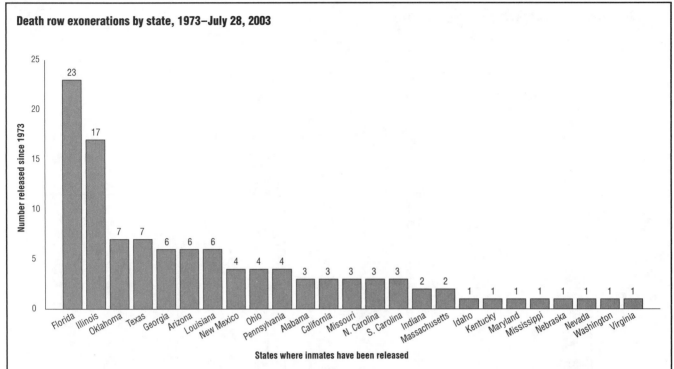

States where inmates have been released

SOURCE: Figure constructed by Gale Group staff from the graphic "Death Row Exonerations by State (Total: 99; as of 1/3/02)" and additional Death Penalty Information Center text data, in *Innocence and the Death Penalty,* Death Penalty Information Center, Washington, DC, 2003 [Online] http://www.deathpenaltyinfo.org/article.php?did=412&scid=6 [accessed October 19, 2003]. Reproduced with permission.

based on the testimony of two eyewitnesses who separately claimed they saw Porter commit the crimes. By 1998 Porter had exhausted all his appeals. On September 21, 1998, two days before Porter's scheduled execution, the defense lawyer filed an emergency petition with the Illinois Supreme Court, arguing that the defendant was mentally retarded (he had an IQ of 51) and did not understand what was about to happen to him. The court granted Porter a stay of execution to determine his mental competency.

In the meantime, an investigative journalism class taught by David Protess (Northwestern University, Medill School of Journalism, Evanston, IL) had chosen Porter's case to review. The professor, his students, and a private investigator, Paul Ciolino, uncovered evidence of Porter's innocence. The first eyewitness (the second one had died) confessed to giving false testimony. The group tracked down the wife of the real murderer in Milwaukee (the couple had moved soon after Porter's arrest) and were able to convince her to confess to being present when her husband shot the victims. Next, the investigator succeeded in obtaining a videotaped confession from the murderer, Alstory Simon. On March 11, 1999, Porter's conviction was reversed; he had been on death row for 17 years.

DNA TESTING

The National Commission on the Future of DNA Evidence, in *Postconviction DNA Testing: Recommendations*

for Handling Requests (National Institute of Justice, Washington, D.C., September 1999), observed how, in *Herrera v. Collins* (506 U.S. 390, 1993), the Supreme Court noted that newly discovered evidence does not constitute grounds for a federal *habeas* relief if there is no evidence of a constitutional violation occurring during state criminal proceedings. Leonel Torres Herrera, 10 years after his initial trial, alleged that he was innocent of a double murder, presenting "actual evidence" that his brother, who had since died, had committed the crime. The commission, however, noted that today, with the availability of DNA testing, "the possibility of demonstrating actual innocence has moved from the realm of theory to the actual."

The science of deoxyribonucleic acid (DNA) testing is improving rapidly. When DNA testing was first used in criminal trials starting in the mid-1980s, DNA samples had to be not only fresh but contain thousands of cells. As DNA technology has become more sophisticated, scientists are able to test a single cell for DNA patterns that could link suspects to hair or semen found on a victim. Today a crime laboratory can identify unique DNA patterns in a tiny sample of just 100 to 200 cells. DNA testing has played a substantial role in proving the innocence of a number of persons wrongly convicted. As of November 30, 2003, the DPIC reported that 12 of the 111 inmates released from death row since 1973 were exonerated by DNA evidence.

When biological material has been left at the scene of the crime, DNA testing could, in some cases, establish with near certainty a defendant's innocence or guilt. DNA, which stores the genetic code of the human body, is found in saliva, skin tissue, bones, blood, semen, and the root and shaft of hair. Biological samples that were difficult to test in the 1980s may yield more accurate information where previous results had proved inconclusive.

In 1996 David Protess and another group of students at Northwestern University's Medill School of Journalism helped uncover new evidence that proved the innocence of four black men who were convicted for a 1978 gang rape and double murder. Two received life imprisonment while the other two were sentenced to death. DNA tests helped prove the men's innocence. In March 1999 the four men received a $36 million settlement from Cook County, Illinois, to resolve a lawsuit charging police misconduct. In a Florida case, Frank Lee Smith was sentenced to death in 1986 for the rape and murder of an eight-year-old girl. DNA testing performed in 2000 proved Smith's innocence. However, Smith had died of cancer the previous year while awaiting execution.

Backlog of DNA Testing

In December 2000 Congress authorized the U.S. Department of Justice to provide state crime laboratories more than $30 million to analyze the backlog of DNA samples that had been collected but never tested. Under the DNA Analysis Backlog Reduction Act of 2000 (Public Law 106-546), states would receive funding to conduct tests on about a million samples collected from criminals and crime scenes that had never been analyzed. Each test costs about $2,000 to perform. Of this number, about 180,000 rape kits nationwide had not been tested. In August 2001 U.S. Attorney General John Ashcroft announced that, in addition to the state initiative, the Department of Justice had authorized the collection of DNA samples from about 20,000 to 30,000 federal, military, and District of Columbia offenders.

The Report to the Attorney General on Delays in Forensic DNA Analysis (National Institute of Justice [NIJ], Washington, D.C., March 2003) revealed that a task force assembled by the NIJ found a continuing backlog in the testing of DNA samples collected at crime scenes. While an estimated 350,000 rape and homicide DNA samples needed testing, just 10 percent of the samples were in forensic crime laboratories. Most of the evidence samples were in the custody of law enforcement agencies because most laboratories lacked the proper storage facilities for preventing damage to the evidence.

Even if the laboratories had the proper storage facilities, the analysis of DNA samples could not take place because of the shortage of trained forensic scientists. Newly hired scientists need on-the-job training that requires an experienced scientist to spend time working one-on-one with new hires. The task force found that even when these problems were confronted, public crime laboratories could not retain their staff because of their lower compensation, compared to that paid by private companies.

Most States Provide Postconviction DNA Testing

At the hearing on the Innocence Protection Act of 2002 before the U.S. Senate Committee on the Judiciary on October 16, 2002, Senator Orrin Hatch reported that virtually every state provides access to DNA testing for postconviction defendants. Twenty-six states had enacted specific statutory provisions for DNA testing. Six states— Colorado, Connecticut, Mississippi, Nevada, South Carolina, and South Dakota—relied on general state laws and/or legal decisions in offering DNA testing, while Alabama and Ohio provided for the testing through an administrative policy or program. Georgia, New Hampshire, Wyoming, and the federal government had no statute or other means of providing postconviction DNA testing.

To disprove the claim that numerous death row inmates were in desperate need of getting access to DNA testing to prove their innocence, Senator Hatch presented a detailed chart illustrating the total number of death row inmates in each state and the number of those who had requested DNA testing and been denied. The chart showed that out of 3,554 death row inmates nationwide, just 18 had requested and been denied DNA testing. This translated to 0.51 percent of all death row state inmates. Furthermore, of the 23 federal defendants currently on death row, not one sought a DNA test to prove his or her innocence. (See Table 7.9.)

As of November 30, 2003, a total of 32 death penalty states had statutes that provided DNA testing to death row defendants. In 2003 Colorado, Connecticut, Georgia, and Nevada passed legislation providing for postconviction DNA testing. In Mississippi a bill for DNA testing failed to pass. New Hampshire and South Dakota did not enact any postconviction DNA testing law but offered testing pursuant to court decisions. South Carolina had a DNA testing bill pending. Alabama remained without a postconviction DNA testing statute or any pending legislation for the passage of such a statute. As in 2002 South Carolina offered postconviction DNA testing through administrative policy. Wyoming, however, did not pass legislation, introduce any bill, or have any court decision that provided for postconviction DNA testing. The federal Innocence Protection Act of 2003, with a provision for DNA testing, remained pending.

FAIRNESS AND THE DEATH PENALTY

Racial Questions

Death penalty cases raise a fairness issue. Opponents of the death penalty claim that minorities and poor

TABLE 7.9

Denials of DNA testing to death row inmates, as of December 31, 2001

Fed./State	Post-conviction DNA testing procedure	No. of death row inmates As of 12/31/01	Denied DNA test
Federal	No policy because no inmate has ever requested a DNA test	23	0
Alabama	Administrative policy	181	0
Arkansas	ACA § 16-112-201-205; 207	40	0
Arizona	Az. St §13-4240	121	0
California	Ca. Pen. Code § 1405	606	1
Colorado	Case by case basis	6	0
Connecticut	Conn. Gen. Stat. § 52-582 (2001)	7	0
Delaware	Del. Code. Ann. Tit. 11 § 4504	15	0
Florida	Fl. St. § 925.11	370	0
Georgia	No statute	121	0
Idaho	Id. St. 1949.02 and 1927.19	22	1
Illinois	Il. St. Ch. 725 § 5/116-3	160	1
Indiana	In. 35-38-7-5	36	0
Kansas	KSA 21-25-12	4	0
Kentucky	KRS Ch. 422 HB 4	37	0
Louisiana	La. C.Cr.P. Art. 926.1	90	0
Maryland	Md. Crim. Proc. § 8-201	14	0
Missouri	Rev. St. Mo. 547.035	70	1
Mississippi	Judicially created standard in *Ellis v. State*, 97-M-01326.	66	0
Montana	Can be provided by MCA 46-21-102	6	0
Nebraska	Ne. St. § 29-4120	7	0
New Hampshire	No statute or provision	0	0
New Jersey	NJ St. 2a:84A-32a	14	0
New Mexico	NM St § 31-1A-1	3	0
New York	NY C. Cr. P. § 440.30	5	0
North Carolina	NC Gen. Stat. 15A-269	215	0
Nevada	By court order	87	3*
Ohio	Voluntary AG program	204	0
Oklahoma	OK Stat. Tit. 22 § 1371	103	1
Oregon	OR St. T. 14 Ch. 138	25	0
Pennsylvania	42 P.A.C.S. 9543.1	244	0
South Carolina	Case by case basis	73	1
South Dakota	Judicially created standard in *Jenner v. State*, 590 N.W.2d 463 (S.D. 1999).	5	1
Tennessee	Tn. Code Ann. 40-30-401	95	0
Texas	Tx. Code Crim. Pro. 64.01-05	431	8
Utah	Ut. Code Ann. 78-35A § 301-304	11	0
Virginia	Va. Code § 19.2-327.1	24	0
Washington	R.C.W. 10.73.170	11	0
Wyoming	No statute	2	0
Total		**3554**	**18 (.51%)**

*Estimate.

SOURCE: Orrin Hatch, "Attachment D: Denials of DNA Testing to Death Row Inmates," in *Minority Views on S. 486* (The Innocence Protection Act of 2002), U.S. Senate Committee on the Judiciary, Washington, DC, October 16, 2002 [Online] http://www.prodeathpenalty.com/Articles/MINORVIEWS. PDF [accessed October 20, 2003]

defendants are more likely to be convicted and receive the death penalty than white and wealthy defendants. In 1987, on appeal, the lawyers for Warren McCleskey, a convicted murderer, brought before the Supreme Court the Baldus study (by Professors David C. Baldus, George Woodworth, and Charles Pulanski), an analysis of 2,000 cases in Georgia in the 1970s.

This study showed that black defendants who were convicted of killing whites were more likely to receive death sentences than white murderers or blacks who killed blacks. The justices, in *McCleskey v. Kemp* (481 U.S. 279, 1987), rejected the study, declaring that "apparent disparities ... are an inevitable part of our criminal justice system" and that there were enough safeguards built into the legal system to protect every defendant.

In 1998 Dr. Baldus and others, expanding on the Baldus study, found evidence of race-of-victim disparities in 26 out of 29 death penalty states ("Racial Discrimination and the Death Penalty in the Post-*Furman* Era: An Empirical and Legal Analysis with Recent Findings from Philadelphia," *Cornell Law Review,* Vol. 83). The researchers found that the race of the victim was related to whether capital punishment was imposed. A defendant was more likely to receive the death penalty if the victim was white than if the victim was black.

These studies were consistent with a 1990 U.S. government study of capital punishment. The U.S. General Accounting Office (GAO), in *Death Penalty Sentencing: Research Indicates Pattern of Racial Disparities* (Washington, D.C.), reviewed 28 studies on race and the death penalty. The GAO reported that "in 82 percent of the studies, the race of the victim was found to influence the likelihood of being charged with capital murder or receiving the death penalty." The GAO found that when the victim was white, the defendant, whether white or black, was more likely to get the death sentence.

GAO added that in the small number of horrendous murders, death sentences were more likely to be imposed, regardless of race. Nevertheless, when the offender killed a person while robbing him or when the murderer had a previous record, the race of the victim played a role. The studies also showed that for crimes of passion, the convicted person (regardless of race) rarely received the death penalty.

In testimony before the Illinois House of Representatives' hearing on the state's system of capital punishment in September 1999, Richard C. Dieter, Executive Director of the Death Penalty Information Center (Washington, D.C.), noted,

Ten out of 12 people who have been released from Illinois's death row are members of a minority. Most are African American. That doesn't prove bias, but it should raise concerns. Illinois's death row is made up of approximately 156 individuals, 97 of whom are Black—that's 62 percent in a state where the Black population is less than 15 percent. Again, those figures do not prove any racial bias, but such a glaring disproportion is evidence that something is wrong at some level of society. If race is playing a role in who is sentenced to death, then it can also be playing a role in who is wrongly convicted.

Some persons claim that district attorneys, who alone decide which case to try as a death penalty case, may be motivated by politics or racial prejudice to impose the death penalty on a minority. Professor Jeffrey Pokorak of St. Mary's University School of Law, in "Probing the Capital Prosecutor's Perspective: Race of the Discretionary Actors" (*Cornell Law Review,* Vol. 83 [1998]), found that 97.5 percent (1,794 out of 1,838 prosecutors in the 38 states with capital punishment) were white. Only 1.2 percent each were black or Hispanic.

Racial Justice Legislation

In 1998 Kentucky became the first state to enact a racial justice law (Racial Justice Act, SB171), prohibiting the execution of a convicted person when evidence shows racial discrimination in prosecution or sentencing. Other states that have considered similar legislation include Florida, Georgia, Indiana, Nebraska, New Mexico, North Carolina, Ohio, Oregon, and Texas. As of November 30, 2003, however, no other state had passed similar legislation.

FIRST FEDERAL STUDY OF RACIAL AND ETHNIC BIAS

In July 2000 President Bill Clinton ordered the Department of Justice to review the administration of the federal death penalty system. This order came in the aftermath of a request for clemency by Raul Juan Garza, scheduled to be executed by the federal government on August 5, 2000. Garza's lawyer contended that it was unfair to execute his client because the federal death penalty discriminated against members of minorities.

On September 12, 2000, the Justice Department released *The Federal Death Penalty System: A Statistical Survey (1988–2000),* providing information on the federal death penalty since the passage of the first federal capital punishment law in 1988 (the Anti-Drug Abuse Act). From 1988 to 1994 prosecutors in the 94 federal districts were required to submit to the U.S. attorney general for review and approval only those cases in which the U.S. attorney sought the death penalty. During this period the U.S. attorneys sought the death penalty in 52 cases and received authorization in 47 cases.

In 1995 the Justice Department adopted a new protocol, requiring U.S. attorneys to submit for review all cases in which a defendant was charged with a crime subject to the death penalty, regardless of whether they intended to seek authorization to pursue the death penalty. These cases were first reviewed by the attorney general's Review Committee on Capital Cases, a committee of senior Justice Department lawyers.

The period 1995–2000, which provides a more extensive picture of the Justice Department's internal decision process as it pertains to the federal death penalty, showed that between January 27, 1995, and July 20, 2000, at every phase of the federal process, minority defendants were overrepresented. Of the 682 defendants whose cases were submitted for review by federal prosecutors, 19.6 percent were white, 47.5 percent were black, and 28.6 percent were Hispanic. The prosecutors recommended seeking the death penalty for 183 of 682 cases submitted for review. Of these 183 cases, about two-thirds (44.3 percent blacks and 21.3 percent Hispanics) were members of minorities. The attorney general reviewed 588 of the cases and authorized the U.S. attorneys to seek the death penalty in 159 cases. Of the 159 defendants, 44.7 percent were black and 20.1 percent were Hispanic. Only about 28 percent were white. (See Table 7.10.)

Racial Disparity in Plea Bargaining

It should be noted that the attorney general's decision to seek the death penalty may be changed up until the jury has returned a sentencing verdict. This change may be sought by the defense lawyer, the U.S. attorney, the Review Committee, or by the attorney general. A plea agreement is one avenue that may result in the withdrawal of the death penalty. This means that the defendant enters into an agreement with the U.S. attorney resulting in a guilty plea, saving him or her from the death penalty. From 1995 to 2000, after the attorney general sought the death penalty for 159 defendants, 51 defendants entered into plea agreements. Almost twice as many white defendants (48 percent, or 21 out of 44) as blacks (25 percent, or 18 of 71) received a plea agreement. About 28 percent (9 of 32) of Hispanics entered into a plea agreement. (See Table 7.10.)

Government Defends Data

The National Institute of Justice observed that, "generally speaking, once submitted for review [to obtain a death penalty authorization], minorities proceeded to the next stages in the death penalty process at lower rates than whites." The institute claimed that the attorney general authorized the death penalty for a larger proportion of whites being considered (38 percent, or 44 of 115), compared to 25 percent (71 of 287) of black defendants and 20 percent (32 of 160) of Hispanic defendants. (See Table 7.10.)

SECOND FEDERAL STUDY OF RACIAL AND ETHNIC BIAS

On June 6, 2001, the Justice Department released a supplement to the September 2000 report—*The Federal Death Penalty System: Supplementary Data, Analysis and Revised Protocols for Capital Case Review.* That same day Attorney General John Ashcroft told the Judiciary Committee of the U.S. House of Representatives that the report confirmed that the subsequent study of the administration of the federal death penalty showed no indication of racial or ethnic bias.

The follow-up study had been ordered by his predecessor, Attorney General Janet Reno. In addition to the

TABLE 7.10

Distribution of defendants within each stage of the federal death penalty process, 1995–2000

STAGE	TOTAL #	%	White #	%	Black #	%	Hispanic #	%	Other #	%
Submitted by U.S. attorneys	682	100.0%	134	19.6%	324	47.5%	195	28.6%	29	4.3%
No recommendation	5	100.0%	1	20.0%	1	20.0%	3	60.0%	0	0.0%
Recommendation not to seek death penalty (DP)	494	100.0%	85	17.2%	242	49.0%	153	31.0%	14	2.8%
Recommendation to seek DP	183	100.0%	48	26.2%	81	44.3%	39	21.3%	15	8.2%
Considered by review committee	618	100.0%	119	19.3%	301	48.7%	172	27.8%	26	4.2%
No recommendation	15	100.0%	4	26.7%	6	40.0%	4	26.7%	1	6.7%
Recommendation not to seek DP	420	100.0%	68	16.2%	215	51.2%	125	29.8%	12	2.9%
Recommendation to seek DP	183	100.0%	47	25.7%	80	43.7%	43	23.5%	13	7.1%
Considered by attorney general (AG)	588	100.0%	115	19.6%	287	48.8%	160	27.2%	26	4.4%
Decision deferred or pending	12	100.0%	3	25.0%	4	33.3%	4	33.3%	1	8.3%
Authorization not to seek DP	417	100.0%	68	16.3%	212	50.8%	124	29.7%	13	3.1%
Authorization to seek DP	159	100.0%	44	27.7%	71	44.7%	32	20.1%	12	7.5%
Authorized by AG to seek DP	159	100.0%	44	27.7%	71	44.7%	32	20.1%	12	7.5%
DP notice withdrawn – plea agreement	51	100.0%	21	41.2%	18	35.3%	9	17.6%	3	5.9%
DP notice withdrawn – subsequent AG decision	11	100.0%	1	9.1%	3	27.3%	5	45.5%	2	18.2%
DP notice dismissed or trial terminated	4	100.0%	0	0.0%	1	25.0%	3	75.0%	0	0.0%
Pending trial or completion of trial	51	100.0%	11	21.6%	23	45.1%	13	25.5%	4	7.8%
Not convicted of capital charge	1	100.0%	0	0.0%	1	100.0%	0	0.0%	0	0.0%
Convicted of capital charge	41	100.0%	11	26.8%	25	61.0%	2	4.9%	3	7.3%
Convicted of capital charge	41	100.0%	11	26.8%	25	61.0%	2	4.9%	3	7.3%
Jury verdict – DP not recommended	21	100.0%	7	33.3%	12	57.1%	0	0.0%	2	9.5%
Jury verdict – DP recommended	20	100.0%	4	20.0%	13	65.0%	2	10.0%	1	5.0%
Sentenced to death	20	100.0%	4	20.0%	13	65.0%	2	10.0%	1	5.0%
DP recommended by jury but not yet imposed	2	100.0%	0	0.0%	0	0.0%	2	100.0%	0	0.0%
DP vacated by court, further action pending	4	100.0%	1	25.0%	3	75.0%	0	0.0%	0	0.0%
Death sentence pending	14	100.0%	3	21.4%	10	71.4%	0	0.0%	1	7.1%

SOURCE: "Table 1A: Distribution of Defendants Within Each Stage of the Federal Death Penalty Process (1995–2000)," in *The Federal Death Penalty System: A Statistical Survey (1988–2000)*, U.S. Department of Justice, Washington, DC, September 12, 2000

682 cases submitted by federal prosecutors for review in the first study of the federal death penalty, another 291 cases were analyzed, for a total of 973 cases. These included cases that should have been submitted for review for the first report but were not, those in which the defendant eventually entered into a plea agreement for a lesser sentence, and cases in which the death penalty could have been sought but was not. Among the 973 defendants, 17 percent (166) were white, 42 percent (408) were black, and 36 percent (350) were Hispanic.

According to the supplement, from 1995 to 2000, of the 973 defendants eligible for capital charges, federal prosecutors requested authorization to pursue the death penalty against 81 percent of whites, 29 percent of blacks, and 56 percent of Hispanics. The attorney general ultimately authorized seeking the death penalty for 27 percent of the white defendants, 17 percent of the black defendants, and 9 percent of the Hispanic defendants.

Critics of the supplementary report pointed out that the second federal review failed to address many issues. Following the release of the September 2000 survey, then Attorney General Reno ordered a study to find out how death penalty cases are taken into the federal system when there is joint state and federal jurisdiction. The June report did not cover this issue. Instead, the report described a

National Institute of Justice (NIJ) meeting on January 10, 2001, in which researchers and practitioners agreed that such a study "would entail a highly complex, multi-year research initiative" and that "even if such a study were carried out, it could not be expected to yield definitive answers concerning the reasons for disparities in federal death penalty."

Testifying before the Senate Judiciary Committee on June 11, 2001, Professor David C. Baldus (Joseph B. Tye Distinguished Professor of Law, College of Law, University of Iowa) reported that he was one of the researchers at the NIJ January 2001 meeting. Baldus claimed that, while it was true he and others at the meeting agreed that the study ordered by Attorney General Reno would likely take two years to complete, the consensus was that "such a study would provide the best possible evidence on the question." Baldus further pointed out that quite some time had elapsed since that meeting and the first report, and still the Justice Department had not taken any steps to initiate such a study.

On July 20, 2001, the NIJ published a solicitation for research of the federal death penalty, including the decision-making factors that determine whether a homicide case is prosecuted in the federal or state system, as well as issues of race/ethnicity and geography in the imposition of the death penalty. This allows researchers to apply for government grants in order to complete the requested research, but such research has yet to be undertaken.

The American Civil Liberties Union (ACLU) noted that, unlike the September 2000 report, the new Justice Department report did not include information on whether the supplemental 291 cases were from all or just some districts and, therefore, whether or not they represented all of the death penalty-eligible cases between 1995 and 2000. The ACLU also noted that, while the report found that federal prosecutors were less likely to submit cases of black and Hispanic defendants to the attorney general for death penalty authorizations and that the attorney general authorized capital punishment for more whites than blacks and Hispanics, there was no information about the decision-making process behind prosecuting on the federal level and of offering plea agreements.

STUDIES OF THE U.S. DEATH PENALTY SYSTEM

Liebman Study

James S. Liebman, Jeffrey Fagan, and Valerie West conducted the first study of its kind—a statistical study of modern American capital appeals—for the U.S. Senate Judiciary Committee. The study, called *A Broken System: Error Rates in Capital Cases, 1973–1995* (June 12, 2000), examined all death penalty sentences (5,760) imposed in the United States over a 20-year period.

On direct appeal, the state high courts reviewed 4,578 death sentences. It should be noted that the authors use "death sentences" and "capital judgments" interchangeably. The study found that two of every three death sentences (68 percent) reviewed by the courts all across the country were found to have serious errors. For every 100 death sentences, 41 were returned to the courts during state appeal because of serious errors. Of the 59 death sentences that reached the second state appeal, another 6 went back to court because of errors. At the third level of appeal—with the federal courts—21 more cases were remanded to the lower courts because of more errors found. All in all, of the original 100 death penalty sentences, 68 had serious errors that required retrial. Of the 68 persons who were retried, 82 percent (56 persons) were found not deserving of the death penalty. Another five inmates were found innocent of the capital crime for which they received the death sentence.

THE LIEBMAN STUDY IS ANALYZED. Critics have found "errors" in the Liebman study. Appearing before the U.S. Senate Committee on the Judiciary hearing on "Reducing the Risk of Executing the Innocent: The Report of the Illinois Governor's Commission on Capital Punishment" (June 12, 2002), Senator Strom Thurmond (R-SC) warned,

A Columbia University report known as the Liebman study is often cited as proof that capital punishment in this country is deeply flawed. This study ... alleged that from 1973 to 1995, 70 percent of death penalty convictions were reversed on appeal. The implication is that 70 percent of the time, innocent people were sentenced to death. This study should be viewed carefully because during the time period addressed by this study, the Supreme Court issued a series of retroactive rules that nullified a number of verdicts. These reversals were not based on the actual innocence of defendants, but rather were based on procedural rules.

Then Nevada Attorney General Frankie Sue Del Papa also took issue with Liebman's conclusions. According to the attorney general, Liebman claimed that, in Nevada, of the 108 death sentences, 34 were reversed, accounting for an error rate of 38 percent. (The correct percentage is 31.5 percent.) The attorney general's researchers found 152 cases with 30 death sentence reversals for an error rate of 19.7 percent. Liebman also used a two-year period to determine the reversal rate of federal *habeas appeals*. He reached an overall error rate of 50 percent after finding two reversals out of four that underwent federal review. Del Papa's office found 17 federal reviews with four reversals for a 23.5 percent error rate. According to Del Papa,

Liebman creates the impression that the reversals are due to innocence, but most are attorney or judge procedural errors. Some are cases where juries followed the existing law, but later the Supreme Court changed it, and constitutional changes are applied retroactively on death cases, to give the defendant every benefit. Liebman also failed to report that after a new trial or penalty hearing, in 12 of those 31 cases death sentences were imposed again. In 13 cases, inmates received "life-in-prison" sentences. Those were not inmates found to be innocent of their murders!

Latzer Study

Barry Latzer and James N. G. Cauthen noted that their reexamination of the Liebman study found that about one-fourth (27 percent)—and not two-thirds (68 percent)—of capital convictions were reversed between 1973 and 1995. In "Capital Appeals Revisited" (*Judicature,* Vol. 84, Number 2, September-October 2000), the authors noted that the Liebman study did not differentiate between reversals of convictions and reversals of death sentences.

Latzer and Cauthen conducted their own investigation, based on the theory that many of the appeals resulted in reversed sentences but not reversed convictions. The study covered the period 1990–99, using reversal data in the same 26 states studied by Liebman and his colleagues. Latzer and Cauthen wanted more recent data of the death penalty system that would provide more complete reversal rate differences.

The authors found that, of the 837 death penalty reversals in state-level direct appeal or postconviction review, 61 percent were sentence reversals, and 39 percent were conviction reversals (reversals addressing the guilt or innocence of the defendant). Using Liebman's conclusion that 5 of 10 capital judgments were reversed at either the direct-appeal phase or postconviction review phase, Latzer and Cauthen applied this finding to their study and concluded that, of the five reversals, three were sentence reversals and two were conviction reversals.

The authors also investigated reversals at the federal level, using data from the Ninth Circuit Court of Appeals, the largest of the circuit courts. Of the 29 capital cases reversed by the court during the 10-year period, 21 (72.4 percent) were sentence reversals, and 8 (27.7 percent) were conviction reversals. This was consistent with the authors' findings regarding direct-appeal and postconviction sentence reversals. Using Liebman's finding that 68 of 100 capital judgments were reversed, Latzer and Cauthen concluded, "If 68 of 100 capital decisions are reversed after direct, post-conviction, and federal *habeas corpus* review, and 39 percent of these are conviction reversals, then convictions in 26.52 (39 percent of 68) of 100 capital decisions are reversed."

STATES' IMPOSITION OF THE DEATH PENALTY

Several states have commissioned studies of their death penalty system. These states include Arizona, Connecticut, Delaware, Illinois, Indiana, Maryland, Nebraska, Nevada, North Carolina, Texas, and Virginia. Results of some of these follow.

Texas

In 1999 the Texas legislature passed a bill that would have required appointment of counsel for indigent representation; then Governor George W. Bush, however, vetoed the legislation. On June 14, 2001, Governor Rick Perry signed the Texas Fair Defense Act (Senate Bill 7), providing, for the first time, state funding for indigent defense services. The $12 million yearly appropriation will help establish public defender offices. Two lawyers will be provided in capital cases, unless the state indicates in writing that it will not seek the death penalty. The law also limits judges' powers by requiring appointments be made from a rotating list of qualified lawyers. Moreover, courts must pay reasonable fees, including necessary overhead reimbursements.

Under the new law, death penalty lawyers have to attend annual training on capital defense in order to remain on the rotating list. In addition, Senate Bill 7 establishes a Texas Task Force on Indigent Defense to be responsible for setting standards for lawyers for different cases. The task force will also monitor the operation of the public defender programs in the counties. The task force and the county capital appointment committee will review the list of lawyers who handle capital cases.

The Texas Fair Defense Act was passed as a result of findings by Texas Appleseed, a nonpartisan legal advocacy group. On December 12, 2000, Texas Appleseed reported that, unlike other active death penalty states, Texas had been "virtually alone" in not having a statewide program to assist indigent defendants with legal representation (*The Fair Defense Report: Analysis of Indigent Defense Practices in Texas,* Texas Appleseed Fair Defense Project, Austin, TX). As of November 20, 2000, among states that most actively imposed the death penalty, Texas was one of two states that did not fund indigent defense representation (Arizona was the other state). Texas was also the only state that had no statewide oversight commission, public defender agencies, and capital trial unit.

Texas Appleseed pointed out that Texas did not have an oversight commission that could have developed standards for appointment and compensation of lawyers in capital cases. In some states, a similar commission further monitors the performance of defense counsel and the judges' fee decisions.

Many death penalty states have a specialized statewide capital trial unit that assists court-appointed private defense lawyers. In addition, nine states—Colorado, Connecticut, Delaware, Maryland, Missouri, New Hampshire, New Jersey, New Mexico, and Wyoming—have a public defender program, most of which provide public defenders in every county statewide. Texas, however, used private lawyers appointed by judges on a case-by-case basis. These lawyers lacked the support of a public defender system that could have made available the expertise of other lawyers more experienced in capital cases, as well as the training programs that such a system provides.

Maryland

On January 7, 2003, the University of Maryland released a state-commissioned study of the use of the death penalty in the state (Raymond Paternoster et al., *An Empirical Analysis of Maryland's Death Sentencing System with Respect to the Influence of Race and Legal Jurisdiction*). The researchers reviewed 1,311 death-eligible cases out of 6,000 murder cases prosecuted between 1978 and 1999. Of the 1,311 death-eligible cases, state attorneys filed a formal notice to seek the death penalty in 353 cases (27 percent). Of the 353 cases, state attorneys dropped the death penalty notice in 140 cases (40 percent). The death penalty notice was retained in 213 cases (60 percent), out of which 180 cases (84.5 percent) proceeded to the penalty phase.

The researchers examined the four decision stages in the death penalty sentencing system—the prosecutor's decision to seek the death penalty, the prosecutor's decision to drop or stick with the death penalty notice, the case's proceeding to a penalty trial, and the court's decision to impose the death sentence. The researchers "found no evidence that the race of the defendant matter[ed] in the processing of capital cases in the state." However, the race of the victim had an impact on whether the prosecutor sought the death penalty. Prosecutors were more likely to seek the death penalty for killers of white victims and were more likely to stick with their death penalty notification when the victims were white. However, the researchers found that

> Among the subset of cases where a death notice "sticks" (i.e., is not retracted), the effect of the victim's race on whether the case progresses to a penalty trial is not statistically significant (although the sign of the effect suggests that white victims are more likely to receive a penalty trial if they make it to this stage). Among the subset of cases where the case actually does reach a penalty trial, the victim's race does not have a significant impact on the imposition of a death sentence.

The study also revealed that jurisdictions affected whether state attorneys sought the death penalty. A defendant in Baltimore County was 26 times more likely to be sentenced to death than a defendant in Baltimore City. A defendant was 14 times more likely to get the death penalty in Baltimore County than in Montgomery County and 7 times more likely to get the death penalty in Prince George's County.

North Carolina

On April 16, 2001, Isaac Unah and John Charles Boger released the most comprehensive study of North Carolina's death penalty system in the state's history (*Race and the Death Penalty in North Carolina, an Empirical Analysis: 1993–1997, Initial Findings*, University of North Carolina at Chapel Hill and the Common Sense Foundation, NC). The researchers studied all 3,990 homicide cases between 1993 and 1997, including defendants who received death sentences, as well as those sentenced to life imprisonment.

On first analysis of all homicide cases, the researchers found that, overall, the death-sentencing rate where white victims were involved was almost twice as high (3.7 percent) as the rate where the victims were nonwhite (1.9 percent). In addition, the death-sentencing rate for nonwhite defendants/white victims (6.4 percent) was nearly 2.5 times higher than the rate for white defendants/white victims (2.6 percent).

When the researchers confined their investigation to death-eligible cases (those imposing the death penalty, such as a case involving the murder of a police officer), race determined whether the defendant received the death sentence. The death-sentencing rate in all death-eligible cases was much higher in white-victim cases (8 percent) than in cases in which the victims were nonwhite (4.7 percent). As with all cases, nonwhite defendants in white-victim homicides received the death sentence at a higher

rate (11.6 percent) than white defendants who murdered whites (6.1 percent).

After the initial analysis, Dr. Unah and Professor Boger performed a more comprehensive investigation involving 502 defendants, collecting 113 factors about each crime. These factors included the circumstances of the homicide, the evidence, the charges brought against the defendant, the character and background of the defendant and the victim, the presence or absence of aggravating or mitigating circumstances as specified under the law, as well as the presence or absence of aggravating or mitigating circumstances not specified under the law. The researchers also looked into other factors that might have influenced the imposition of the death penalty, such as the coming reelection of the district attorney prosecuting the crime. In the end, the researchers found that race—specifically the race of the victim—indeed played a role in the imposition of capital punishment in North Carolina from 1993 to 1997. On average, the odds of receiving the death penalty were increased by a factor of 3.5 times when the victim was white.

Nebraska

In May 1999 the Nebraska legislature became the first in the country to pass a bill proposing a two-year moratorium on executions. The bill also called for a study, during the moratorium, to determine the fairness of the administration of the death penalty. Governor Mike Johanns vetoed the bill. The governor also vetoed the proposed study, but the legislature overrode his veto.

On July 25, 2001, the Nebraska Commission on Law Enforcement and Criminal Justice released its findings of the state death penalty (David C. Baldus, George Woodworth, Gary L. Young, and Aaron M. Christ, *The Disposition of Nebraska Capital and Non-Capital Homicide Cases [1973–1999]: A Legal and Empirical Analysis*). The researchers reviewed more than 700 homicide cases that resulted in a conviction. They then closely examined the decision-making process in 177 death-eligible cases, 27 of which received the death sentence. The study did not find racial bias in the use of the death penalty. White defendants (15 percent) were just as likely as nonwhite defendants (16 percent) to receive the death penalty. The study also concluded that there was no significant evidence of unfair treatment based on the victim's race—17 percent of defendants who murdered white victims and 11 percent of defendants who murdered minority victims were sentenced to death.

The study found, however, that death-eligible defendants who murdered victims of "high socioeconomic status" were nearly four times as likely to receive the death sentence than those who murdered poor victims, even when similar crimes had been committed. In addition, the study found geographic disparities in seeking the death penalty. Prosecutors in rural capital trials were more likely to seek the death penalty than their urban counterparts (31 percent versus 20 percent).

COSTS OF THE DEATH PENALTY

Most death penalty opponents advocate life imprisonment without the chance of parole as an alternative to the death sentence. Some people, however, believe that capital punishment costs the taxpayers less than a life sentence without parole. Several studies have found that the death penalty costs more than life imprisonment without parole. Hugo Adam Bedau, in *The Case against the Death Penalty* (American Civil Liberties Union, Washington, D.C., 1997), found that a "murder trial normally takes longer when the death penalty is at issue than when it is not. Litigation costs—including the time of judges, prosecutors, public defenders, and court reporters, and the high costs of briefs—are mostly borne by the taxpayer."

In January 2000 the *Palm Beach Post* estimated that the death penalty cost Florida $51 million more than what it would cost to incarcerate all first-degree murderers without parole. According to the Department of Legislative Services of Maryland's General Assembly, it cost approximately $2.3 million to move a death row defendant through the system. In contrast, keeping the same inmate in prison cost about $19,200 annually, totaling about $768,000 for 40 years' confinement. Texas spent an estimated $2.3 million per death penalty case, about three times the cost of keeping a Texas inmate in prison for 40 years.

North Carolina

Phillip J. Cook and Donna B. Slawson, professors of public policy at Duke University, in *The Costs of Processing Murder Cases in North Carolina* (1993), studied the total costs of every death penalty case in the state for more than two years. They found that in North Carolina, the cost to try a noncapital murder case and imprison a convicted murderer for 20 years was $166,000. The cost to try a capital murder case, convict, and execute a prisoner after 10 years of imprisonment averaged $329,000. A noncapital murder case thus saved the state and local governments an estimated $163,000.

Only one-third (31 percent) of the capital murder trials, however, resulted in a sentence of death. Only about 10 percent of those condemned to death were actually executed. Many of those sentenced to death had retrials or new sentencing trials, which had different results than their original trials. Professors Cook and Slawson estimated that the extra cost for each case in which the defendant was sentenced to death was about $216,000. The extra cost per case in which the defendant was executed was more than $2.16 million.

Some of the costs incurred in a capital murder case—providing indigent defendants with two lawyers instead of

one (which is their right), calling more expert witnesses, and filing more briefs—might not have been incurred in a noncapital murder trial in North Carolina. The appeals process had nine steps, some of which could be repeated.

New York

The *New York Law Journal* investigated the costs of the death penalty in New York since its reinstatement in 1995 (Daniel Wise, "Capital Punishment Proves to be Expensive," Vol. 227, April 30, 2002). Defense costs amounted to $68.4 million so far. No national system is in place to track prosecution costs; however, the state Division of Criminal Justice Services paid counties that prosecuted capital cases $5.1 million between 1995 and March 2001. Each year the allocation for the New York Court of Appeals increased by more than $533,000 to allow for the salary of an extra clerk for each of the seven judges. The New York Prosecutors Training Institute, which assists district lawyers in capital cases, costs $1.2 million annually to operate. The defense for Darrel Harris, the first person to be sentenced to death under New York's 1995 law, had so far spent about $1.7 million, while the Capital Defender Office spent $1.2 million just to prepare the brief. The Department of Correctional Services spent $1.3 million to construct a new death row, allocating another $300,000 annually to guard it.

California

A study of the California system suggested a minimum cost of $500,000 per case (this included all capital cases, not just those ending with a death sentence). In 1994 California set up the Office of Public Defender, which worked exclusively on appeals for poor defendants on death row at an annual cost of $8 million. Because the office cannot handle all the defendants, the state offered private attorneys contracts for $75,000 to $200,000 to handle cases. Despite these efforts, about one-third of the prisoners on death row do not have lawyers to represent them in the appeals process. Many death penalty cases are on hold because lawyers cannot be found to handle the appeals.

Connecticut

Connecticut's Commission on the Death Penalty submitted a report to the state General Assembly on January 8, 2003 ("Study Pursuant to Public Act No. 01-151 of the Imposition of the Death Penalty in Connecticut") that included the cost of prosecuting capital cases. As of January 2002 Connecticut had seven death row inmates and had not executed any. The last execution occurred in 1960. Since Connecticut has not carried out an execution, the commission did not present any comparison between the cost of implementing the death penalty and keeping an inmate in prison without the possibility of parole. Nonetheless, the commission was able to illustrate the defense costs for persons sentenced to death (following

TABLE 7.11

Average amount of non-attorney compensation in capital and non-capital homicide cases, 1997

	Case type	Avg. amount of non-attorney comp.	Avg. total cost of representation (attorney and non-attorney)
Non-capital	Homicides	$ 1,515	$ 9,159
Capital	Auth. denied	$10,094	$ 55,773
	Auth. granted	$51,889	$218,113
	Capital trial	$53,143	$269,139
	Plea	$51,028	$192,333
	Drug cases	$52,218	$244,186

SOURCE: "Average Amount of Non-Attorney Compensation in Capital and Non-Capital Homicide Cases," in *Federal Death Penalty Cases: Recommendations Concerning the Cost and Quality of Defense Representation,* Judicial Conference of the United States, Committee on Defender Services, Subcommittee on Federal Death Penalty Cases, Washington, DC, 1998

TABLE 7.12

Average number of attorney hours billed in capital and non-capital homicide cases, 1992–97

	Case Type	In Court Hours	Out of Court Hours	Avg. Total Attorney Hours Per Representation
Non-Capital	Homicides	18	100	117
Capital	Auth. Denied	38	391	429
	Auth. Granted	231	1,233	1,464
	Capital Trial	409	1,480	1,889
	Plea	61	1,201	1,262
	Drug Cases	277	1,343	1,619

SOURCE: "Average Number of Attorney Hours Billed in Capital and Non-Capital Homicide Cases," *Federal Death Penalty Cases: Recommendations Concerning the Cost and Quality of Defense Representation,* Judicial Conference of the United States, Committee on Defender Services, Subcommittee on Federal Death Penalty Cases, Washington, DC, 1998

trial and sentencing), compared to the defense costs incurred by defendants receiving life imprisonment without parole (also following trial and sentencing).

The commission reviewed the cases of the seven men on death row from 1973 to 2002. The defense costs ranged from nearly $102,000 to $1.07 million, with an average cost of about $380,000 per case. The prisoners serving life sentences without parole included those incarcerated from 1989 to 2001. Their defense costs ranged from $86,000 to $321,000, with an average cost of about $202,000 per inmate. In 2000–01 the Division of Public Defender Services spent approximately $2 million for capital cases.

Federal Death Penalty Costs

Since the passage of the Violent Crime Control and Law Enforcement Act (Public Law 103-322; also known as the Federal Death Penalty Act of 1994), the number of federal prosecutions, including crimes punishable by death, has risen. The Subcommittee on Federal Death Penalty Cases of the Committee on Defender Services of the Judicial Conference of the United States, in *Federal Death Penalty Cases: Recommendations Concerning the Cost and Quality of Defense Representation* (Washington, D.C., 1998), estimated that about 560 federal death penalty cases were filed between 1991 and 1997. The numbers increased each year. In 1991 there were 12 cases, rising nearly tenfold to 118 in 1995, and reaching 159 and 153 cases in 1996 and 1997, respectively.

Although the decision to charge a crime punishable by death is made by the local federal prosecutor, the U.S. attorney general alone authorizes the seeking of the death penalty. Between 1988 and December 1997, the U.S. attorney general authorized seeking capital punishment in 111 cases. The attorney general's decision to authorize

seeking the death penalty makes a substantial difference in the cost of representing a defendant. From 1990 to 1997 the average total cost (for counsel and related services) per representation of a sample of cases in which the defendant was not charged with capital homicide was $9,159. In contrast, in those cases in which the defendant was charged with an offense punishable by death and the attorney general authorized seeking the death penalty, the average cost was $218,113. This included cases resolved by a guilty plea as well as cases resolved by a trial. In contrast, the average total cost per representation in which the defendant was charged with an offense punishable by death and the attorney general did not authorize seeking the death penalty was $55,773. (See Table 7.11.)

The decision whether to go to trial or to enter a guilty plea also affects the cost of representing the alleged offender. Between 1988 and 1997, of the 111 cases in which the attorney general sought the death sentence, 41 were tried for capital charges. Cases that ended in capital trials cost an average of $269,139, compared to $192,333 for cases resolved with a guilty plea. (See Table 7.11.)

Since a death penalty case differs from other cases in that a defendant's life is at stake, the defense generally devotes more time to the case. One time-consuming aspect of defense involves prolonged jury selection. While jury selection in noncapital cases may take a couple of days, in capital cases it may take several months. Table 7.12 shows the difference in the number of billable hours in capital and noncapital homicide cases as compiled by the Subcommittee on Federal Death Penalty Cases.

Costs of Federal Case in Non-Death Penalty State

Federal law can be enacted in any U.S. state or territory, even in a jurisdiction that does not have the death penalty. In March 2002 Michigan became the first non-death penalty state in which a federal jury sentenced a person to death. Marvin Gabrion had been convicted of the murder of 19-year-old Rachel Timmerman.

In 1997 Timmerman's body, tied with chains and handcuffs and secured to cinder blocks, was found in Oxford Lake in Michigan's Manistee National Forest. Authorities said she was drowned while still alive. Timmerman was scheduled to testify against Marvin Gabrion for raping her in 1996. Authorities also believed Gabrion was involved in the disappearance of Timmerman's one-year-old daughter. Since Rachel Timmerman was found on federal property, the government authorized the death penalty.

The federal government's decision to pursue the death penalty meant that taxpayers nationwide had to foot the bill. Ed White of the *Grand Rapids Press* reported on May 24, 2002, that the defense costs amounted to more than $730,000. A major portion of the expenses (over $537,000) went toward attorney fees. According to Chief Justice Robert Holmes Bell of the U.S. District Court of the Western District of Michigan, one of two federal judges who oversaw the budget, defending federal death penalty cases usually costs over $1 million each. That price tag does not include the cost of prosecuting the case. However, prosecutors typically do not make an accounting of their expenses. The *Grand Rapids Press* reported that although the U.S. Attorney's Office disclosed it spent at least $316,201, it did not say what the total additional costs were. These included, among other things, staff salaries and Federal Bureau of Investigation expenses.

CHAPTER 8

PUBLIC ATTITUDES TOWARD CAPITAL PUNISHMENT

Like all statistics, those contained in public opinion polls should be viewed cautiously. The way a question is phrased can influence the respondents' answers. Many other factors may also influence a response in ways that are often difficult to determine. Respondents might never have thought of the issue until asked, or they might be giving the pollster the answer they think the pollster wants to hear. Organizations that survey opinions do not claim absolute accuracy. Their findings are approximate snapshots of the attitudes of the nation at a given time.

The surveys presented here have been selected from numerous polls taken on capital punishment. The Gallup Organization and Harris Interactive (formerly Louis Harris and Associates, Inc.), to name two such organizations, are well-respected in their fields, and their surveys are accepted as representative of public opinions. A typical, well-conducted survey claims accuracy to about plus or minus three points.

ACCEPTABLE PENALTY FOR MURDER

In December 1936, the first time the Gallup Organization polled Americans regarding their attitudes toward the death penalty for murder, about three in five respondents (59 percent) favored the death penalty. For the next three decades support for capital punishment fluctuated, dropping to its lowest point in 1966 (42 percent). Starting in early 1972 support for capital punishment steadily increased, peaking at 80 percent in 1994. Since then support for capital punishment has mainly declined, dropping to an average of 67 percent in 2001, rising to 71 percent in 2002, and then declining to an average of 69 percent in 2003. (See Figure 8.1 and Figure 8.2.) On October 6 to 8, 2003, the Gallup poll found that 64 percent of Americans favored the death penalty for persons convicted of murder.

The lowest proportion to support capital punishment for murder was 42 percent in 1966, a period of civil rights

and anti–Vietnam War marches, "flower children," and the peace movement. It was also the only time in the 67 years (as of October 2003) of Gallup polling that those who opposed capital punishment (47 percent) outnumbered those who favored it.

On June 3–4, 2003, nearly 7 of 10 (69 percent) registered voters surveyed across the nation by the FOX News/Opinion Dynamics Poll said that they favored the death penalty for persons convicted of premeditated murder. Twenty-three percent opposed the death penalty for convicted murderers, while 8 percent were not sure. In January 1998 a higher proportion (74 percent) of those surveyed indicated they supported the death penalty for

FIGURE 8.1

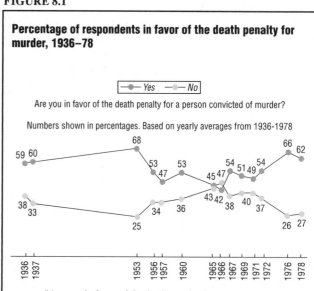

Percentage of respondents in favor of the death penalty for murder, 1936–78

Are you in favor of the death penalty for a person convicted of murder?

Numbers shown in percentages. Based on yearly averages from 1936-1978

SOURCE: "Are you in favor of the death penalty for a person convicted of murder? (Numbers shown in percentages. Based on yearly averages from 1936–1978 and 1981–2003)," in *Death Penalty,* Copyright © 2003–The Gallup Organization, Princeton, NJ, October 6–8, 2003 [Online] http://www.gallup.com/poll/topics/death_pen.asp [accessed October 27, 2003]. Reproduced with permission.

FIGURE 8.2

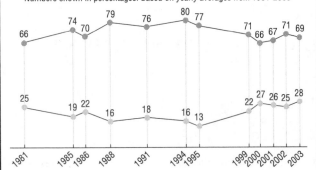

Percentage of respondents in favor of the death penalty for murder, 1981–2003

Are you in favor of the death penalty for a person convicted of murder?

Numbers shown in percentages. Based on yearly averages from 1981-2003

SOURCE: "Are you in favor of the death penalty for a person convicted of murder? (Numbers shown in percentages. Based on yearly averages from 1936–1978 and 1981–2003)," in *Death Penalty*, Copyright © 2003–The Gallup Organization, Princeton, NJ, October 6–8, 2003 [Online] http://www.gallup.com/poll/topics/death_pen.asp [accessed October 27, 2003]. Reproduced with permission.

TABLE 8.1

Support for capital punishment by gender, race, age, and other characteristics, 2001

By demographic characteristics, United States, 2001[a]

Question: "Do you believe in capital punishment, that is, the death penalty, or are you opposed to it?"

	Believe in it	Opposed to it	Not sure/ refused
National	67%	26%	7%
Sex			
Male	74	22	4
Female	62	30	8
Race, ethnicity			
White	73	22	6
Black	46	43	10
Hispanic	63	33	4
Age			
18 to 24 years	72	23	5
25 to 29 years	66	23	11
30 to 39 years	71	24	5
40 to 49 years	63	33	4
50 to 64 years	66	28	6
65 years and older	67	22	11
Education			
College post graduate	53	40	7
College graduate	66	29	5
Some college	70	26	3
High school graduate or less	69	22	8
Income			
$75,000 and over	61	34	5
$50,000 to $74,999	73	25	2
$35,000 to $49,999	73	19	8
$25,000 to $34,999	65	27	8
$15,000 to $24,999	66	21	13
Less than $15,000	67	29	4
Region			
East	65	31	4
Midwest	74	20	6
South	63	28	9
West	70	23	8
Politics			
Republican	85	12	2
Democrat	54	36	10
Independent	68	25	6

[a] Percents may not add to 100 because of rounding.

SOURCE: Kathleen Maguire and Ann L. Pastore, eds., "Table 2.62: Attitudes toward the death penalty," in *Sourcebook of Criminal Justice Statistics 2001*, Bureau of Justice Statistics, Washington, DC, 2002

---

convicted killers. Eighteen percent were against the death penalty, and 8 percent were not sure.

DEATH PENALTY VERSUS LIFE IMPRISONMENT WITH NO PAROLE

Some people say they support the death penalty because a person sentenced to life imprisonment may get out on parole at some time in the future. In January 2003 an ABC News/*Washington Post* poll of the American public showed that 64 percent supported the death penalty for those convicted of murder. When the respondents were given the alternative choice of a life sentence without parole for convicted murderers, the numbers of those favoring the death sentence dropped to 49 percent. Another 45 percent chose life without parole for convicted killers.

On January 11, 2003, Governor George Ryan of Illinois commuted 167 death sentences to life imprisonment without the possibility of parole. The same ABC News/*Washington Post* poll surveyed people in the 38 death penalty states. The respondents were told that Governor Ryan's action was a result of his belief that too many mistakes occurred in capital cases, and were then asked if they would support or oppose a similar blanket commutation by their governor. Thirty-nine percent indicated they would support such an action, while 58 percent said they would oppose it.

As of October 31, 2003, of the 38 states with the death penalty, just three—Kansas, New Mexico, and Texas—do not give the juries the option of sentencing an inmate to imprisonment without the possibility of parole. The federal government and the military also provide this option.

Seven of 10 Texans Favor Life without Parole

In April 2003 the Texas Senate refused to debate legislation that would have given juries the sentencing option of life without parole. Currently Texas juries have two sentencing options—death or life in prison with the possibility of parole after 40 years. Interestingly, a Scripps Howard Texas poll conducted in February 2003 found that 72 percent of Texans favored amending the capital law to allow juries the choice of sentencing a convicted murderer to life without parole.

WHO SUPPORTS THE DEATH PENALTY?

A Harris Poll released on August 17, 2001, found that men (74 percent) were more likely than women (62 percent) to support capital punishment. Whites (73 percent) tended to favor the death penalty more than Hispanics (who may be of any race; 63 percent) and blacks (46 percent). Republicans (85 percent) were more likely than independents (68 percent) and Democrats (54 percent) to believe in the death penalty. (See Table 8.1.)

The percentage of those believing in the death penalty varied with age and income. Those in the 18–24 and 30–39 age groups were most likely to favor the death penalty. More than 7 of 10 (73 percent) of persons earning $35,000 to $74,999 favored the death penalty. Support for the death penalty also varied with the degree of education, with those having a postgraduate degree favoring it the least. In contrast to previous years, people living in the South were the least likely to favor the death penalty (63 percent). (See Table 8.1.) In 1999, when the Harris Poll asked the same question in different regions nationwide, three-quarters (74 percent) of those living in the South said that they believed in the death penalty.

CRIMES DESERVING THE DEATH PENALTY

In June 2000 a *Newsweek* poll conducted by Princeton Survey Research Associates found that, overall, nearly two of five Americans (38 percent) favored the death penalty for persons convicted of the most brutal murders, mass murders, and serial killings. More non-Hispanic whites (40 percent) than nonwhites (33 percent) supported the death penalty for such heinous crimes. Another 23 percent of the general public preferred the death penalty for persons convicted of murder, other especially violent crimes, and major drug dealing. A larger proportion of non-Hispanic whites (24 percent) than nonwhites (15 percent) favored the death penalty for these crimes. About 12 percent of respondents thought any murder (be it brutal or less brutal) should be punished by death. However, almost one-fifth (19 percent) of the American public opposed the death penalty in all cases.

On July 23–24, 2002, 71 percent of registered voters who responded to a FOX News/Opinion Dynamics Poll said they supported the death sentence as punishment for those guilty of kidnapping and murdering a child.

DEATH PENALTY FOR SELECTED MURDERERS

A May 2002 Gallup poll surveyed Americans to determine whether they favored the death penalty for certain individuals. Nearly 7 out of 10 respondents (68 percent) supported the death penalty for women. About one-fourth (26 percent) favored the death penalty for those who were juveniles when they committed the crime, and almost one-fifth (19 percent) favored the death penal-

TABLE 8.2

Percentages of respondents favoring or opposing the death penalty for various groups of offenders

DO YOU FAVOR OR OPPOSE THE DEATH PENALTY FOR — [RANDOM ORDER]? HOW ABOUT FOR — [INSERT NEXT ITEM]?

	Favor	Oppose	No opinion
Women 2002 May 6-9	68%	29	3
The mentally ill 2002 May 6-9	19%	75	6
The mentally retarded 2002 May 6-9	13%	82	5
Juveniles 2002 May 6-9	26%	69	5

SOURCE: "Do you favor or oppose the death penalty for—[RANDOM ORDER]? How about for—[INSERT NEXT ITEM]?" in *Death Penalty,* Copyright © 2003–The Gallup Organization, Princeton, NJ, October 6–8, 2003 [Online] http://www.gallup.com/poll/topics/death_pen.asp [accessed October 27, 2003]. Reproduced with permission.

ty for those who are mentally ill. A lower proportion (13 percent) thought mentally retarded murderers should receive the death sentence. (See Table 8.2.)

Since 1976, when the United States reinstituted capital punishment, Texas has executed 12 inmates who were minors when they committed the crime (as of November 30, 2003). Three such executions occurred in 2002. A Scripps Howard Texas poll in February 2003 revealed that 60 percent of Texans supported the death penalty for those who murdered when they were 17 years old, a higher percentage than the year before (51 percent). In 2003, 34 percent opposed executing offenders who were minors when the crime was committed, slightly lower than in 2002 (37 percent).

On April 3, 2003, Oklahoma executed Scott Allen Hain, who was 17 when he and Robert Lambert, age 21, burned two people alive in a car trunk in 1987. A University of Oklahoma poll released after the execution showed that almost 63 percent of Oklahomans favored a legislative ban on executing offenders who were juveniles at the time of the crime if given the alternative choice of life without parole. As of January 9, 2004, Lambert, with a claim of mental retardation, remained on death row.

A Fox News/Opinion Dynamics Poll of June 6–7, 2001, found that more than two-thirds (67 percent) of Americans opposed the death penalty for persons convicted of premeditated murder if those persons have been found to be mentally retarded. About 19 percent supported the death penalty for convicted mentally retarded persons, and 14 percent were not sure.

REASONS FOR SUPPORTING THE DEATH PENALTY

On May 19–21, 2003, Gallup researchers asked capital punishment supporters why they favored the death

TABLE 8.3

Why respondents favor the death penalty for persons convicted of murder, June 1991 to May 2003

WHY DO YOU FAVOR THE DEATH PENALTY FOR PERSONS CONVICTED OF MURDER? [OPEN-ENDED]

[Based on —715—who favor the death penalty for persons convicted of murder]

	May 19-21, 2003	Feb 19-21, 2001	Feb 14-15, 2000	Jun. 13-16, 1991
	%	%	%	%
An eye for an eye/They took a life/ Fits the crime	37	48	40	40
They deserve it	13	6	5	5
Save taxpayers money/Cost associated with prison	11	20	12	12
Deterrent for potential crimes/ Set an example	11	10	8	8
They will repeat crime/Keep them from repeating it	7	6	4	4
Biblical reasons	5	3	3	3
Depends on the type of crime they commit	4	6	6	6
Serve justice	4	1	3	2
Fair punishment	3	1	6	6
If there's no doubt the person committed the crime	3	2	—	—
Would help/benefit families of victims	2	1	—	—
Support/believe in death penalty	2	6	—	—
Don't believe they can be rehabilitated	2	2	1	1
Life sentences don't always mean life in prison	1	2	—	—
Relieves prison overcrowding	1	2	—	—
Other	4	3	10	10
No opinion	2	1	3	3

SOURCE: "Why do you favor the death penalty for persons convicted of murder [Open-ended]? Based on—715—Who Favor the Death Penalty for Persons Convicted of Murder," in *Death Penalty*, Copyright © 2003–The Gallup Organization, Princeton, NJ, October 6–8, 2003 [Online] http://www .gallup.com/poll/topics/death_pen.asp [accessed October 27, 2003]. Reproduced with permission.

penalty for people convicted of murder. Over one-third (37 percent) felt that the death penalty was the appropriate punishment for murder. Eleven percent believed the death penalty saved taxpayers money. (Contrary to popular belief, studies show that the death penalty costs more than life imprisonment without parole.) Another 11 percent thought that putting a murderer to death would serve as a deterrent, that is, set an example so that others would not commit similar crimes. (See Table 8.3.)

SUPPORT FOR CAPITAL PUNISHMENT VARIES WITH SPECIFIC CASES

John Walker Lindh

American-born John Walker Lindh was captured by U.S. soldiers in November 2001 in Afghanistan while fighting for the Taliban. ABCNews.com conducted a poll on December 5–9, 2001, asking Americans what they thought the United States should do with Lindh. More than half (55 percent) indicated he should be charged with a crime. Of this group of respondents, one-third (34 percent) felt Lindh should be tried for treason, which is pun-

ishable by death. Sixteen percent chose a lesser charge. In June 2002 Lindh entered into a plea agreement to cooperate with U.S. authorities in investigating al Qaeda, which the government believes is responsible for the September 11, 2001 terrorist attacks on the United States. He was sentenced to 20 years in prison.

Andrea Yates

On June 20, 2001, Andrea Pia Yates of Houston, Texas, admitted to police that she drowned her five children. Respondents to a June 28, 2001, Gallup Poll were split over whether Yates should be sentenced to death if convicted of killing her children (44 percent for and 43 percent against). Nearly two-thirds (63 percent) of the respondents believed that the defendant's postpartum depression at the time of the murders should be taken into consideration during her trial.

On October 23–31, 2001, a *Houston Chronicle*/KHOU-TV poll of registered voters in Harris County, Texas, revealed that nearly three times as many respondents (57.3 percent versus 19.4 percent for the death sentence) thought Andrea Yates should receive a life sentence.

Three of ten Americans (30 percent) polled by a FOX News/Opinion Dynamics Poll on February 26–27, 2002, thought Andrea Yates should be sentenced to death. A larger proportion of men (35 percent) than women (27 percent) chose the death penalty for the defendant. While the respondents were equally split on a sentence of life in prison (23 percent) and life in a psychiatric hospital (22 percent), just 12 percent said Yates should be sent to a psychiatric hospital until she's well. In March 2002 a Texas jury found Yates guilty of capital murder and sentenced her to life in prison.

Buford Furrow

Although most Americans generally favor the death penalty, they tend to be more lenient when a survey mentions a specific offender. In August 1999, after Buford Furrow killed a postal carrier during a shooting spree in a Jewish community center in Los Angeles, a CNN/*USA Today*/Gallup Poll survey found that 55 percent of the American public favored the death penalty for Furrow if he were convicted. This figure is 16 percentage points lower than the 71 percent of general support for capital punishment that same year.

Karla Faye Tucker

In 1998 a *Dallas Morning News* survey found that although most (75 percent) Texans generally favored capital punishment, less than half (45 percent) supported the death penalty for Karla Faye Tucker, the second woman to be executed in the nation since the reinstatement of the death penalty in 1976. Tucker was convicted of beating two people to death with a pickax.

Timothy McVeigh

Timothy McVeigh was initially scheduled to be executed on May 16, 2001, for the 1995 Oklahoma City bombing that killed 168 people. U.S. Attorney General John Ashcroft stayed McVeigh's execution when it was discovered that the FBI failed to turn over all documents to McVeigh's counsel. McVeigh was put to death on June 11, 2001. He was the first federal inmate executed since 1963, when Victor Harry Feguer was hanged in Iowa for kidnapping and murder.

Prior to McVeigh's execution, a June 8–10, 2001, Gallup Poll found that about three of five (59 percent) respondents favored the death penalty and felt that McVeigh should be put to death. About one of five (19 percent) respondents opposed the death penalty but believed McVeigh should be executed. A slightly lower proportion (17 percent) indicated that they were against the death penalty and thought that McVeigh should not be executed.

Juan Raul Garza

In the same June 8–10, 2001, Gallup Poll, respondents who were asked similar questions regarding drug kingpin Juan Raul Garza gave slightly different responses. Garza was the second federal inmate set for execution on June 19, 2001, for murder. While nearly as many (50 percent) of the American public who supported the death penalty believed Garza should be executed, just 12 percent of those who opposed the death penalty stated that Garza should be put to death. More than one-fourth (27 percent) of those who opposed the death penalty believed he should not be executed, 10 percent more than those polled regarding McVeigh.

IS THE DEATH PENALTY IMPOSED TOO OFTEN?

Although the United States leads all Western countries in executions, just about one-quarter (23 percent) of Americans surveyed by the Gallup Organization in May 2003 felt the death penalty was imposed too often. More than twice that proportion (48 percent) thought it was not used often enough, while 26 percent thought the level of death penalty imposition was about right.

Two years before, in May 2001, when the Gallup Organization asked the same question, an almost similar proportion (21 percent) said the death penalty was imposed too often. A smaller percentage (38 percent) thought the death penalty was not imposed enough. However, more respondents (34 percent) had said the death penalty was imposed the right amount.

Only One-Third of Americans Support an Increase in Executions

Since 1997 the proportion of Americans supporting an increase in execution of convicted criminals has continued to decline. In August 2001 the Harris Poll reported that about one-third (35 percent) of Americans favored an increase in the number of executions, one-fourth (26 percent) favored a decrease, and 30 percent favored no change. In 1997 over half (53 percent) of the public favored an increase in the use of the death penalty, 14 percent favored a decrease, and 27 percent wanted no change.

DEATH PENALTY FAVORED EVEN IF SOME ARE INNOCENT

In July 2001 the Harris Poll found that virtually all Americans (94 percent) believed that, on average, for every 100 people convicted of murder, approximately 1 in 8 (12 percent) were innocent. Women guessed that this occurred more often (estimate of 14 percent) than men did (9 percent). Blacks estimated that 22 percent of people convicted of murder were innocent, compared to estimates by Hispanics (15 percent) and whites (10 percent). Democrats and those with a high school degree or less were more likely to believe that a higher proportion of innocent people (15 and 14 percent, respectively) were convicted of murder.

Though 94 percent of respondents indicated they believed that at least some of those charged with murder were innocent, the 12 percent error did not seem to qualify as "substantial." When asked if they would still support the death penalty if a "substantial" number of innocent people were convicted of murder, only one-third (36 percent) said they would still support the death penalty. Over half (53 percent) would oppose it under those conditions. Nevertheless, the 36 percent who continued to support the death penalty were a smaller proportion compared to their counterparts in 2000 and 1999 (53 percent and 51 percent, respectively).

MORATORIUM

On January 31, 2000, Illinois governor George H. Ryan declared a moratorium on executions. In March 2001 more than half (53 percent) of Gallup Poll respondents said they favored a moratorium on the death penalty in states with capital punishment. Such a moratorium was opposed by 40 percent.

In April 2001 an ABC News/*Washington Post* survey found that half (51 percent) of Americans believed there should be a moratorium on executions nationwide so that a commission could study whether or not the death penalty is administered fairly. A slightly smaller proportion (43 percent) of the American public believed enough safeguards are in place to prevent unfair or erroneous executions.

DETERRENT OR NOT?

A July 2001 Harris Poll found that about 4 of 10 Americans (42 percent) felt that capital punishment deters (discourages) people from committing murders. However, about 5 of 10 Americans (52 percent) believed capital punishment does not have much effect. In 1976, when the death penalty was reinstated, nearly 6 of 10 (59 percent) Americans thought capital punishment was a deterrent, compared to just over 3 in 10 (34 percent) who thought it had little effect.

In May 2001, a month before Timothy McVeigh was put to death, the Gallup Poll asked the American people if they thought McVeigh's execution would serve as a deterrent to future acts of violence and murder. Two-thirds (66 percent) of respondents did not think so. Less than half that number (30 percent) believed the execution would act as a deterrent.

CHAPTER 9
CAPITAL PUNISHMENT AROUND THE WORLD

UNITED NATIONS RESOLUTIONS

Capital punishment is controversial not only in the United States but also in many other countries of the world. The ethical arguments that fuel the debate in the United States also characterize the discussion in other countries. The United Nations' position on capital punishment is a compromise among those countries that want it completely abolished, those that want it limited to very serious offenses, and those that want it left up to each country to decide. In 1957, after 11 years of debate, a statement on the death penalty was included in the International Covenant on Civil and Political Rights, which the General Assembly adopted in Resolution 2200 (XXI) of December 16, 1966. Article 6 of the Covenant states,

• Every human being has the inherent right to life. This right shall be protected by law. No one shall be arbitrarily deprived of his life.

• In countries that have not abolished the death penalty, sentence of death may be imposed only for the most serious crimes in accordance with the law in force at the time of the commission of the crime and not contrary to the provisions of the present Covenant and to the Convention on the Prevention and Punishment of the Crime of Genocide [systematic killing of a racial, political, or cultural group]. This penalty can only be carried out pursuant to a final judgment rendered by a competent court.

• When deprivation of life constitutes the crime of genocide, it is understood that nothing in this article shall authorize any State Party to the present Covenant to derogate [turn away] in any way from any obligation assumed under the provisions of the Convention on the Prevention and Punishment of the Crime of Genocide.

• Anyone sentenced to death shall have the right to seek pardon or commutation of the sentence [replacement of the death sentence with a lesser sentence]. Amnesty,

pardon, or commutation of the sentence of death may be granted in all cases.

• Sentence of death shall not be imposed for crimes committed by persons below eighteen years of age and shall not be carried out on pregnant women.

• Nothing in this article shall be invoked to delay or prevent the abolition of capital punishment by any State Party to the present Covenant.

The United Nations (UN) has dealt with the death penalty in several other documents and meetings. Among them is General Assembly Resolution 2393 (XXIII) of November 26, 1968, which specifies the following legal safeguards that should be offered to condemned prisoners by countries with capital punishment:

• A person condemned to death shall not be deprived of the right to appeal to a higher judicial authority or, as the case may be, to petition for pardon or reprieve [postponement or cancellation of punishment].

• A death sentence shall not be carried out until the procedures of appeal or, as the case may be, of petition for pardon or reprieve have been terminated.

• Special attention shall be given in the case of indigent [poor] persons by the provision of adequate legal assistance at all stages of the proceedings.

Since then the UN has come out more strongly for eliminating capital punishment. General Assembly Resolution 2857 (XXVI) of December 20, 1971, observed,

In order to guarantee fully the right to life, provided for in Article 3 of the Universal Declaration of Human Rights, the main objective to be pursued is that of progressively restricting the number of offenses for which capital punishment may be imposed, with a view to the desirability of abolishing this punishment in all countries.

The UN Economic and Social Council Resolution 1574 (L) of May 20, 1971, made a similar declaration. In 1984 the Economic and Social Council adopted the *Safeguards Guaranteeing Protection of the Rights of Those Facing the Death Penalty,* including those of persons younger than age 18 at the time the crime was committed. Subsequently, over the years, General Assembly and Economic and Social Council resolutions have called for the eventual abolition of the death penalty.

On December 15, 1989, the UN General Assembly, under Resolution 44/128, adopted the Second Optional Protocol to the International Covenant on Civil and Political Rights, aimed at abolishing the death penalty. This international treaty allows countries to retain the death penalty in wartime as long as they reserve the right to do so at the time they become party to the treaty. As of November 2, 2003, seven countries had endorsed the treaty by signing, indicating their intention to become parties to it at a later date. Signatories are not legally bound by the treaty but are obliged to avoid acts that would go against the treaty. Fifty countries became parties to the protocol by ratification or accession, which means that they were legally bound by the terms of the treaty. Accession is similar to ratification, except that it occurs after the treaty has entered into force. In 1992 the United States ratified the International Covenant on Civil and Political Rights but had not signed the Second Optional Protocol to this treaty as of January 10, 2004.

Recent UN Initiatives

On December 18, 2000, the secretary general of the United Nations, Kofi Annan, received a petition signed by more than 3 million people from more than 130 countries, appealing for an end to executions. Subsequently, the secretary general called for a worldwide moratorium on the death penalty, noting that the taking of life as punishment for crime is "too absolute [and] too irreversible."

Since April 1997 the UN Commission on Human Rights has adopted resolutions calling for a moratorium on executions and an eventual abolition of the death penalty. At the commission's meeting in Geneva, Switzerland, on April 25, 2001, the United States voted against the resolution on the death penalty. Ambassador George E. Moose stated that "[i]nternational law does not prohibit the death penalty when due process safeguards are respected and when capital punishment is applied only to the most serious crimes."

In its 2002 session, the commission, in Resolution 2002/77, asked countries with the death penalty "[t]o ensure that ... the death penalty is not imposed for non-violent acts such as financial crimes, non-violent religious practice or expression of conscience and sexual relations between consenting adults." The part of the resolution referring to sexual relations between consenting adults

resulted from the potential execution of a Nigerian woman, who became pregnant while divorced. She was convicted of adultery and, in March 2002, was sentenced to die by stoning. The man who fathered the child claimed innocence, brought in three men to corroborate his claim as required by law, and was released. On September 25, 2003, the woman was acquitted.

The UN Commission on Human Rights adopted Resolution 2003/67 on April 24, 2003, in Geneva, Switzerland. For the first time, the commission asked countries that retained capital punishment not to extend the application of the death penalty to offenses to which it does not currently apply. It also admonished those countries to inform the public of any scheduled execution and to abstain from holding public executions and inhuman forms of executions, such as stoning. The UN also called on death penalty countries not to impose the death sentence on mothers with dependent children nor on offenders who committed the crime when they were under 18.

RETENTIONIST COUNTRIES

Amnesty International (AI), a human rights organization headquartered in London, United Kingdom, maintains information on capital punishment throughout the world. (AI vehemently opposes the death penalty, considering it the "ultimate form of cruel, inhuman, and degrading punishment.") The organization refers to countries that retain and use the death penalty as retentionist countries; those that no longer use the death penalty are known as abolitionist countries.

As of January 1, 2003, 83 countries and territories in the world retained and used the death penalty as a possible punishment for ordinary crimes. (See Table 9.1.) Ordinary crimes are crimes committed during peacetime. Ordinary crimes that could lead to the death penalty include murder, rape, and, in some countries, robbery or embezzlement of very large sums of money. Exceptional crimes, however, are military crimes committed during exceptional times, mainly wartime. Examples are treason, spying, or desertion (leaving the armed services without permission).

Although many of the retentionist countries had not executed anybody in many years, in 2002, 31 countries carried out at least 1,526 executions. AI reported that of these countries, China, Iran, and the United States accounted for four out of five executions (81 percent). An estimated 1,060 persons were reportedly executed in China, although AI believed the actual number was larger. Iran had at least 113 executions, while the United States counted 71. Sixty-seven countries sentenced more than 3,200 people to death. According to Amnesty International, the actual number of death sentences was much higher than known to the organization.

TABLE 9.1

Countries and territories that retain the death penalty for ordinary crimes, January 2003

Retentionist

Afghanistan	Lebanon
Algeria	Lesotho
Antigua and Barbuda	Liberia
Bahamas	Libya
Bahrain	Malawi
Bangladesh	Malaysia
Barbados	Mauritania
Belarus	Mongolia
Belize	Morocco
Benin	Myanmar
Botswana	Nigeria
Burundi	Oman
Cameroon	Pakistan
Chad	Palestinian Authority
China	Philippines
Comoros	Qatar
Congo (Democratic Republic)	Rwanda
Cuba	Saint Christopher & Nevis
Dominica	Saint Lucia
Egypt	Saint Vincent & Grenadines
Equatorial Guinea	Saudi Arabia
Eritrea	Sierra Leone
Ethiopia	Singapore
Gabon	Somalia
Ghana	Sudan
Guatemala	Swaziland
Guinea	Syria
Guyana	Taiwan
India	Tajikistan
Indonesia	Tanzania
Iran	Thailand
Iraq	Trinidad and Tobago
Jamaica	Tunisia
Japan	Uganda
Jordan	United Arab Emirates
Kazakstan	United States of America
Kenya	Uzbekistan
Korea (North)	Viet Nam
Korea (South)	Yemen
Kuwait	Zambia
Kyrgyzstan	Zimbabwe
Laos	

SOURCE: "4. Retentionist," in *The Death Penalty: List of Abolitionist and Retentionist Countries (1 January 2003)*, AI Index: ACT 50/003/2003, © Amnesty International Publications, 1 Easton Street, London WC1X 0DW, United Kingdom, April 2003 [Online] http://web.amnesty.org/aidoc/aidoc_pdf.nsf/Index/Act500032003ENGLISH/$File/ACT5000303.pdf [accessed October 15, 2003]. Reproduced with permission.

United States

The United States remains the only Western country that practices capital punishment. (The federal government and 38 states have the death penalty.) In September 1997, for the first time, a UN monitor investigated the use of the death penalty in the United States. In his report to the UN Commission on Human Rights, the special investigator accused the United States of unfair, arbitrary, and racist use of capital punishment. He claimed that "allegations of racial discrimination in the imposition of death sentences are particularly serious in southern states, such as Alabama, Florida, Louisiana, Mississippi, Georgia and Texas, known as the 'death penalty belt.'"

FOREIGN NATIONALS. Mark Warren of Human Rights Research (Ontario, Canada), who provides information and expertise on human rights issues to government, nongovernmental organizations, consulates, and lawyers, reported that as of October 1, 2003, 120 foreign nationals representing 29 nationalities were on death row in the United States. Capital punishment opponents claim that the United States generally does not inform foreign nationals under arrest of their right to consult with the consulate of their home country as required by Article 36 of the Vienna Convention on Consular Relations. Article 36 requires local law enforcement to notify all detained foreigners "without delay" of this right. The United States ratified (formally approved and sanctioned) this international agreement in 1969. Since 1976, 20 foreign nationals have been executed.

THE UNITED STATES DEFIES THE UN'S HIGHEST COURT. Angel Francisco Breard, a Paraguayan national, was arrested on charges of attempted rape and capital murder in 1992. In 1993 Breard was sentenced to death for these crimes. Following the denial of his appeals before the Virginia Supreme Court and the U.S. Supreme Court, Breard invoked the provision of the Vienna Convention on Consular Relations. The U.S. District Court, in *Breard v. Netherland* (945 F. Supp. 1255, 1266 [E.D. Va. 1996]), rejected Breard's claim because he had "procedurally defaulted" the claim when he failed to raise it in state court. In addition, the district court concluded that Breard could not show cause and prejudice for this default.

That same year, 1996, the Republic of Paraguay brought suit against Virginia officials for violation of the Vienna Convention because they failed to notify the Paraguayan consulate of Breard's arrest. The district court dismissed the suit, a decision that the appellate court affirmed. On April 3, 1998, the Republic of Paraguay brought the case before the International Court of Justice (ICJ; the UN's highest court), which ruled, on April 9, 1998, that the United States should stay Breard's execution pending the ICJ's final decision. Paraguay had also petitioned the U.S. Supreme Court.

On April 14, 1998, the day of execution, the U.S. Supreme Court, voting 6–3, refused to intervene in the case despite requests for a stay of execution from then–Secretary of State Madeleine Albright. In *Paraguay et al. v. Gilmore* (No. 97-1390 [S-738]), the Court stated,

It is the rule in this country that assertions of error in criminal proceedings must first be raised in state court in order to form the basis for relief in *habeas*.... Claims not so raised are considered defaulted. By not asserting his Vienna Convention claim in state court, Breard failed to exercise his rights under the Vienna Convention in conformity with the laws of the United States and the Commonwealth of Virginia. Having failed to do so, he cannot raise a claim of violation of those rights now on federal *habeas* review.

As for Paraguay's suits (both the original action and the case coming to us on petition for *certiorari* [a petition to the Supreme Court to review the issues brought up in the direct appeal]), neither the text nor the history of the Vienna Convention clearly provides a foreign nation a private right of action in United States courts to set aside a criminal conviction and sentence for violation of consular notification provisions.... Though Paraguay claims that its suit is within an exemption dealing with continuing consequences of past violations of federal rights, we do not agree. The failure to notify the Paraguayan Consul occurred long ago and has no continuing effect.

In November 1998 the United States formally apologized to Paraguay for failing to inform Breard of his right to seek consular assistance. Paraguay withdrew its lawsuit following the apology.

GERMANY SUES THE UNITED STATES. In 1982 German brothers Karl and Walter LaGrand killed a bank employee during a robbery attempt in Tucson, Arizona. They were sentenced to death in 1984. In February 1999 Karl LaGrand was executed. On March 2, 1999, the day before Walter LaGrand's execution, Germany sued the United States at the ICJ. According to Germany, the United States violated Article 36 of the Vienna Convention by failing to inform the defendant without delay after the arrest of his right to contact the German consulate for help. Germany also claimed that Arizona prosecutors violated Article 36 because they knowingly failed to inform Germany of the arrest and conviction until 10 years after the murder. By that time it was too late, under "procedural default," for the defendant to raise the issue of the treaty violation. The U.S. rule of procedural default requires that claims challenging conviction and/or sentence have to be presented at the appropriate appeals stage. Walter LaGrand had not argued for his Article 36 rights in previous court proceedings and, therefore, could not raise a violation of that right in later proceedings.

The ICJ ordered the United States to stay Walter LaGrand's execution, but Arizona let the execution take place. Despite the execution, Germany proceeded with the lawsuit. During a November 2000 hearing before the ICJ, the United States argued that Article 36 does not confer personal rights to individual nationals. In other words, the United States conceded that while it violated its treaty obligations to Germany, it did not violate its obligations to the brothers. The United States added that although German authorities knew of the LaGrand case in 1992, they waited until 1999 to intervene for the brothers.

On June 27, 2001, the ICJ, in *Germany v. United States of America,* ruled 14–1 that the United States had violated its obligations to Germany and to the LaGrand brothers under the Vienna Convention on Consular Relations. The ICJ also ruled that domestic law must not prevent the review of the conviction and sentencing when a defendant's right to consular notification has been violated. In addition, the United States must provide review and remedies should a similar case arise.

MEXICO SUES THE UNITED STATES. In 2003 the International Court of Justice (ICJ) again was asked to settle a case involving the United States and consular notification. On January 9 Mexico sued the United States for allegedly violating the Vienna Convention on Consular Relations with respect to 51 Mexican nationals on U.S. death row *Avena and other Mexican Nationals [Mexico v. United States of America]).* Mexico also asked the court, pending final judgment of the case, to issue provisional measures ordering the United States to abstain from executing any Mexican national or schedule any such execution. The United States argued that Mexico's request for provisional measures should be rejected by the court because they were equivalent to "a sweeping prohibition on capital punishment for Mexican nationals in the United States, regardless of United States law."

On February 5, 2003, the court unanimously issued an order directing the United States to take all necessary measures to ensure that three Mexican nationals, who faced possible execution in the coming months or even weeks, not be executed pending its final decision. The court, however, noted that the other 48 death row inmates were not included in the provisional measures order because they were not in the same situation as the other three men.

Although Judge Shigeru Oda (Japan) voted with the other 14 court members regarding the order for provisional measures, he expressed his doubts about the court's definition of "disputes arising out of the interpretation or application" of the Vienna Convention. He had expressed the same doubts in the *Breard* and *LaGrand* cases. Judge Oda stated that since the United States had admitted its failure to abide by the Vienna Convention, no dispute concerning consular notification existed. He believed the current lawsuit "is essentially an attempt by Mexico to save the lives of its nationals sentenced to death by domestic courts in the United States." Judge Oda observed that the International Court of Justice cannot act as a court of criminal appeal, adding that "if the rights of those accused of violent crimes are to be respected, then the rights of the victims should also be taken into consideration." As of November 30, 2003, final judgment on the case had not been handed down.

China

Human rights groups have found that China executes more persons each year than all other nations combined. In October 1999 the Chinese government passed a law allowing the imposition of the death sentence on leaders of the Falun Gong movement charged with murder and endangering national security. The government claimed the "cult" movement has caused the death of more than 1,000 followers by dissuading them from seeking medical help.

In 2001 a massive increase in executions occurred as a result of a nationwide anticrime campaign called Strike

Hard. Chinese officials had allegedly been very inconsistent in determining which crimes warranted the death penalty. Law enforcement, under pressure to achieve results, sped up the criminal process, reportedly subjecting defendants to torture to extract confessions. It is reported that the general public approves of the death penalty.

Persons convicted of nonviolent offenses, such as tax fraud, bribery, embezzlement, and counterfeiting, have been put to death. During the last Strike Hard campaign in 1996, AI reported, more than 4,400 inmates were shot to death. Between April and July 2001, nearly 3,000 death sentences had been handed down. About 1,780 were executed during those four months alone.

Human rights organizations report that China, which introduced lethal injection in 1997, was using mobile execution buses in Yunnan province in the southwest region of China. The buses are outfitted with a bed and automatic syringe. Amnesty International reported in March 2003 that government officials admitted that four individuals participate in executions—the executor, a court representative, a doctor, and an official from the procuratorate (legal supervisory organ of the state).

Japan

Amnesty International reported that, as of September 30, 2003, at least 118 persons in Japan were under sentence of death. About 50 of these inmates had seen their sentences confirmed. Between 1988 and 1992 the number of prisoners sentenced to death declined, from 12 in 1988 to 5 in 1992. Thirteen inmates were executed from 1982 to 1989. No executions occurred from November 1989 to March 1993 because two Ministers of Justice, who opposed capital punishment, refused to issue execution orders. Executions resumed in March 1993. Between 1993 and 2000, 39 prisoners were put to death by hanging.

Death row inmates are forbidden from meeting with journalists and researchers collecting data on the death penalty. Any information gathered by these persons usually results from significant investigations of their own. Families have limited access to the inmates, many of whom spend their days in solitary confinement.

Japan is also known for its drawn-out process of appeals. A case that drew worldwide attention involved a prisoner who, in 1997, after having been on death row for 30 years, was executed in secrecy. The inmate had committed multiple murders at age 19 (a minor under Japanese law) but was convicted as an adult. The law requires the Justice Ministry to carry out an execution within six months after appeals are finalized. According to human rights organizations, the ministry, nonetheless, arbitrarily sets the execution date.

Many inmates have been on death row for more than 30 years. In 1987, 95-year-old Sadamichi Hirasawa died

TABLE 9.2

Countries that are abolitionist in practice, January 2003

Abolitionist in Practice
Countries that retain the death penalty for ordinary crimes such as murder but can be considered abolitionist in practice in that they have not executed anyone during the past 10 years and are believed to have a policy or established practice of not carrying out executions. The list also includes countries which have made an international commitment not to use the death penalty.

Country	Date (last ex.)[1]
Armenia	
Bhutan	1964[2]
Brunei Darussalam	1957[2]
Burkina Faso	1988
Central African Republic	1981
Congo (Republic)	1982
Gambia	1981
Grenada	1978
Madagascar	1958[2]
Maldives	1952[2]
Mali	1980
Nauru	Ind.
Niger	1976[2]
Papua New Guinea	1950
Russian Federation	1999
Samoa[3]	
Senegal	1967
Sri Lanka	1976
Suriname	1982
Togo	
Tonga	1982

[1]Date of last execution.
[2]Date of last known execution.
[3]No executions since independence.

SOURCE: "3. Abolitionist in Practice," in *The Death Penalty: List of Abolitionist and Retentionist Countries (1 January 2003)*, AI Index: ACT 50/003/2003, © Amnesty International Publications, 1 Easton Street, London WC1X 0DW, United Kingdom, April 2003 [Online] http://web.amnesty.org/aidoc/aidoc_pdf.nsf/Index/Act500032003ENGLISH/$File/ACT5000303.pdf [accessed October 15, 2003]. Reproduced with permission.

while awaiting execution. He had been on death row for 32 years. In September 2003 Tsuneki Tomiyama died of kidney failure after having been on death row for about 39 years. His death sentence was finalized in 1976. Tomiyama was 86 years old, the oldest inmate on death row in 2003. Hakamada Iwao has been in prison for 37 years. He was 67 years old in 2003.

The Japanese government does not announce any pending execution or notify families and lawyers of death row inmates about the impending execution. Even the inmate scheduled to be put to death learns of his or her fate only about two hours before the execution. The government has been known to carry out executions when the Diet (Parliament) is not in session or during holidays in order to avoid parliamentary debate.

Human Rights Features, in "Japan Hanging on to Death Penalty" (Vol. 6, Issue 3, March 31–April 6, 2003), noted that Japanese law does not provide judges with the criteria needed to impose the death penalty. For example, homicide may be punishable by execution, life imprisonment, or a prison term of not less than three years.

TABLE 9.3

Countries whose laws do not provide for the death penalty for any crime, January 2003

Abolitionist for All Crimes

Country	Date (A)[1]	Date (AO)[2]	Date (last ex.)[3]
Andorra	1990		1943
Angola	1992		
Australia	1985	1984	1967
Austria	1968	1950	1950
Azerbaijan	1998		1993
Belgium	1996		1950
Bulgaria	1998		1989
Cambodia	1989		
Canada	1998	1976	1962
Cape Verde	1981		1835
Columbia	1910		1909
Costa Rica	1877		
Cote D'Ivoire	2000		
Croatia	1990		
Cyprus	2002	1983	1962
Czech Republic	1990		
Denmark	1978	1933	1950
Djibouti[5]	1995		
Dominican Republic	1966		
Ecuador	1906		
Estonia	1998		1991
Finland	1972	1949	1944
France	1981		1977
Georgia	1997		1994[4]
Germany	1987		
Guinea-Bissau	1993		1986[4]
Haiti	1987		1972[4]
Honduras	1956		1940
Hungary	1990		1988
Iceland	1928		1830
Ireland	1990		1954
Italy	1994	1947	1947
Kiribati[5]			
Liechtenstein	1987		1785
Lithuania	1998		1995
Luxembourg	1979		1949
Macedonia (former Yug. Rep.)	1991		
Malta	2000	1971	1943
Marshall Islands[5]			
Mauritius	1995		1987
Micronesia (Federated States)[5]			
Moldova	1995		
Monaco	1962		1847
Mozambique	1990		1986
Namibia	1990		1988[4]
Nepal	1997	1990	1979
Netherlands	1982	1870	1952
New Zealand	1989	1961	1957
Nicaragua	1979		1930
Norway	1979	1905	1948
Palau			
Panama			1903[4]
Paraguay	1992		1928
Poland	1997		1988
Portugal	1976	1867	1849[4]
Romania	1989		1989
San Marino	1865	1848	1468[4]
Sao Tome and Principe[5]	1990		
Seychelles[5]	1993		
Slovak Republic	1990		
Slovenia	1989		
Solomon Islands[5]		1966	
South Africa	1997	1995	1991
Spain	1995	1978	1975
Sweden	1972	1921	1910

TABLE 9.3

Countries whose laws do not provide for the death penalty for any crime, January 2003 [CONTINUED]

Abolitionist for All Crimes

Country	Date (A)[1]	Date (AO)[2]	Date (last ex.)[3]
Switzerland	1992	1942	1944
Timor-Leste	1999		
Turkmenistan	1999		
Tuvalu[5]			
Ukraine	1999		
United Kingdom	1998	1973	1964
Uruguay	1907		
Vanuatu[5]			
Vatican City State	1969		
Venezuela	1863		
Yugoslavia	2002		

[1]Date of abolition for all crimes.
[2]Date of abolition for all ordinary crimes.
[3]Date of last execution.
[4]Date of last known execution.
[5]No executions since independence.

SOURCE: "1. Abolitionist for All Crimes," in *The Death Penalty: List of Abolitionist and Retentionist Countries (1 January 2003)*, AI Index: ACT 50/003/2003, © Amnesty International Publications, 1 Easton Street, London WC1X 0DW, United Kingdom, April 2003 [Online] http://web.amnesty.org/aidoc/aidoc_pdf.nsf/Index/Act500032003ENGLISH/$File/ACT5000303.pdf [accessed October 15, 2003]. Reproduced with permission.

Forum 90 is an abolitionist group that monitors capital punishment in Japan. In *The Hidden Death Penalty in Japan* (Sachiho Takahashi and Thomas Mariadason, eds., Tokyo, Japan, June 2001), Forum 90 reported that in addition to the other secret elements of the death penalty in Japan, the general public is not informed of the identities of those executed. Since Japan has no jury system, ordinary citizens find out about an execution only after the Ministry of Justice announces that it has occurred.

The government of Japan claims that the public, as shown by its 1999 poll, approves of the death penalty. Experts, however, point out that this percentage resulted from a problematic polling question. The people were asked whether they agreed that the death penalty system should be abolished in any case or whether the death penalty is necessary through unavoidable circumstances. A majority (79.3 percent) chose the second response.

Some initiatives toward abolishing the death penalty in Japan have begun. In November 2002 the Japan Federation of Bar Associations called for a moratorium on the death penalty and a public debate on the issues of the death penalty system. In July 2003 the Japan Parliamentary League Against the Death Penalty, composed of 122 multiparty members, planned to introduce a bill to suspend executions while a commission is formed to discuss capital punishment. The opposition blocked this effort.

ABOLITIONIST IN PRACTICE

As of January 1, 2003, Amnesty International considered 21 countries as abolitionist in practice. (See Table

TABLE 9.4

Countries that have abolished the death penalty since 1976

1976: **PORTUGAL** abolished the death penalty for all crimes.
1978: **DENMARK** abolished the death penalty for all crimes.
1979: **LUXEMBOURG, NICARAGUA** and **NORWAY** abolished the death penalty for all crimes. **BRAZIL, FIJI** and **PERU** abolished the death penalty for ordinary crimes.
1981: **FRANCE** and **CAPE VERDE** abolished the death penalty for all crimes.
1982: The **NETHERLANDS** abolished the death penalty for all crimes.

1983: **CYPRUS** and **EL SALVADOR** abolished the death penalty for ordinary crimes.
1984: **ARGENTINA** abolished the death penalty for ordinary crimes.
1985: **AUSTRALIA** abolished the death penalty for all crimes.
1987: **HAITI, LIECHTENSTEIN** and the **GERMAN DEMOCRATIC REPUBLIC**[1] abolished the death penalty for all crimes.
1989: **CAMBODIA, NEW ZEALAND, ROMANIA** and **SLOVENIA**[2] abolished the death penalty for all crimes.

1990: **ANDORRA, CROATIA**[2], the **CZECH AND SLOVAK FEDERAL REPUBLIC**[3], **HUNGARY, IRELAND, MOZAMBIQUE, NAMIBIA** and **SAO TOMÉ AND PRÍNCIPE** abolished the death penalty
        for all crimes.
1992: **ANGOLA, PARAGUAY** and **SWITZERLAND** abolished the death penalty for all crimes.
1993: **GUINEA-BISSAU, HONG KONG**[4] and **SEYCHELLES** abolished the death penalty for all crimes. **GREECE** abolished the death penalty for ordinary crimes.
1994: **ITALY** abolished the death penalty for all crimes.
1995: **DJIBOUTI, MAURITIUS, MOLDOVA** and **SPAIN** abolished the death penalty for all crimes.

1996: **BELGIUM** abolished the death penalty for all crimes.
1997: **GEORGIA, NEPAL, POLAND** and **SOUTH AFRICA** abolished the death penalty for all crimes. **BOLIVIA** and **BOSNIA-HERZEGOVINA** abolished the death penalty for ordinary
        crimes.
1998: **AZERBAIJAN, BULGARIA, CANADA, ESTONIA, LITHUANIA** and the **UNITED KINGDOM** abolished the death penalty for all crimes.
1999: **EAST TIMOR (**now **TIMOR-LESTE), TURKMENISTAN** and **UKRAINE** abolished the death penalty for all crimes. **LATVIA**[5] abolished the death penalty for ordinary crimes.
2000: **ALBANIA**[6] abolished the death penalty for ordinary crimes. **COTE D'IVOIRE** and **MALTA** abolished the death penalty for all crimes.

2001: **CHILE** abolished the death penalty for ordinary crimes.
2002: **CYPRUS** and **YUGOSLAVIA (**now **SERBIA AND MONTENEGRO)** abolished the death penalty for all crimes. **TURKEY** abolished the death penalty for ordinary crimes.

Notes:
[1]In 1990 the German Democratic Republic became unified with the Federal Republic of Germany, where the death penalty had been abolished in 1949.
[2]Slovenia and Croatia abolished the death penalty while they were still republics of the Socialist Federal Republic of Yugoslavia. The two republics became independent in 1991.
[3]In 1993 the Czech and Slovak Federal Republic divided into two states, the Czech Republic and Slovakia.
[4]In 1997 Hong Kong was returned to Chinese rule as a special administrative region of China. Amnesty International understands that Hong Kong will remain abolitionist.
[5]In 1999 the Latvian parliament voted to ratify Protocol No. 6 to the European Convention on Human Rights, abolishing the death penalty for peacetime offences.
[6]In 2000 Albania ratified Protocol No. 6 to the European Convention on Human Rights, abolishing the death penalty for peacetime offences.

SOURCE: "Countries Which Have Abolished the Death Penalty Since 1976," in *The Death Penalty: List of Abolitionist and Retentionist Countries (1 January 2003)*, AI Index: ACT 50/003/2003, © Amnesty International Publications, 1 Easton Street, London WC1X 0DW, United Kingdom, April 2003 [Online] http://web.amnesty.org/aidoc/aidoc_pdf.nsf/Index/Act500032003ENGLISH/$File/ACT5000303.pdf [accessed October 15, 2003]. Reproduced with permission.

9.2.) They have death penalty laws for such crimes as murder but have not carried out any execution for the past 10 years or more. Some of these nations have not executed anyone for the past 50 years or more. Others have made an international commitment not to impose the death sentence.

Roger Hood, in *The Death Penalty—A Worldwide Perspective* (3rd ed., Oxford University Press, Inc., New York, 2002), noted that just as countries that are abolitionist in practice have eventually outlawed capital punishment, some countries that have not carried out executions for at least 10 years might resume executions at some time in the future. The author gave as examples 10 countries that have resumed executions since 1994: the Bahamas, Bahrain, Burundi, Guinea, Guatemala, the Philippines, St. Christopher and Nevis, Trinidad and Tobago, Qatar, and the United States, where the federal government resumed executions in 2001, 38 years after the last execution.

ABOLITIONIST COUNTRIES

In 1863 Venezuela became the first nation to outlaw the death penalty. Since that time many countries have abolished capital punishment. Several countries, however, including Argentina, Brazil, and Spain, restored it after previously rejecting it. Argentina revoked the death penalty in 1921 and then again in 1972, reinstating it in 1976 after a military takeover. Then, in 1984 it abolished capital punishment again for ordinary crimes. Brazil abolished the death penalty in 1882, restored it in 1969, and revoked it again in 1979 for ordinary crimes.

Similarly, Spain repealed the death penalty in 1932, brought it back for certain crimes in 1934, totally restored it in 1938, and then abolished it again in 1978 for ordinary crimes. Finally, in 1985, Spain outlawed the death penalty for all crimes. The switching back and forth between abolition and the reimposition of capital punishment often reflects these countries' shift between democracy and dictatorship.

As of January 1, 2003, 76 countries had abolished the death penalty for all crimes. (See Table 9.3.) Since 1976, when the United States reinstated the death penalty after a nine-year moratorium, many countries have stopped imposing capital punishment. Belgium and the United Kingdom, the last two Western European democracies to have the death sentence, abolished it for all crimes in 1996 and 1998, respectively. In reality, Belgium has not executed any prisoner since 1950. The last two executions in the United Kingdom occurred in 1964. Hong Kong

TABLE 9.5

Countries that are abolitionist for ordinary crimes only, January 2003

Abolitionist for Ordinary Crimes Only

Countries whose laws provide for the death penalty only for exceptional crimes such as crimes under military law or crimes committed in exceptional circumstances, such as wartime crimes.

Country	Date (AO)[1]	Date (last ex.)[2]
Albania	2000	
Argentina	1984	
Bolivia	1997	1974
Bosnia-Herzegovina	1997	
Brazil	1979	1855
Chile	2001	1985
Cook Islands		
El Salvador	1983	1973[3]
Fiji	1979	1964
Greece	1993	1972
Israel	1954	1962
Latvia	1999	1996
Mexico		1937
Peru	1979	1979
Turkey	2002	1984

[1]Date of abolition for ordinary crimes.
[2]Date of last execution.
[3]Date of last known execution.

SOURCE: "2. Abolitionist for Ordinary Crimes Only," in *The Death Penalty: List of Abolitionist and Retentionist Countries (1 January 2003)*, AI Index: ACT 50/003/2003, © Amnesty International Publications, 1 Easton Street, London WC1X 0DW, United Kingdom, April 2003 [Online] http://web.amnesty.org/aidoc/aidoc_pdf.nsf/Index/Act500032003ENGLISH/$File/ACT5000303.pdf [accessed October 15, 2003]. Reproduced with permission.

returned to Chinese jurisdiction in July 1997. Having abolished capital punishment in 1993, the former British colony remains abolitionist. In 1999 East Timor (now Timor-Leste), Turkmenistan, and Ukraine became abolitionist nations for all crimes. In 2000 Cote d'Ivoire and Malta also abolished the death penalty for all crimes. In 2002 Cyprus and Yugoslavia (now Serbia and Montenegro) abolished the death penalty for all crimes. (See Table 9.4 for a list of the countries that have abolished the death penalty since 1976.)

Abolitionist Countries for Ordinary Crimes Only

Fifteen countries do not impose the death penalty for ordinary crimes committed during peacetime, though they may impose it for exceptional crimes. (See Table 9.5.) Since 1997 six countries—Bolivia (1997), Bosnia-Herzegovina (1997), Latvia (1999), Albania (2000), Chile (2001), and Turkey (2002)—have joined this group.

Capital Punishment Is Seldom Reintroduced

Amnesty International notes that once a country abolishes capital punishment, it seldom brings it back. Between 1985 and January 1, 2003, more than 50 countries either enacted laws abolishing the death penalty or, having revoked it for ordinary crimes, eventually outlawed it for all crimes. During this period just four abolitionist countries reimposed the death penalty—Nepal, the

Philippines, Gambia, and Papua New Guinea. Nepal, which reinstated the death penalty for murder, abolished it for all crimes in 1997. Gambia and Papua New Guinea remained abolitionist in practice. Although they retained the death penalty for ordinary crimes, Gambia last carried out an execution in 1981, and Papua New Guinea last put an offender to death in 1950.

After banning capital punishment in 1987, the Philippines reintroduced it in 1993. In February 1999 the first execution since 1976 took place, followed by six others. In March 2000 then-President Joseph Estrada suspended all executions in honor of the Christian Jubilee year. In October 2001 newly elected President Gloria Macapagal-Arroyo lifted the moratorium on the death penalty in light of the rising numbers of kidnapping cases for ransom money. The president restored the moratorium in late 2003, saying she might commute the death sentence to life imprisonment. More than 1,000 persons were under sentence of death as of November 30, 2003.

DEATH PENALTY AGAINST MINORS

According to Amnesty International, between 1990 and 2000 seven countries—the Democratic Republic of Congo, Iran, Nigeria, Pakistan, Saudi Arabia, the United States, and Yemen—had executed offenders who were under the age of 18 when they committed their crime. Since then, Pakistan (2000) and Yemen (2001) have raised the age for the imposition of the death penalty to 18. From 1990 to April 2003, 33 inmates were executed for crimes committed when they were minors. Of these, 19 executions occurred in the United States. In 2002 Texas was the only jurisdiction that executed inmates (three) who committed their crime as minors. As of November 30, 2003, one inmate who was a minor at the time of crime was executed in Oklahoma.

Those countries were said to violate international human rights agreements when they impose the death sentence on minor offenders. The International Covenant on Civil and Political Rights, the UN Convention on the Rights of the Child, the African Charter on the Rights and Welfare of the Child, and the American Convention on Human Rights all ban the imposition of the death sentence on persons who were less than 18 years old at the time of the crime. In addition, the UN Convention on the Rights of the Child further prohibits the sentence of life without the possibility of parole for those younger than 18. Today virtually all countries in the world either have statutes prohibiting the execution of minors or are believed to be abiding by the provisions of one or another of the aforementioned treaties.

Although the United States ratified the International Covenant on Civil and Political Rights on 1992, it has reserved the right to execute juveniles. While signing an international treaty is just a general endorsement of the treaty's provisions, ratifying that treaty signifies that a country is legally bound by its terms. In reserving the right to execute offenders who were juveniles when they committed the crime, the United States stated "[that it] reserves the right, subject to its Constitutional constraints, to impose capital punishment on any person (other than a pregnant woman) duly convicted under existing or future laws permitting the imposition of capital punishment, including such punishment for crimes committed by persons below eighteen years of age." The United States has signed but not ratified the United Nations Convention on the Rights of the Child and the American Convention on Human Rights.

CHAPTER 10

THE DEBATE—CAPITAL PUNISHMENT SHOULD BE MAINTAINED

PORTIONS OF THE MINORITY VIEWS BY SENATOR ORRIN HATCH (R-UT) INCLUDED IN THE REPORT ON THE INNOCENCE PROTECTION ACT OF 2002 (S. 486) BY SENATOR PATRICK LEAHY (D-VT) TO THE SENATE, 107TH CONGRESS, OCTOBER 16, 2002

S. 486 is presented by the Majority as a bill to ensure access to DNA testing and competent counsel in capital proceedings. While such goals are laudable, the Majority Report raises broader issues relating to the overall fairness of the death penalty system in this country, the need for a national moratorium, and the need to address other "defects of capital punishment systems nationwide...." Some who have injected these larger concerns into the debate over S. 486 are simply attempting to frustrate the administration of the death penalty in our country by alleging, without any credible evidence, that there is a significant risk that innocent persons have been or will be executed. By attaching itself to this claim, the Majority has lent credence to a minority of activist groups that has little concern for the overall safety of the public and the significant benefits to our society of a swift, accurate, and fair death penalty system.

Contrary to the Majority's view, we submit that the death penalty system in our country is accurate. Suggestions to the contrary are contradicted by the fact that no credible evidence has been provided to suggest that a single innocent person has been executed since the Supreme Court imposed the heightened protections in 1976. The death penalty system now includes numerous layers of court review, which ensure that errors are identified and corrected. In fact, the death penalty system saves lives by incapacitating dangerous offenders who, if freed, would pose a significant risk that they will kill again. Moreover, there is substantial evidence that the death penalty is a significant deterrent; states that impose the death penalty have reduced murder rates, while states that do not impose the death penalty have experienced increases in murder

rates. For convicted murderers who are already serving life without parole sentences, the death penalty is a critical deterrent to the murder of prison guards, nurses, and other inmates. Moreover, the possibility of the death penalty has served a vital national security interest by encouraging those guilty of espionage against the United States, like Aldrich Ames and Robert Hanssen, to cooperate and provide full disclosure of the damage they caused....

... We disagree with the underlying premise for much of S. 486—that the death penalty system in our country is "broken" and needs to be fixed. In our view, the death penalty system in our country continues to play a vital role in protecting the public from vicious criminals by deterring and punishing murderers. Moreover, aside from the protection of the public and the just punishment of the guilty, our death penalty system vindicates the right of victims and their families to see that justice is done. All too often, the value of a swift, certain, and reliable death penalty is challenged by a vocal minority of special interest groups seeking to advance their own anti–death penalty agenda by proffering unreliable studies and generalizations based on isolated incidents. Death penalty opponents pursue their cause without even considering the public benefits of the death penalty....

The death penalty system in our country has been built on "super due process," a term used by former Supreme Court Justice Lewis Powell to describe the procedural system for imposing and reviewing death penalty cases. We have an elaborate system of appeals in capital cases, which typically involves multiple levels of state and federal review, ultimately landing at the United States Supreme Court. Over the past 25 years, procedural protections have been adopted to reduce as much as possible the likelihood that error will be committed or, if committed, that it will go undetected. Neither the Majority nor any death penalty opponents has cited any credible evidence that any innocent person has been executed since the Supreme Court reinstated the death penalty in 1976....

The likely explanation for the absence of errors in capital cases during the past quarter century is the greater care taken by the courts to assure the correct resolution of such cases and, particularly, the painstaking reviews that occur in cases in which the death sentence is actually imposed.

More significantly, death penalty opponents undervalue the important benefit of the death penalty—it saves lives. Through a combination of deterrence, incapacitation, and the imposition of just punishment, a swift, certain and accurate death penalty system protects a significant number of innocent lives.

... Death penalty opponents attack capital punishment by focusing on the alleged risk that we will execute an innocent person or that we already have executed an innocent person. While there is no credible evidence to support these claims, there is overwhelming evidence that capital punishment saves a substantial number of innocent lives, deterring probably thousands of murders in the United States every year. The recent and most comprehensive academic studies, our nation's historical experience, and criminals' own account of their motives and behavior all point in the same direction: that the death penalty is a substantial deterrent to homicide....

TESTIMONY OF KENT SCHEIDEGGER, LEGAL DIRECTOR, CRIMINAL JUSTICE LEGAL FOUNDATION, BEFORE THE UNITED STATES SENATE COMMITTEE ON THE JUDICIARY HEARING ON "REDUCING THE RISK OF EXECUTING THE INNOCENT: THE REPORT OF THE ILLINOIS GOVERNOR'S COMMISSION ON CAPITAL PUNISHMENT," JUNE 12, 2002

... The correct identification and sufficient punishment of murderers is a matter of the greatest importance. Indeed, there is no more important function of the state governments than the protection of their citizens from murder. The performance of this function, while also protecting the wrongly accused, deserves the closest attention and greatest care. Regrettably, there has been a great deal of misleading information circulating on the subject of capital punishment, so I welcome the opportunity to make at least a start at getting the truth out today.

The focus of today's hearing is on the actual guilt or innocence of the defendant. This change of focus is most welcome and long overdue. For three decades, the American people have suffered inordinate delays and exorbitant expense in extended litigation over issues which have nothing to do with guilt, which are not in the Constitution as originally enacted and understood, and which often involve sentencing policy decisions of dubious merit. Congress should certainly be concerned with further reducing the already small possibility of conviction of the innocent, whether the penalty be death or life in prison. At the same time, it should take care not to exacerbate, and if

possible to reduce, the interminable delays and erroneous reversals that are presently the norm in that vast majority of capital cases that involve no question whatever of the identity of the perpetrator. I suggest that the Congress set a national goal of reducing to four years the median time from sentence to execution and establish a standing commission to periodically review the system and recommend changes to achieve that goal. Four years is more than sufficient to weed out the very few cases of real doubt of identity, but short enough that the American people would finally have the benefits of [an] effective death penalty system: justice for the worst murders, certainty the murderer will not kill again, and the life-saving deterrent effect of such a system.

The specific topic of today's hearing is the Report of the [Illinois] Governor's Commission on Capital Punishment. Regrettably, that report shows little of the balance needed for this important topic. Particularly disturbing is the summary manner in which the report dismisses deterrence. While the subject has long been controversial and will likely remain so, the flurry of recent studies finding a deterrent effect cannot be brushed off. A sophisticated econometric analysis at Emory University estimated that each execution saves 18 innocent lives. Another study at the University of Colorado estimated a lower but still very substantial 5 to 6 fewer homicides for each execution. Even using the lowest of these figures, a national moratorium would kill hundreds of innocent people each year. Indeed, a study at the University of Houston estimated that a temporary halt in executions in Texas to resolve a legal question cost over 200 lives in a single state. There are, of course, other studies to the contrary. Even so, any public official considering a halt to or severe restriction of capital punishment must consider the very substantial possibility that such an action will result in the deaths of a great many innocent people.

One of the commission's recommendations is to narrow the scope of offenses eligible for capital punishment. Some amount of narrowing is indeed in order, but the drastic limitations in the report are not justified by any concerns with actual innocence. In particular, the recommendation that murder of the rape victim by a rapist no longer be a capital offense should be rejected out of hand. This is the kind of case where the deterrent effect is most needed, since without capital punishment the rapist is looking at a long prison sentence whether he kills the victim or not. It is also the kind of case where DNA is most likely to eliminate any doubt of identity.

On a positive note, the report does acknowledge that many of the reversed judgments in capital cases are "based on legal issues that had little to do with the trial itself," and are often the result of new rules created by the state and federal supreme courts after the trial. This is an important fact for the Congress to consider when it is confronted with misleading statistics of the so-called "error rate" in capital cases....

STATEMENT OF FRANK KEATING, GOVERNOR OF OKLAHOMA, AT THE CONFERENCE OF THE PEW FORUM ON RELIGION & PUBLIC LIFE (A CALL FOR RECKONING: RELIGION AND THE DEATH PENALTY), HELD AT THE UNIVERSITY OF CHICAGO DIVINITY SCHOOL, CHICAGO, ILLINOIS, JANUARY 25, 2002

... I had never been to the Republic of Ireland and I arrived as a guest to participate in a debate on the subject of capital punishment....

... [S]everal of the things I said came as somewhat of a surprise to my Irish listeners. The impression they had was that the United States is a killing field, that we execute everyone for everything, and that it is a killing field largely focused on minorities. When I explained to them that the United States' problem is its incredible violence, our problem as a country is that we—in many cities and in many rural areas—treat life cheaply. For example, the big shock was when the prime minister of Ireland said that the year previously they had had 40 homicides in Ireland. We had 60 in Oklahoma City; they had 40 homicides in the entire country the year previous.

When some who were Catholics pointed out that the pope felt that capital punishment should be rare if nonexistent, I said, "Well, in the United States, believe it or not, that is practically true." Between 1977 and the time of my speech—and it's changed somewhat obviously unfortunately on the high side of homicides since then—we had something like 480,000 homicides and 629 executions. So for 480,000 deaths, we executed 629 people, something like 1/12th of 1 percent of the killings resulting in executions. If you applied that same standard to the Republic of Ireland, they wouldn't execute anybody either, because 1/12th of 1 percent of 40 people is zero. There is no one out there.

In the state of Oklahoma in the heartland of America, right in the middle of the United States we had 8,000 homicides since 1977 and 30 executions, something like 1/2 of 1 percent of the killings in our state resulting in executions.

Thirdly, the Irish listeners were surprised that there was anguish on the part of those of us who consider ourselves conservative. I'm a pro-life conservative. I believe in the quality of each individual life, in the goodness of every human being and the right of everyone to stand tall, to do that which he or she can do in this magnificent free society in which we live. But they were surprised that there was anguish and debate—and in our many different religioned environment (only 3 percent of the people in my state are Catholic)—that we have a very vigorous debate on capital punishment....

My friends were also surprised that in my state the average time between conviction and execution was ten years. They thought that if somebody committed a crime, somebody was quickly executed. They were also surprised to learn that nationally that statistic was a little bit less than ten years, but it's nearly double digits the number of years that pass between the time a killing results in a conviction to the time of execution.

Yes, it is true, I said, that we have offenses certainly at the federal level for trafficking large amounts of narcotics, treason, where the death sentence can be applied, but for all practical purposes certainly at the state level capital punishment is reserved for people who kill other human beings.

They also were surprised that a life sentence was not a life sentence. In my life I have been an FBI agent, I've been a state prosecutor, I've been a United States Attorney, I supervised all the federal prosecutions in the United States and many of the law enforcement agencies, most federal law enforcement agencies in the country, including the U.S. Bureau of Prisons. It came as a surprise to them that we had situations where people were sentenced to life in prison without parole and it didn't mean that, that people were released, people escaped, people killed other people while in prison, and that happens, by the way, far more frequently than we think.

... I must confess that probably some of the most ardent capital punishment advocates are people like me who have seen up close and [sic] person the flotsam, the jetsam of those who horribly, cruelly treat other people.

Timothy McVeigh killed 168 of our neighbors and friends in Oklahoma City, including 19 children. Now, people say when you debate the death penalty you shouldn't get into emotions, you shouldn't talk about individuals, but you have to because that's what it is all about, people doing horrible incredibly sick, evil things to other people.

And to have someone like Timothy McVeigh making a political statement, knowing that there was a daycare center in a building and blowing it up and seeing the wreckage, the carnage that resulted, the anguish, the agony, the destruction of lives and livelihoods and happiness and future that resulted, I am unforgiving.

I think, of course, that we want to make sure we have the right person. I think, of course, that that individual has the rights and the full panoply of the criminal justice system, including a first-rate defense. But when it is over, in my judgment, the law should be carried out, if that is what a judge or a jury decides. That does not cause me much disquiet. I don't have a sleepless night.

Now, for those to say, "But isn't there a chance that you would execute the innocent," there's no evidence of that. Even Barry Scheck [of the Innocence Project] admitted that that, as far as he knows, has never occurred; there's no evidence of it. But, yes, that is something that all of us have to be very concerned about. I would like to think that it's enough that ten to 12 years pass between conviction and execution, that the average number of appeals is something like 12 in both the state and the federal system, that no governor, no pardon or parole board wants to execute an innocent person. Why? Because the guilty person would be free.

... What we have done in Oklahoma is to require that every felony case and certainly every capital case have, at our expense, DNA testing. And I think that's very sound. Now, many cases don't have DNA testing available because there is no evidence in the case that would be subject to such testing.

Secondly, I have said that if the Pardon and Parole Board recommends to me clemency, and I have granted clemency in some cases, I think "proof beyond a reasonable doubt" with respect to capital cases is too low a standard. I've said that publicly at home and I apply it in my own case. If the governor is asked to determine yes or no on a particular capital event, then what is my burden? Basically, whatever burden I seek to establish, there is nothing written.

As Justice Scalia notes, in the federal system we define "proof beyond a reasonable doubt." State systems generally don't. In Oklahoma we don't. But in the federal system, it is defined as proof of such a convincing character that you would rely up on it unhesitatingly in the most important of your affairs.

Is that a high enough standard when you're taking another person's life? I think there should be a moral certainty standard, which I apply to myself. If I don't have in these cases a confession or physical evidence, if I don't have that even higher standard than proof beyond a reasonable doubt, I'm willing and do commute.

But once that standard is established in my own mind—and this is not easy, because you're dealing with another human being—if that standard is applied, I with no hesitation can deny clemency, because I believe if we love and elevate human life—that means innocent human life—for those who would intentionally, with malice, with violence, take another human being's life, that person has forfeited the right to live....

STATEMENT OF STEVEN D. STEWART, PROSECUTOR, CLARK COUNTY, INDIANA, NOVEMBER 7, 2001

Along with two-thirds of the public, I believe in capital punishment. I believe that there are some defendants who have earned the ultimate punishment our society has to offer by committing murder with aggravating circumstances present. I believe life is sacred. It cheapens the life of an innocent murder victim to say that society has no right to keep the murderer from ever killing again. In my

view, society has not only the right, but the duty to act in self defense to protect the innocent.

Nevertheless, the value of the death penalty in our current system of justice is a limited one and should not be overstated. Because the death sentence is so rarely carried out, whatever deterrent value that exists is lessened in years of appeals and due process. Because of the unlimited power of judges, juries, and prosecutors to show mercy, the difference between those who receive the death penalty and those who do not is minimal. Finally, because the system allows it, the financial costs to state and local governments can be staggering.

In spite of these shortcomings, it is my view that pursuing a death sentence in appropriate cases is the right thing to do. There is no adequate and acceptable alternative. Life Without Parole does not eliminate the risk that the prisoner will murder a guard, a visitor, or another inmate, and we should not be compelled to take that risk. It is also not unheard of for inmates to escape from prison. The prisoner will not be eligible for parole until the next legislative session, when the parole laws can be changed. Considering that a defendant sentenced to "life imprisonment" across the country actually serves on the average less than 8 years in prison, it is a good bet that "life without parole" will not have the meaning intended as years go by.

No system of justice can produce results which are 100 percent certain all the time. Mistakes will be made in any system, which relies upon human testimony for proof. We should be vigilant to uncover and avoid such mistakes. Nevertheless, the risk of making a mistake with the extraordinary due process applied in death penalty cases is very small, and there is no credible evidence to show that any innocent persons have been executed at least since the death penalty was reactivated in 1976. The estimated 50–85 inmates "exonerated" and released from death row, as trumpeted by antideath penalty activists, should be considered in context of over 7,000 death sentences handed down since 1973. The inevitability of a mistake should not serve as grounds to eliminate the death penalty any more than the risk of having a wreck should make automobiles illegal. At the same time, we should never ignore the risks of allowing the inmate to kill again. Our "system" was created by legislators and judges. In order for the death penalty to remain a meaningful and effective punishment, those same legislators and judges need to make necessary changes to reflect the will of the people in a democratic society.

STATEMENT OF PRESIDENT GEORGE W. BUSH ABOUT THE EXECUTION OF TIMOTHY MCVEIGH, JUNE 11, 2001

This morning, the United States of America carried out the severest sentence for the gravest of crimes. The victims of the Oklahoma City bombing have been given not vengeance, but justice. And one young man met the fate he chose for himself six years ago. For the survivors of the crime and for the families of the dead, the pain goes on. The final punishment of the guilty cannot alone bring peace to the innocent. It cannot recover the loss or balance the scales, and it is not meant to do so.

Today, every living person who was hurt by the evil done in Oklahoma City can rest in the knowledge that there has been a reckoning. At every point from the morning of April 19, 1995, to this hour, we have seen the good that overcomes evil. We saw it in the rescuers who saved and suffered with the victims. We have seen it in a community that has grieved and held close the memory of the lost. We have seen it in the work of detectives, marshals, and police. And we have seen it in the courts. Due process ruled. The case was proved. The verdict was calmly reached. And the rights of the accused were protected and observed to the full, and to the end. Under the laws of our country, the matter is concluded. Life and history bring tragedies, and often they cannot be explained. But they can be redeemed. They are redeemed by dispensing justice, though eternal justice is not ours to deliver.

By remembering those who grieve, including Timothy McVeigh's mother, father, and sisters, and by trusting in purposes greater than our own, may God in his mercy grant peace to all, to the lives that were taken six years ago, to the lives that go on, and to the life that ended today.

STATEMENT OF REPRESENTATIVE HENRY J. HYDE (R-IL), CHAIRMAN, HOUSE OF REPRESENTATIVES JUDICIARY COMMITTEE, DECEMBER 10, 1997

With regard to the issue of capital punishment, it is my view that the death penalty, if imposed fairly and without undue delay, can serve [as] a deterrent purpose in our criminal justice system. There are some cases of murder that are so heinous and brutal that society must impose its ultimate penalty. These cases would include terrorism, treason, hijacking resulting in the death of a hostage, or the killing of a police [officer] or prison guard acting in the line of duty. If, under careful deliberation, it is determined that such a crime has occurred and the defendant in the crime has been proven guilty beyond a reasonable doubt, then I would support the imposition of capital punishment.

Society has a right to impose whatever punishment it collectively determines befits the violation of its laws. Denying society the ability to impose the death penalty on those convicted of murder devalues the lives of its citizens.

STATEMENT OF REPRESENTATIVE ROBERT K. DORNAN (R-CA), DECEMBER 4, 1995

As a U.S. congressman, one of my primary concerns is the rule of law. Over the last 30 years, our nation has experienced a crippling decline in effective law enforcement resulting from the erosion of the concept of swift and sure punishment for law breakers. This has resulted from multiple causes, including a politicized judiciary, which all too often has been more sympathetic to the criminal than the victim, and as well, to a general judicial philosophy which has become more concerned with questions of procedure than the search for truth....

As a conservative, I believe there are certain crimes for which the death penalty is justified. Some individuals commit crimes so reprehensible that they forfeit their right to live in society. And some commit crimes so heinous that they do not deserve to be supported for life by the society they injured. These are the people who should be sentenced to death. The death penalty should remain our most severe punishment and should be used only in extraordinary cases. But as has always been the standard in our justice system, the punishment should fit the crime.

STATEMENT OF REPRESENTATIVE SAM JOHNSON (R-TX), NOVEMBER 8, 1995

Regarding capital punishment, I continue to believe that the best way to prevent crime is to target repeat offenders. Criminals must understand the consequences of their actions. We should make prisoners serve out their entire sentences and enforce stiffer penalties, such as capital punishment against felons convicted of heinous crimes, such as rape, murder, and drug-related deaths. I am aware of the need for individual responsibility in determining the death penalty's applicability, and we must always be diligent not to punish the innocent. However, in spite of these risks, I believe that capital punishment is a morally justifiable, necessary, and effective punishment.

Thirty-six states currently administer capital punishment. Texas alone has executed 99 criminals in the past seven years. The people of Texas have made it known that violent crime will not be tolerated.

STATEMENT OF SENATOR JESSE HELMS (R-NC), NOVEMBER 6, 1995

Although I wish that the death penalty was never necessary, I do believe that it should be available to our courts to punish those responsible for especially violent crimes. I believe that the death penalty protects society from further harm by the offender. I also think that it is useful in deterring others from committing similar crimes.

American society will be increasingly plagued by violent crime without the use of the death penalty. In order to combat crime, we must give our police officers and judges the support and encouragement necessary to get tough with criminals. The death penalty is one step in the *right* direction.

EXCERPTS FROM JUSTICE ANTONIN SCALIA'S CONCURRING OPINION IN THE SUPREME COURT DECISION *CALLINS V. COLLINS* (510 U.S. 1141, 1994), DENYING REVIEW OF THE DEATH PENALTY CASE (IN RESPONSE TO JUSTICE HARRY A. BLACKMUN'S DISSENT)

The Fifth Amendment provides that "no person shall be held to answer for a capital crime, unless on a presentment or indictment of a Grand Jury ... nor be deprived of life ... without due process of law." This clearly permits the death penalty to be imposed and establishes beyond doubt that the death penalty is not one of the "cruel and unusual punishments" prohibited by the Eighth Amendment.

Convictions in opposition to the death penalty are often passionate and deeply held. That would be no excuse for reading them into a Constitution that does not contain them, even if they represented the convictions of a majority of Americans. Much less is there any excuse for using that course to thrust a minority's views upon the people. Justice Blackmun ... describ[es] with poignancy the death of a convicted murderer by lethal injection. He chooses ... one of the less brutal of the murders—the murder of a man ripped by a bullet suddenly and unexpectedly, with no opportunity to prepare himself and his affairs, and left to bleed to death on the floor of a tavern. The death-by-injection, which Justice Blackmun describes, looks pretty desirable next to that. It looks even better next to some of the other cases currently before us, which Justice Blackmun did not select as the vehicle for his announcement that the death penalty is always unconstitutional—for example, the case of the 11-year-old girl raped by four men and then killed.... How enviable a quiet death by lethal injection compared with that! If the people conclude ... that ... brutal deaths may be deterred by capital punishment, indeed, if they merely conclude that justice requires such brutal deaths to be avenged by capital punishment, the creation of false, untextual, and unhistorical contradictions within the "Court's Eighth Amendment jurisprudence" should not prevent them.

STATEMENT OF PAUL G. CASSELL, ASSOCIATE PROFESSOR OF LAW, UNIVERSITY OF UTAH, SALT LAKE CITY, BEFORE THE SENATE JUDICIARY COMMITTEE, APRIL 1, 1993

The paucity [smallness of number] of examples of innocent defendants who have been executed provides compelling evidence that the risk of mistaken execution is virtually non-existent. If opponents of the death penalty are able to produce no better examples of mistaken executions [in the testimony], then the overwhelming majority of Americans who support capital punishment can rest assured that the criminal justice system is doing an admirable, if not indeed perfect, job of preventing the execution of innocent defendants....

Capital sentences, when carried out, save innocent lives by permanently incapacitating murderers. Some persons who commit capital homicide will slay other innocent persons if given the opportunity to do so. The death penalty is the most effective means of preventing such killers from repeating their crimes. The next most serious penalty, life imprisonment without possibility of parole, prevents murderers from committing some crimes but does not prevent them from murdering in prison.

At least five federal prison officers have been killed since December 1982, and the inmates in at least three of the incidents were already serving life sentences for murder....

While the innocent lives saved through the incapacitative effect of capital punishment are important, the penalty also saves far more innocent lives through its general deterrent effect....

Logic supports the conclusion that the death penalty is the most effective deterrent for some kinds of murders—those that require reflection and forethought by persons of reasonable intelligence and unimpaired mental facilities. Many capital offenses are quintessential [the most typical] contemplative offenses. Murder for hire, treason, and terrorist bombings all require extensive planning. It stands to reason that capital punishment deters such persons more than the next most serious penalty, life imprisonment without parole.

Anecdotal evidence in support of the deterrent value of capital sentences comes from examples of persons who have been deterred from murdering, or risking a murder, because of the death penalty. For instance, Justice McComb of the California Supreme Court collected from the files of the Los Angeles Police Department 14 examples within a four-year period of defendants who, in explaining their refusal to take a life or carry a weapon, pointed to the presence of the death penalty....

Statistical studies support the proposition that capital sentences, like other criminal sanctions, have a deterrent effect. To be sure, some statistical surveys, often conducted by opponents of the death penalty, have found no such effect....

One of the most recent substantial econometric studies [applying statistical methods to economics to study problems] was performed by Professor Stephen K. Layson of the University of North Carolina at Greensboro, who analyzed data for the United States from 1936 to 1977. Layson concluded that increases in the probability of execution reduced the homicide rate. Specifically, Layson found that, on average, each execution deterred approximately 18 murders....

Through the imposition of just punishment, civilized society expresses its outrage and sense of revulsion toward those who, by contravening [violating] its laws, have not only inflicted injury upon discrete [separate and distinct] individuals, but also weakened the bonds that hold communities together. Certain crimes constitute such outrageous violation of human and moral values that they demand retribution. It was to control the natural human impulse to seek revenge and, more broadly, to give expression to deeply held views that some conduct deserves punishment, that criminal laws, administered by the state, were established. The rule of law does not eliminate feelings of outrage but does provide controlled channels for expressing such feelings. People can rely on society to sanction criminal conduct and to carry out deserved punishments....

The death penalty's retributive function thus vindicates the fundamental moral principle that a criminal should receive his or her just deserts. Through the provision of just punishment, capital punishment affirms the sanctity of human life and thereby protects it.

... The system imposes a vast array of due process protections to assure that no innocent person is convicted of a crime.

STATEMENT OF MIRIAM SHEHANE, STATE PRESIDENT, VICTIMS OF CRIME AND LENIENCY, MONTGOMERY, ALABAMA, BEFORE THE SENATE JUDICIARY COMMITTEE, APRIL 1, 1993

My daughter, Quenette, was brutally murdered in 1976....

Time will not permit nor will I burden you with the gory details of how one of the defendants described her hours of torture and final death, but the memory is imprinted in my mind permanently. The three men who killed her were arrested and brought to trial—literally seven trials over a period of six years.... The frustrations the families go through when they think justice will soon prevail, only to receive jolt after jolt as they learn the case is going back for trial due to technicalities, [are] enough to cause fatal health problems.

... As you know, 36 states have determined that the death penalty is the most appropriate punishment for certain brutal and vicious murders. As the parent of a murder victim, I feel this punishment is not only fair, it is essential. What is not fair is when this punishment is prolonged by extensive appeals, stays, and postponements. We victims need a closure to our grief. I did not rejoice when Wallace Norrell was executed July 13, 1990, for murdering Quenette, but I certainly felt relief. I could not have a sense of completion and finally put my dear Quenette to rest if I didn't [sic] have to worry about two others being released at some point....

I can assure you that the system, as it now operates, gives far more consideration to death row inmates than it affords the victims and their families. What are the safeguards for the victim when a murderer is tried, acquitted by a jury, but can never be retried no matter how much evidence is produced in the future? Are the scales of justice earnestly balanced when a convicted murderer is not executed for 13.5 years? Lest we forget, in addition to the extensive appeals of the courts, every state with a capital punishment statute has a procedure for executive clemency.

STATEMENT OF BRUCE FEIN, PRIVATE ATTORNEY SPECIALIZING IN CONSTITUTIONAL AND COMMUNICATIONS LAW, BEFORE THE HOUSE JUDICIARY COMMITTEE, MAY 23, 1990

Although the death penalty certainly is not the answer to the worrisome ... levels of crime today, it is an important tool, I think, in creating a right kind of moral climate that suggests there are certain standards of behavior that must be accepted in order to avoid degeneration of society, anarchy, and a level of bestiality....

We must recognize that death laws have tongues. They speak to a moral universe that places some kind of conduct simply beyond the level of decent mankind....

It seems to me as well that certainly when you speak of the need for a death penalty for [killing] prison wardens, that would not threaten somebody who is already in prison under a life term with no possibility of parole, and who has very little incentive to do anything to control his conduct, to try to escape, to kill to escape because there isn't any further punishment that is available if death is not an option.

I think we owe a certain decency toward our prison wardens who undertake very dangerous positions to have that death penalty option there.

STATEMENT OF JOHN C. SCULLY, COUNSEL, WASHINGTON LEGAL FOUNDATION, WASHINGTON, D.C., BEFORE THE HOUSE JUDICIARY COMMITTEE, MAY 3, 1990

The overwhelming majority of Americans, black and white, support the death penalty. The Supreme Court has consistently upheld the constitutionality of the death penalty. The drug-war killings and the other murders that occur daily in our country demonstrate the need for the death penalty. The death penalty is a deterrent to future murders. Finally, some murders are so shocking that it is evident that there is no other punishment that fits the crime.

Yet, the will of the majority of the people is regularly frustrated by the opponents of the death penalty who repeatedly devise new and often bizarre forms of lethal attacks upon the death penalty. The rejection by the U.S. Supreme Court of the statistical disparity-death-by-racial-quota theory has led the anti–death penalty advocates to seek a legislative vehicle to attack the death penalty....

WLF [Washington Legal Foundation] strongly opposes racial discrimination in the justice system. Individuals sentenced to death should and do have the right and opportunity to challenge any act of racial discrimination in the justice system.

... The BJS [Bureau of Justice Statistics] report showed that for every 1,000 whites arrested on homicide charges, approximately 16 were given a death sentence, while fewer than 12 blacks were sent to death row for every 1,000 blacks arrested for homicide. This means that white murderers are 36 percent more likely to be sentenced to death than their black counterparts.

Does that mean that white murderers are the victims of racial discrimination? Of course not. There are numerous individual circumstances that comprise each murder case; those circumstances make it impossible to use statistics to prove discrimination in a manner similar to that utilized in employment discrimination cases.

... Studies, unable to show racial discrimination against blacks by examining the race of the defendant, also examined the race of the victim. The Baldus study concluded that for some types of murders, if the victim of the crime was white, then the murderer was more likely to receive a death sentence than if the victim was black.

The race-of-the-victim theory, if accepted, means that even a white murderer can level charges of racism at a jury that sent him to death row for killing a white person....

The Katz study showed that the black defendant/white victim cases are the most aggravated of the four defendant-victim racial combinations. The interracial nature of this kind of homicide minimized the possibility that the killing arose due to a family dispute or fight between friends, neighbors, or relatives.

The black defendant/black victim homicides occurred most frequently and were characterized by poor defendants who kill family members, friends, or other acquaintances during a fight or argument. Those types of murders generally have the most mitigating circumstances.

The white defendant/white victim homicides reflected a mix between killings precipitated by a dispute similar to those precipitating black-on-black homicides, but with a substantial percent (about one-third) of the killings comparable to the black-on-white homicides.

Only 27 of the 1,082 cases were characterized as white defendant/black victim homicides. The relatively small number of such homicides made them difficult for Katz to classify.

STATEMENT OF JAMES C. ANDERS, SOLICITOR, FIFTH JUDICIAL CIRCUIT OF SOUTH CAROLINA, BEFORE THE SENATE JUDICIARY COMMITTEE, SEPTEMBER 19, 1989

I believe that in certain cases, the death penalty can be shown to be the only rational and realistic punishment for

an unspeakable crime.... Obviously, the most basic right a citizen has is the right to be secure in his person, the right to be safe from physical or economic harm from another. Laws to protect citizens and advance the harmony of society are founded upon these principles. To enforce these laws, created in the best interest of society as a whole, there has to be a deterrent for a breach of the law. Therefore, deterrence is the first aim of a system of punishment.

Deterrence is only one side of the punishment coin, however. An equally fundamental reason to punish lies in society's compelling desire to see justice done. Punishment expresses the emotions of the society wronged, the anger and outrage felt, and it solidifies and reinforces the goals, values, and norms of acceptable behavior in the society....

The deterrent effect of the death penalty is the favorite criticism of the opponents of capital punishment. The social scientists' studies have been mixed at best, and there is no authoritative consensus on whether or not the death penalty deters anyone from committing a crime. Threats of punishment cannot and are not meant to deter everybody all of the time. They are meant to deter most people most of the time. Therefore, the death penalty can only be a deterrent if it is meted out with a reasonable degree of consistency. The deterrence effect lies in the knowledge of the citizenry that it will more likely than not be carried out if the named crime is committed.

Even if one is not fully convinced of the deterrent effect of the death penalty, he or she would surely choose the certainty of the convicted criminal's death by execution over the possibility of the deaths of new victims.

Death penalty opponents argue that if life is sacred, then the murderer's life, too, is sacred ... and for the state to punish him by execution is barbaric and causes the state to bend to the murderer's level. The only similarity between the unjustified taking of an innocent life and the carrying out of a convicted murderer's execution is the end result—death. The death penalty is a legal sentence, enacted by the legislatures of various states, which presumably reflect their constituents' desires. It is a penalty that can finally be carried out only after a trial where the defendant is afforded all of his constitutional rights....

Death penalty opponents are also troubled by the studies that purport to show that the death penalty is applied capriciously [unpredictably] that it discriminates racially and economically.... Assuming that premise for the sake of argument, is that a rational reason to abolish the death penalty? Is the fact that some guilty persons escape punishment sufficient to let all guilty persons escape it?

... If the death penalty can deter one murder of an innocent life or if it can make a statement to the community about what will and will not be tolerated, then it is justified.

Opponents of the death penalty advocate the life sentence in prison as a viable alternative to execution.... Early release programs, furloughs, and escape combine to place a shockingly high number of convicted murderers back on the streets in record time.

The life without parole sentence is no solution either. First, the possibility of escape cannot be completely eliminated, even in the most secure of institutions.... Second, the life without parole sentence places a tremendous burden on prison administrators. Faced with controlling inmates who have already received the worst punishment society can mete out, they can only throw their hands up in frustration. Lastly, the true lifer is not only capable of continuing to murder, but may actually be more likely to do so. Every prison in the country has its own stories of the lifer who killed another inmate over a cigarette or a piece of chicken.

STATEMENT OF ROBERT B. KLIESMET, PRESIDENT, INTERNATIONAL UNION OF POLICE ASSOCIATIONS, BEFORE THE SENATE JUDICIARY COMMITTEE, SEPTEMBER 19, 1989

Street cops, in their pragmatic view, believe, as does 86 percent of the public, that the death penalty is a viable deterrent for persons convicted of certain crimes. A search of the literature shows there are a number of studies and articles that show a direct deterrent effect by imposing and carrying out the death penalty. One study goes as far as to point out that for each execution for a homicide, up to 15 lives can be saved through the deterrent effect. The safety of society, which is the real goal of the criminal justice system, is being compromised by saving the life of a convicted offender. This compromise is a needless sacrifice of a blameless victim's life.

STATEMENT OF REPRESENTATIVE NEWT GINGRICH (R-GA), JANUARY 31, 1988

[The state] should use the death penalty for such serious crimes as murder and treason. Criminals might think twice before committing such acts if they knew that the consequences of their actions could result in the death penalty. People must be held accountable for the crimes they commit. I don't believe we can just slap someone on the hand and hope [he or she] never misbehave[s] again.

Right now, there are over a thousand prisoners on death row. Many of them have been there since the early 1970s because our current criminal justice system encourages them to seek endless appeals in order to delay their sentence of death.

I believe this is wrong. That's why I'm working on legislation to establish a unified appeals process that would place a two-year time limit on appeals to federal courts. This would prevent persons convicted of crimes from deliberately dragging out their appeals simply to delay the death sentence.

STATEMENT OF SENATOR JOHN P. EAST (R-NC), JANUARY 16, 1986

With the tougher attitude towards crime that we have taken in the past five years, the murder rate has gone down, but day after day we still read newspaper accounts of murders, many of which are carried out with chilling cruelty and detachment. The American people deserve continued protection from this wave of killing, protection often denied them by a system that often still gives lenient penalties to the most vicious criminals.

Death is the only suitable penalty for reprehensible crimes, such as premeditated murder. Murder does not simply differ in magnitude from extortion or theft. It differs in kind as well, and its punishment also should differ in kind. Murderers have not simply injured their victims, but they have weakened the most important bond that holds communities together—respect for life. By imposing the supreme penalty in cases of murder, society expresses its moral outrage at such a crime; it sends a signal that innocent human life is precious; and it declares that such life cannot be violated without a like consequence to the killer. By imposing the death penalty, it also deters other would-be murderers, and it prevents the murderer from killing again.

I am convinced that there needs to be a federal death penalty statute. In particular, we need to be able to impose the death penalty for the assassination of high government officials. We also need to provide for capital punishment in cases where convicted killers, already confined in a federal prison and serving life sentences, commit murder again. At present, such people have no incentive not to kill because they are already suffering the severest penalty that federal law has to offer. As a result, the number of gruesome murders at federal correctional institutions is on the rise.

TESTIMONY OF ERNEST VAN DEN HAAG, ADJUNCT PROFESSOR OF SOCIAL PHILOSOPHY, NEW YORK UNIVERSITY, BEFORE THE SUBCOMMITTEE ON CRIMINAL LAW AND PROCEDURES OF THE SENATE JUDICIARY COMMITTEE, MARCH 15, 1972

It is suggested that the death penalty discriminates against the poor and the black.... If true, ... the suggestion would be nonetheless wholly irrelevant. It concerns the unfair way in which the penalty is distributed, not the fairness or unfairness of the penalty.

Any penalty ... could be unfairly or unjustly applied. The vice is not in the penalty, but in the process by which it is inflicted. It is unfair to inflict unequal penalties on equally guilty parties, or on any innocent parties, regardless of what the penalty is.... You should try to correct the judicial processes by which, it is alleged, the penalties are unfairly inflicted....

All penalties—including fines, prison sentences, and the death penalty—are deterrent roughly in proportion to their severity.... Were that not the case, we would certainly not have varied penalties, but might impose a uniform penalty of $5 for any crime whatsoever. We impose penalties roughly differentiated because we feel that crimes of different gravity deserve different punishment.

On the basis of the statistics available, no logical conclusion one way or the other can be reached. It cannot be proven that the death penalty is additionally deterrent; it cannot be proven either that it is not.

No penalty can deter the irrational, perhaps. But penalties do influence those who are rational enough to be influenced. In this respect the data suggest the death penalty has been very effective, precisely because very few murders are committed by rational persons.

CHAPTER 11

THE DEBATE—CAPITAL PUNISHMENT SHOULD BE ABOLISHED

STATEMENT OF SENATOR RUSSELL FEINGOLD (D-WI) ON THE FEDERAL DEATH PENALTY ABOLITION ACT FROM THE SENATE FLOOR, FEBRUARY 13, 2003

[T]oday I introduce the Federal Death Penalty Abolition Act of 2003. This bill would abolish the death penalty at the Federal level. It would put an immediate halt to executions and forbid the imposition of the death penalty as a sentence for violations of Federal law.

Since 1976, when the death penalty was reinstated by the Supreme Court, there have been 830 executions across the country, including two at the Federal level. At the same time, 103 people on death row were later found innocent and released from death row. Exonerated inmates are not only removed from death row, but they are usually released from prison altogether. Apparently, these people never should have been convicted in the first place. While death penalty proponents claim that the death penalty is fair, efficient, and a deterrent, the fact remains that our criminal justice system has failed and has resulted in at least 103 very grave mistakes.

... Since January 25, 2001, when I last introduced this bill, the Federal Government resumed executions for the first time in almost 40 years, and 138 people have been executed nationwide. In this new year, we have begun our use of capital punishment at an alarming pace. We are only in the second week of February, and there have already been 10 executions this year. And yet this one-to-eight error rate looms. Is it possible that those 10 people are representative of the one-to-eight error rate that has plagued the death penalty since it was reinstated in 1976? Is it possible that in the last six weeks, as we have debated a war in Iraq, funding levels for Federal programs, and judicial nominations, our nation has killed an innocent person?

... That our society relies on killing as punishment is disturbing enough. Even more disturbing, however, is that the States' and Federal Government's use of the death penalty is often not consistent with principles of due process, fairness, and justice. These principles are the foundation of our criminal justice system. It is more clear than ever before that we have put innocent people on death row. In addition, statistics show that those States that have the death penalty are more likely to put people to death for killing white victims than for killing black victims.

After the death penalty was reinstated in 1976, the Federal Government first resumed death penalty prosecutions after enactment of a 1988 Federal law that provided for the death penalty for murder in the course of a drug-kingpin conspiracy. The Federal death penalty was then expanded significantly in 1994, when the omnibus crime bill allowed its use to apply to a total of some 60 Federal offenses. Since 1994, Federal prosecutions seeking the death penalty have now accelerated.

... While the Federal death penalty system is clearly plagued by flaws, there are 38 States across our Nation that also authorize the use of capital punishment. And like the Federal system, those systems are not free from error.

... Maryland and Illinois are not exceptions to a rule, nor anomalies in an otherwise perfect system. In fact, since reinstatement of the modern death penalty, 81 percent of capital cases across the country have involved white victims, even though only 50 percent of murder victims are white. Nationwide, more than half of the death row inmates are African Americans or Hispanic Americans.

There is evidence of racial disparities, inadequate counsel, prosecutorial misconduct, and false scientific evidence in death penalty systems across the country. While the research done in Maryland and Illinois has yielded shocking results, there are 36 other States that authorize the use of the death penalty, most of them far more frequently. Twenty-one of the 38 States that authorize capital punishment have executed more inmates than

Maryland, and 13 of those States have carried out more executions than Illinois. So while we are closer to uncovering the unthinkable truth about the flaws in the Maryland and Illinois death penalty systems, there are 36 other states with systems that are most likely plagued with the same flaws. And yet, the killing continues.

At the beginning of 2003, at the beginning of a new century and millennium with hopes for great progress, I cannot help but believe that our progress has been tarnished by our Nation's not only continuing, but increasing use of the death penalty. We are a Nation that prides itself on the fundamental principles of justice, liberty, equality and due process. We are a Nation that scrutinizes the human rights records of other nations. We are one of the first nations to speak out against torture and killings by foreign governments. We should hold our own system of justice to the highest standard.

Over the last two years, some prominent voices in our country have done just that. And they are not just voices of liberals, or of the faith community. They are the voices of Justice Sandra Day O'Connor, Reverend Pat Robertson, George Will, former FBI Director William Sessions, Republican Governor George Ryan, and Democratic Governor Parris Glending [sic]. The voices of those questioning our application of the death penalty are growing in number, and they are growing louder.

And while we examine the flaws in our death penalty system, we cannot help but note that our use of the death penalty stands in stark contrast to the majority of nations, which have abolished the death penalty in law or practice. There are now 111 countries that have abolished the death penalty in law or in practice. The European Union denies membership in the alliance to those nations that use the death penalty. In fact, it passed a resolution calling for the immediate and unconditional global abolition of the death penalty, and it specifically called on all states within the United States to abolish the death penalty. This is significant because it reflects the unanimous view of a group of nations with which the United States enjoys the closest of relationships.

...As we begin a new year and another Congress, our society is still far from fully just. The continued use of the death penalty shames us. The penalty is at odds with our best traditions. It is wrong and it is immoral. The adage "two wrongs do not make a right," applies here. Our nation has long ago done away with other barbaric punishments like whipping and cutting off the ears of suspected criminals. Just as our nation did away with these punishments as contrary to our humanity and ideals, it is time to abolish the death penalty as we seek justice in this new century. And it's not just a matter of morality. The continued viability of our justice system as a truly just system requires that we do so. And our Nation's striving to remain the leader and defender of freedom, liberty and equality demands that we do so.

... I ask my colleagues to join me in taking the first step in abolishing the death penalty in our great Nation. I also call on each State that authorizes the use of the death penalty to cease this practice. Let us step away from the culture of violence and restore fairness and integrity to our criminal justice system.

STATEMENT OF MARYLAND ATTORNEY GENERAL J. JOSEPH CURRAN, JR., NEWS CONFERENCE AT LAWYERS MALL, ANNAPOLIS, MARYLAND, JANUARY 30, 2003

Over the past forty years, there have been three executions in our State. Over the next few months, seven men are poised to be executed. In the fractured history of the death penalty in Maryland, this is a watershed moment.

I have long opposed human executions on moral grounds, and I stand today with clergy and others from many different faiths who share this view. I believe that we should hold ourselves to a higher moral standard than those who commit these unspeakable wrongs. Serious questions are also being raised about racial and geographic disparities in our application of the death penalty.

But I am here to talk today about what I believe is the most compelling issue: the inevitability of mistake.

We are blessed in Maryland with dedicated police officers, prosecutors, judges, and lawyers, all who labor every day to make our criminal justice system work. But despite our best efforts, this system makes mistakes. It is a human institution, and humans are not infallible. Any trial judge and any trial lawyer will tell you—mistakes happen. People are imperfect, the system is imperfect. Mistakes are inevitable.

With appeals and reviews, we catch many of them. We hope to catch most of them. But we do not catch all of them.

Since the Supreme Court reinstated capital punishment in 1976, 821 people have been executed. During the same time period, 103 people have been exonerated, the most recent just this week in Florida. Those 103 were lucky. The mistake that led to their wrongful death sentence was found and corrected. Others are not so lucky. We will never know how many mistakes were not caught in time.

I support with the strongest conviction the need to severely punish those who have committed these unspeakable wrongs. They have taken a life. They have caused incomprehensible suffering for the victims' families. They have forfeited the right to live among us.

We now have a way to punish them which we lacked when we reinstated the death penalty. Life without parole puts people away for the rest of their lives, with no hope or possibility of ever getting out. Let me be absolutely clear: they die in prison.

But, there is one pivotal difference between death in prison and the death penalty. That is the chance to correct a mistake. It is a terrible injustice to wrongfully incarcerate an innocent person. We have just witnessed such an injustice with Bernard Webster, who was recently exonerated from a rape conviction after serving 20 years in prison. But at least we were able to set him free, to correct the mistake. The death penalty allow[s] no such possibility.

So let me say it again: Capital punishment comes only at the intolerable risk of killing an innocent person. This is unworthy of us.

Therefore, today I call for abolition of the death penalty.

A JOINT STATEMENT, *TO END THE DEATH PENALTY*, BY THE NATIONAL JEWISH/ CATHOLIC CONSULTATION (COSPONSORED BY THE NATIONAL COUNCIL OF SYNAGOGUES AND THE BISHOPS' COMMITTEE FOR ECUMENICAL AND INTERRELIGIOUS AFFAIRS OF THE NATIONAL CONFERENCE OF CATHOLIC BISHOPS), DECEMBER 3, 1999

"A Sanhedrin [Jewish court of law] that puts one person to death once in seven years is called destructive. Rabbi Eliezer ben Azariah says: Or even once in seventy years. Rabbi Tarfon and Rabbi Akiba say: Had we been the Sanhedrin, none would ever have been put to death." *Mishnah Makkot, 1:10 (2nd Century, C.E.)*

"A sign of hope is the increasing recognition that the dignity of human life must never be taken away, even in the case of someone who has done great evil. Modern society has the means of protecting itself, without definitively denying criminals the chance to reform. I renew the appeal for a consensus to end the death penalty, which is both cruel and unnecessary." *Pope John Paul II, January 27, 1999, St. Louis, Missouri*

Almost two millennia separate these two statements, which together embody the collective wisdom and moral insights of our two ancient religious traditions, Rabbinic Judaism and Roman Catholicism, on a burning issue of our time, capital punishment. At our meeting of March 23, 1999, we religious leaders, Catholic and Jewish, probed and shared our own traditions with each other. [The National Jewish/Catholic Consultation has been meeting twice a year since 1987.] The result was a remarkable confluence of witness on how best in our time to interpret the eternal word of God.

Both traditions begin with an affirmation of the sanctity of human life. Both, as the above statements imply, acknowledge the theoretical possibility of a justifiable death penalty, since the Scriptures mandate it for certain offenses. Yet both have, over the centuries, narrowed

those grounds until, today, we would say together that it is time to cease the practice altogether. To achieve this consensus [majority opinion], we analyzed the statements of our respective bodies going back to the late 1970s and we agree that in them we found a growing conviction that the arguments offered in defense of the death penalty are less than persuasive in the face of the overwhelming mandate in both Jewish and Catholic traditions to respect the sanctity of human life.

Some would argue that the death penalty is needed as a means of retributive justice [exacting punishment for offense done] to balance out the crime with the punishment. This reflects a natural concern of society, and especially of victims and their families. Yet we believe that we are called to seek a higher road even while punishing the guilty, for example through long and in some cases life-long incarceration, so that the healing of all can ultimately take place.

Some would argue that the death penalty is needed as a deterrent to crime. Yet the studies that lie behind our statements over the years have yet to reveal any objective evidence to justify this conclusion. Criminals tend to believe they will escape any consequences for their behavior, or simply do not think of consequences at all, so an escalation of consequences is usually irrelevant to their state of mind at the time of the crime.

Some would argue that the death penalty will teach society at large the seriousness of crime. Yet we say that teaching people to respond to violence with violence will, again, only breed more violence.

Some would argue that our system of justice, trial by jury, can ensure that capital punishment will be meted out equitably [fairly] to various groups in society and that the innocent will never be convicted. This is the least persuasive argument of all. Statistics, however weighted, indicate that errors are made in judgment and convictions. Recent scientific advances, such as DNA testing, may reveal that persons on death row, despite seemingly "overwhelming" circumstantial evidence, may in fact be innocent of the charges against them. Likewise, suspiciously high percentages of those on death row are poor or people of color. Our legal system is a very good one, but it is a human institution. Even a small percentage of irreversible errors is increasingly seen as intolerable. God alone is the author of life.

The strongest argument of all is the deep pain and grief of the families of victims and their quite natural desire to see punishment meted out to those who have plunged them into such agony. Yet it is the clear teaching of our traditions that this pain and suffering cannot be healed simply through the retribution of capital punishment or by vengeance. It is a difficult and long process of healing, which comes about through personal growth and God's grace. We agree that much more must be done by the religious community and by society at large to solace and care for the grieving families of the victims of violent crime.

...We affirm that we came to these conclusions because of our shared understanding of the sanctity of human life. We have committed ourselves to work together, and each within our own communities, toward ending the death penalty.

STATEMENT OF SAMUEL JORDAN, DIRECTOR, PROGRAM TO ABOLISH THE DEATH PENALTY, AMNESTY INTERNATIONAL U.S.A., MARCH 4, 1998

The death penalty as imposed in the United States has the power to mislead even the most attentive social observer. Despite its fatal brutality, the death penalty is permitted by the Constitution, honored by custom, and upheld by the courts—as was slavery. Beneath the veneer, the practice of executions is accompanied by a resolute defiance of internationally accepted standards of human rights and fairness.

Repeatedly, studies have shown that capital punishment is imposed arbitrarily with disproportionate weight given to race—of the victim. Although African-Americans account for 50 percent of the homicide victims in the nation, 82 percent of death row offenders have been convicted for the murder of whites. Poverty as well as race often determines the allocation of the death sentence. Inadequate, inexperienced representation for indigent [poor] defendants characterizes most capital litigation. In addition, imposition of the death penalty often costs as much as three times the expense of lifetime incarceration. The system of executions has also sought to lower the age of offenders against whom it may be applied, thus ensnaring juveniles. And sadly, there are no reliable statistics on the numbers of mentally deficient victims of the executioner.

Many organizations have begun to support the call for a moratorium on the death penalty. They argue that the same conditions persist today, which led the U.S. Supreme Court to order a moratorium on executions in 1972 in the landmark case, *Furman v. Georgia*. The resumption of executions after *Gregg v. Georgia* in 1976 has not been marked by the abatement of racial disparities, arbitrariness, and substandard representation in the judicial process leading to the death sentence.

While the moratorium effort draws attention to the shortcomings of the judicial process, we must not rely upon the courts alone to settle matters of public morality and human rights. The role of the abolitionist in the struggle to rid our nation of the death penalty is not unlike the task that confronted abolitionists in the era of chattel slavery [slaves were treated as personal property] in the United States. The answer will not be found in the law. Laws which permit executions must be changed. They must reflect instead an attempt by our society to respect and

enhance the dignity of human life without regard to race, wealth, and prestige.

The first challenge for the modern abolitionist is to topple the death penalty from its pedestal of broad, popular acceptance and to expose it for what it is, a brutal and dehumanizing rationale for legal murder. Next, we must demand that all sectors of the society, especially religious organizations, take command of the moral and humanitarian dimensions of this issue. In the end, to be successful, we must drive a wedge between those who promote capital punishment for selfish reasons, including vote totals and public image, and those who might honestly believe that there is a connection between the death penalty and fairness.

Meeting these challenges will release enormous social energies which can be employed to change the laws. Only then will we join the 101 of the 194 nations of the world which have abandoned the practice of state-sanctioned killing. We deserve a criminal justice system free of the ritual of human sacrifice.

STATEMENT OF RICHARD C. DIETER, EXECUTIVE DIRECTOR, DEATH PENALTY INFORMATION CENTER, WASHINGTON, D.C., DECEMBER 31, 1997

As the number of executions reached a record high, the discriminatory nature of the death penalty became more apparent. Of the 74 executions this year, only 10 percent were punishment for the murder of a black person, yet blacks are victims in about 50 percent of the murders committed in the U.S. Their deaths rarely merit the attention and the expenditures associated with the death penalty. Since the death penalty was reinstated, six white defendants have been executed for murdering a black person, while 112 black people have been executed for the murder of a white person.

Lack of competent representation continued to contribute to the arbitrariness of the death penalty. Exzavious Gibson, a poor black man in Georgia, went before the Georgia courts to appeal his death sentence without a lawyer to plead his case. He lost the appeal. In Mississippi, a federal civil rights suit was filed on behalf of death row inmates against the state, which provides no money and no attorneys for the post-conviction appeals process. The suit cited the results of psychological testing given to the inmates, which showed that one-third suffered from mental retardation. The inmates also were given the Law School Admission Test to test the assumption that they could act as their own lawyers (none of the inmates scored above the 1 percent level)....

... In the past, representation in Georgia and Mississippi might have been provided by the death penalty resource centers, which were established to help with appeals. But federal funding for these centers in 20 states around the country was cut off in 1996, leaving many inmates unrepresented.

The increasing frequency of executions in the U.S. has done little to settle the issue in the eyes of the public. Opposition has moved from candlelight vigils outside of penitentiaries to national and international critiques of the continuing arbitrariness and inequity in the implementation of the death penalty. Public disillusionment with the political promises made for capital punishment is evidenced in the high support for alternatives to executions. While the trend toward more executions will likely continue because of the vast number of people on death row and the shorter appeals process, there are signs that the public may be shifting its focus away from the death penalty as a solution to crime.

STATEMENT OF REPRESENTATIVE HENRY B. GONZALEZ (D-TX) IN THE HOUSE OF REPRESENTATIVES, JUNE 30, 1995

I believe that the death penalty is an act of vengeance veiled as an instrument of justice. Not only do I believe that there are independently sufficient moral objections to the principle of capital punishment to warrant its abolition, but I also know that the death penalty is meted out to the poor, to a disproportionate number of minorities, and does not either deter crime or advance justice.

Violent crimes have unfortunately become a constant in our society.... The sight of any brutal homicide excites a passion within us that demands retributive [exacting punishment for offense done] justice.... We cannot allow ourselves to punish an irrational action with an equally irrational retaliation—murder is wrong, whether it is committed by an individual or by the state.

... The United Nations Universal Declaration of Human Rights states, "No one shall be subjected to torture or to cruel, inhuman, or degrading treatment or punishment." The death penalty is torture, and numerous examples exist, emphasizing the cruelty of the execution....

... Studies fail to establish that the death penalty either has a unique value as a deterrent or is a more effective deterrent than life imprisonment. We assume that perpetrators will give greater consideration to the consequences of their actions if the penalty is death, but the problem is that we are not always dealing with rational actions. Those who commit violent crimes often do so in moments of passion, rage, and fear—times when irrationality reigns.

... Proponents advocate that some crimes simply deserve death. This argument is ludicrous. If a murderer deserves death, I ask why then do we not burn the arsonist or rape the rapist? Our justice system does not provide for such punishments because society comprehends that it must be founded on principles different from those it condemns. How can we condemn killing while condoning execution?

... In practice, capital punishment has become a kind of grotesque lottery. It is more likely to be carried out in some states than in others.... The death penalty is far more likely to be imposed against blacks than whites.... It is most likely to be imposed upon the poor and uneducated—60 percent of death row inmates never finished high school....

... There are moves in Congress to speed up the execution process by limiting and streamlining the appeals process. But when the statistics show how arbitrarily the death penalty is applied, how can we make any changes without first assuring fairness?... There are no do-overs in this business when mistakes are made.

EXCERPTS FROM JUSTICE HARRY A. BLACKMUN'S DISSENTING OPINION IN THE SUPREME COURT DECISION *CALLINS V. COLLINS* (510 U.S. 1141, 1994), DENYING REVIEW OF THE DEATH PENALTY CASE

Twenty years have passed since this Court declared that the death penalty must be imposed fairly, and with reasonable consistency, or not at all, and, ... despite the effort of the states and courts to devise legal formulas and procedural rules to meet this daunting challenge, the death penalty remains fraught with arbitrariness, discrimination, caprice, and mistake.... Experience has taught us that the constitutional goal of eliminating arbitrariness and discrimination from the administration of death ... can never be achieved without compromising an equally essential component of fundamental fairness—individualized sentencing....

From this day forward, I no longer shall tinker with the machinery of death. For more than 20 years, I have endeavored—indeed, I have struggled—along with a majority of this Court, to develop procedural and substantive rules that would lend more than the mere appearance of fairness to the death penalty endeavor. Rather than continue to coddle the Court's delusions that the desired level of fairness has been achieved and the need for regulation eviscerated [removed], I feel morally and intellectually obligated simply to concede that the death penalty experiment has failed. It is virtually self-evident to me now that no combination of procedural rules or substantive regulations ever can save the death penalty from its inherent constitutional deficiencies.... The problem is that the inevitability of factual, legal, and moral error gives us a system that we know must wrongly kill some defendants, a system that fails to deliver the fair, consistent, and reliable sentence of death required by the Constitution....

There is little doubt now that *Furman*'s essential holding was correct. Although most of the public seems to desire, and the Constitution appears to permit, the penalty of death, it surely is beyond dispute that, if the death penalty cannot be administered consistently and rationally, it may not be administered at all.

Delivering on the *Furman* promise, however, has proved to be another matter. *Furman* aspired to eliminate the vestiges of racism and the effects of poverty in capital sentencing; it deplored the "wanton" and "random" infliction of death by a government with constitutionally limited power. *Furman* demanded that the sentencer's discretion be directed and limited by procedural rules and objective standards in order to minimize the risk of arbitrary and capricious sentences of death.

... It soon became apparent that discretion could not be eliminated from capital sentencing without threatening the fundamental fairness due a defendant when life is at stake. Just as contemporary society was no longer tolerant of the random or discriminatory infliction of the penalty of death, ... evolving standards of decency required due consideration of the uniqueness of each individual defendant when imposing society's ultimate penalty....

... While one might hope that providing the sentencer with as much relevant mitigating [lessening the gravity of crime] evidence as possible will lead to more rational and consistent sentences, experience has taught otherwise. It seems that the decision whether a human being should live or die is so inherently subjective—rife with all of life's understandings, experiences, prejudices, and passions—that it inevitably defies the rationality and consistency required by the Constitution....

STATEMENT OF SENATOR CAROL MOSELEY-BRAUN (D-IL) BEFORE THE SENATE JUDICIARY COMMITTEE, APRIL 1, 1993

The Supreme Court's recent holding in the *Herrera* case, that a death row inmate's claim of actual innocence does not entitle him to *habeas* relief (a prisoner's petition to be heard in federal court), is deeply troubling in an era when Congress and state legislatures are rushing to make more and more crimes punishable by death yet simultaneously curtailing the right to appeal at both the state and federal levels....

When human judgment becomes infallible, our system will be infallible. Until then, those who would strip the system of vital safeguards lead us ever closer to the day when, in the name of the state, we will execute an innocent man. And that, in the word of Justice Brennan's dissent in the *Herrera* case, "comes perilously close to simple murder."

STATEMENT OF WALTER MCMILLIAN, MONROEVILLE, ALABAMA, BEFORE THE SENATE JUDICIARY COMMITTEE, APRIL 1, 1993

My name is Walter McMillian. I was sentenced to die in the electric chair and spent nearly six years on death row in Alabama awaiting execution for a murder that I did not commit, a murder that I knew nothing about, a murder that

I had nothing to do with. Today, the state of Alabama has acknowledged that I am an innocent man and that I was wrongfully convicted. What happened to me could have happened to you, or to anyone else. I was convicted and sentenced to death on the false testimony of one man. I am here today to urge you to do all that is in your power to prevent what happened to me from happening to anyone else.

TESTIMONY OF JULIUS L. CHAMBERS, DIRECTOR-COUNSEL, NAACP LEGAL DEFENSE AND EDUCATIONAL FUND, INC., BEFORE THE HOUSE JUDICIARY COMMITTEE, MARCH 14, 1990

Passage of the proposed death penalty bills would not advance—but would instead retard—resolution of the vexing problems associated with urban crime. While holding up the mirage of fighting and deterring crime, these death penalty bills would surely result in furthering the historical and well-documented racial disparities in the imposition of capital punishment in the United States.

Our concern is squarely grounded in the stark reality, which black people have traditionally faced. For more than three centuries, the weight of the death penalty in this country has been borne far more heavily by blacks than by whites....

... There is no question that the financial cost of sentencing a single person to death is astronomical.... For example, the GAO [General Accounting Office] noted that one study done on "death penalty costs in New York estimated it would cost at least $1.8 million to defend and prosecute a capital case." By contrast, the cost of feeding and housing the defendant convicted in that same case for a period of 40 years would only be $602,000. The proposed statutes are absolutely silent as to where the millions of dollars would come from to "foot the bill...."

Perhaps the true purpose of the bills is to divert the public's attention away from considering measures which could truly serve to fight crime. One commentator correctly observed that ... "the death penalty debate enables public officials and legislators to falsely assert that they are being tough on crime because they favor the death penalty." More emphasis should be placed on the less glamorous side of fighting crime. Most major cities in the country, for example, cannot afford to offer adequate treatment to young offenders who have become ensnared with the drug world.

TESTIMONY OF HENRY SCHWARZSCHILD, DIRECTOR, AMERICAN CIVIL LIBERTIES UNION CAPITAL PUNISHMENT PROJECT, BEFORE THE HOUSE JUDICIARY COMMITTEE, MARCH 14, 1990

The American Civil Liberties Union ... hold[s] capital punishment to be inherently cruel and unusual punishment, barred by the Eighth Amendment of the Constitution. We conclude, furthermore, that in its application, the death penalty violates the due-process-of-law clause of the Fifth Amendment and the equal-protection-of-the-law clause of the Fourteenth. These judgments are grounded in the evidence that the retention of the death penalty in no way contributes to a lessening of the incidence of violent crime, that executions are a barbaric spectacle inflicted upon isolated individual criminal offenders in circumstances redolent with arbitrariness, racial and sex discrimination, as well as status bigotry, that entirely innocent persons are unavoidably executed on occasion, and that the death penalty is not only staggeringly expensive to administer but radically distorts the entire scheme of criminal sentencing.

No one—I want to emphasize—opposes the death penalty because we think that violent crime is not so terrible or that punishment for it should not be proportionately severe. It is the *limits* of severity that is in controversy, not deep anguish about violent crime; that latter, we all, of course, share. When 200 years ago Western countries, including ours, abolished medieval forms of criminal punishment—drawing and quartering, boiling in oil, burning at the stake, gibbeting [hanging], and their like—we did so not because crimes were no longer thought to be so bad or because criminals had become nicer people: Those brutal forms of execution were abolished because we had come to think of *ourselves* as too civilized to do that sort of thing to another human being, no matter who he or she was or what [he or she] had done. *That,* and not the baseless claim that execution makes for less crime, is the issue.

THE REVEREND GUILLERMO CHAVEZ, CHAIRMAN, NATIONAL INTERRELIGIOUS TASK FORCE ON CRIMINAL JUSTICE, BEFORE THE HOUSE JUDICIARY COMMITTEE, NOVEMBER 7, 1985

I question the notion of "standards of decency" as an accepted rationale upon which to base public policy. We need to remember that, about 200 years ago, slaveholding was not considered offensive to the then-current "standards of decency."

... As people of religious and ethical conscience, we seek the restoration and the renewal of wrongdoers, not their deaths. Capital punishment makes it possible for human error or prejudice to send innocent persons to their death. It eliminates forever the healing possibilities of human love and respect. Penal history provides us with prominent examples of innocent persons falsely condemned. Our Judeo-Christian heritage affirms that for the state to assume the power of absolute judgment is to assume a power that belongs only to God.

Another issue that concerns us is that the value of life, when confronted with the death penalty, is cheapened. In this regard, we are especially concerned with what the death penalty does to a society that inflicts it.

As the United Presbyterian Church has declared, "The use of the death penalty tends to brutalize the society that condones it." In denying the humanity of those we put to death, even those guilty of the most terrible crimes, including espionage or treason, we deny our own humanity, and life is further cheapened. Nothing is achieved by taking one more life or adding one more victim.

REMARKS OF SUPREME COURT JUSTICE THURGOOD MARSHALL AT A JUDICIAL CONFERENCE OF THE SECOND CIRCUIT IN HERSHEY, PENNSYLVANIA, SEPTEMBER 6, 1985

Capital defendants frequently suffer the consequences of having trial counsel who are ill-equipped to handle capital cases. Death penalty litigation has become a specialized field of practice, and even the most well-intentioned attorneys often are unable to recognize, preserve, and defend their client's rights. Often trial counsel simply are unfamiliar with the special rules that apply in capital cases. Counsel—whether appointed or retained—often are handling their first criminal cases, or their first murder cases, when confronted with the prospect of a death penalty. Though acting in good faith, they inevitably make very serious mistakes.... The federal reports are filled with stories of counsel who presented *no* evidence in mitigation [lessening of the gravity of the crime] of their client's sentences because they did not know what to offer or how to offer it, or had not read the state's sentencing statute.

... The Court has not yet recognized that the right of effective assistance must encompass a right to counsel familiar with death penalty jurisprudence at the trial stage. Instead, in all but the most egregious [outstanding for undesirable qualities] case, a court cannot or will not make a finding of ineffective assistance of counsel, because counsel has met what the Supreme Court has defined as a minimal standard of competence for criminal lawyers. As a consequence, many capital defendants find that errors by their lawyers preclude presentation of substantial constitutional claims, but that such errors—with the resulting forfeitures of rights—are not sufficient in themselves to constitute ineffective assistance.

Contrary to popular perceptions, all capital defendants have *not* spent years filing frivolous claims in federal courts. Many of these defendants have not yet filed *any* federal claims when their execution dates are set. We simply cannot allow this inaccurate view to blind us to reality or to accept the hasty review process on the ground that defendants already have had the benefits of an untruncated [lengthy] review process. Until an execution date is set and the situation becomes urgent, capital defendants simply have been unable to secure counsel.

Once the execution date is set, the race is on. Prisoners who have not yet sought state or federal *habeas corpus* relief have roughly one month to do so.... But the new attorney often has no knowledge of the record, has not met the client, and has only a few days to read hundreds of pages of transcripts and prepare a petition. This peti- tion, hastily prepared, must include all claims that the defendant might raise, because subsequent petitions will likely be declared abusive of the process if they entertain collateral attacks.

IMPORTANT NAMES AND ADDRESSES

American Bar Association
Criminal Justice Section
740 15th St. NW
10th Fl.
Washington, DC 20005-1019
(202) 662-1000
FAX: (202) 662-1501
URL: http://www.abanet.org/crimjust/home.
html

American Civil Liberties Union
Capital Punishment Project
122 Maryland Ave. NE
Washington, DC 20002
(202) 675-2319
E-mail: capitalpunishment@dcaclu.org
URL: http://www.aclu.org/death-penalty

Amnesty International U.S.A.
National Office
322 Eighth Ave.
New York, NY 10001
(212) 807-8400
FAX: (212) 627-1451
E-mail: admin-us@aiusa.org
URL: http://www.amnestyusa.org

Amnesty International U.S.A.
The Program to Abolish the
Death Penalty
600 Pennsylvania Ave. SE
5th Fl.
Washington, DC 20003
(202) 544-0200
FAX: (202) 546-7142
E-mail: padp@aiusa.org
URL: http://www.aiusa.org/abolish

Bureau of Justice Statistics
U.S. Department of Justice
810 Seventh St. NW
Washington, DC 20531
(202) 307-0765
Toll-free: (800) 732-3277

E-mail: askbjs@ojp.usdoj.gov
URL: http://www.ojp.usdoj.gov/bjs

Criminal Justice Legal Foundation
P.O. Box 1199
Sacramento, CA 95816
(916) 446-0345
E-mail: cjlf@cjlf.org
URL: www.cjlf.org

Death Penalty Information Center
1320 18th St. NW
5th Fl.
Washington, DC 20036
(202) 293-6970
FAX: (202) 822-4787
E-mail: dpic@deathpenaltyinfo.org
URL: http://www.deathpenaltyinfo.org

Federal Bureau of Investigation
J. Edgar Hoover Building
935 Pennsylvania Ave. NW
Washington, DC 20535-0001
(202) 324-3000
URL: http://www.fbi.gov

Federal Bureau of Prisons
Office of Public Affairs
320 First St. NW
Washington, DC 20534
(202) 307-3198
E-mail: webmaster@bop.gov
URL: http://www.bop.gov

Innocence Project
Benjamin N. Cardozo School of Law
100 Fifth Ave., 3rd Fl.
New York, NY 10011
E-mail: info@innocenceproject.org
URL: http://www.innocenceproject.org

International Association of Chiefs
of Police
515 N. Washington St.
Alexandria, VA 22314

(703) 836-6767
FAX: (703) 836-4543
Toll-free: (800) THE-IACP (843-4227)
E-mail: information@theiacp.org
URL: http://www.theiacp.org

Justice for All
URL: http://www.jfa.net

Justice Research and
Statistics Association
777 N. Capitol St. NE
Suite 801
Washington, DC 20002
(202) 842-9330
FAX: (202) 842-9329
E-mail: cjinfo@jrsa.org
URL: http://www.jrsa.org

Murder Victims' Families
for Reconciliation
2161 Massachusetts Ave.
Cambridge, MA 02140
(617) 868-0007
FAX: (617) 354-2832
E-mail: info@mvfr.org
URL: http://www.mvfr.org

NAACP Legal Defense and Educational
Fund, Inc.
99 Hudson St.
Suite 1600
New York, NY 10013
(212) 965-2200
FAX: (212) 226-7592
E-mail: dfins@naacpldf.org
URL: http://www.naacpldf.org

National Association of Criminal
Defense Lawyers
1150 18th St., NW
Suite 950
Washington, DC 20036
(202) 872-8600
FAX: (202) 872-8690
E-mail: assist@nacdl.com

URL: http://www.nacdl.org

National Center for Victims of Crime
2000 M St. NW
Suite 480
Washington, DC 20036-3398
(202) 467-8700
FAX: (202) 467-8701
Toll-free: (800) 394-2255
URL: http://www.ncvc.org

National Criminal Justice Reference Service
P.O. Box 6000
Rockville, MD 20849-6000
(301) 519-5500
FAX: (301) 519-5212
Toll-free: (800) 851-3420
E-mail: askncjrs@ncjrs.org
URL: http://www.ncjrs.org

National District Attorneys Association
99 Canal Center Plaza
Suite 510
Alexandria, VA 22314
(703) 549-9222
FAX: (703) 836-3195

URL: http://www.ndaa.org

Pro-Death Penalty.com
URL: http://www.prodeathpenalty.com

The Sentencing Project
514 10th St. NW
Suite 1000
Washington, DC 20004
(202) 628-0871
FAX: (202) 628-1091
URL: http://www.sentencingproject.org

U.S. Commission on Civil Rights Public Affairs Unit
624 9th St. NW
Washington, DC 20425
(202) 376-8312
E-mail: wwwadmin@uscrr.gov
URL: http://www.usccr.gov

U.S. Department of Justice
950 Pennsylvania Ave. NW
Washington, DC 20530-0001
E-mail: askdoj@usdoj.gov
URL: http://www.usdoj.gov

U.S. House Committee on the Judiciary
2138 Rayburn House Office Bldg.
Washington, DC 20515
(202) 225-3951
E-mail: judiciary@mail.house.gov
URL: http://www.house.gov/judiciary

U.S. Senate Committee on the Judiciary
224 Dirksen Senate Office Bldg.
Washington, DC 20510
(202) 224-5225
FAX: (202) 224-9102
URL: http://judiciary.senate.gov

U.S. Sentencing Commission Office of Public Affairs
1 Columbus Circle NE
Washington, DC 20002-8002
(202) 502-4500
E-mail: pubaffairs@ussc.gov
URL: http://www.ussc.gov

U.S. Supreme Court
1 First St. NE
Washington, DC 20543
(202) 479-3211
URL: http://www.supremecourtus.gov

RESOURCES

The U.S. Department of Justice collects statistics on death row inmates as part of its National Prisoner Statistics (NPS) program. Based on voluntary reporting, the NPS program collects and interprets data on state and federal prisoners. Begun by the U.S. Bureau of the Census in 1926, the program was transferred to the Federal Bureau of Prisons in 1950, to the now-defunct Law Enforcement Assistance Administration (LEAA), and then to the Bureau of Justice Statistics (BJS) in 1979.

Since 1972 the Bureau of the Census, as the collecting agent for the LEAA and the BJS, has been responsible for compiling the relevant data. The BJS annually prepares a bulletin titled *Capital Punishment,* which provides an overview of capital punishment in the United States. The BJS *Sourcebook of Criminal Justice Statistics,* prepared by the Hindelang Criminal Justice Research Center of the State University at Albany, New York, is the most complete compilation of criminal justice statistics.

The Department of Justice has released two reports on the federal death penalty. They are *The Federal Death Penalty System: A Statistical Survey (1988–2000)* (2000) and *The Federal Death Penalty System: Supplementary Data, Analysis and Revised Protocols for Capital Case Review* (2001). *The Report to the Attorney General on Delays in Forensic DNA Analysis* (2003) and *Postconviction DNA Testing: Recommendations for Handling Requests* (1999), both by the National Institute of Justice, were helpful in the preparation of this book. *Federal Death Penalty Cases: Recommendations Concerning the Cost and Quality of Defense Representation,* prepared by the Subcommittee on Death Penalty Cases of the Committee on Defender Services of the Judicial Conference of the United States (1998), provides information on the cost of federal death penalty cases.

The NAACP Legal Defense and Educational Fund, Inc. (LDF; New York, NY), is a private institution that maintains statistics on capital punishment. LDF is strongly opposed to the death penalty. Despite its name, LDF is not part of the National Association for the Advancement of Colored People (NAACP), although it was founded by that organization. Since 1957 LDF has had a separate board of directors, program, staff, office, and budget. LDF publishes *Death Row U.S.A.,* a periodic compilation of capital punishment statistics and information, including the names of all those currently on death row. Data from this quarterly release were helpful in preparing this book.

The Death Penalty Information Center (DPIC; Washington, D.C.), a nonprofit organization, provides the media and general public with information and analysis regarding capital punishment. The DPIC, which is against the death penalty, serves as a resource to those working on this issue. Its reports and charts on capital punishment were used in preparing this book.

Amnesty International is the Nobel Prize–winning human rights organization headquartered in London, United Kingdom. It strongly opposes the death penalty. Amnesty International maintains information on the death penalty and torture throughout the world and periodically publishes its findings. Its publication *The Death Penalty: List of Abolitionist and Retentionist Countries (1 January 2003)* provided data on the status of capital punishment worldwide.

Charts and data from the *Death Penalty for Female Offenders: January 1, 1973, to December 31, 2000* (2001), *Death Penalty for Female Offenders: January 1, 1973, through June 30, 2003* (2003), and *The Juvenile Death Penalty Today: Death Sentences and Executions for Juvenile Crimes: January 1, 1973–September 30, 2003* (2003) by Professor Victor L. Streib of the Claude W. Pettit College of Law of the Ohio Northern University (Ada, OH) were used in the preparation of this book.

Other studies used in this book include the *Study Pursuant to Public Act No. 01-151 of the Imposition of the*

Death Penalty in Connecticut by the State of Connecticut Commission on the Death Penalty (2003); *Critique of DPIC List "Innocence: Freed from Death Row"* by Ward A. Campbell (2002); *Case Histories: A Review of 23 Individuals Released from Death Row* by the Florida Commission on Capital Cases (2002); "Capital Punishment Proves to be Expensive" by Daniel Wise (*New York Law Journal,* Vol. 227, April 30, 2002); *A Broken System: Error Rates in Capital Cases, 1973–1995* (2000) by James S. Liebman, Jeffrey Fagan, and Valerie West; "Capital Appeals Revisited," *Judicature,* Vol. 84, Number 2, September–October 2000, by Barry Latzer and James N. G. Cauthen; *The Fair Defense Report: Analysis of Indigent Defense Practices in Texas* (2000) by the Texas Appleseed Fair Defense Project (Austin, TX); *Race and the Death Penalty in North Carolina, an Empirical Analysis: 1993–1997, Initial Findings* (2001) by Isaac Unah and John Charles Boger (University of North Carolina at Chapel Hill and the Common Sense Foundation, NC); and *The Disposition of Nebraska Capital and Non-Capital Homicide Cases (1973–1999): A Legal and Empirical Analysis* (2001) by David C. Baldus, George Woodworth, Gary L. Young, and Aaron M. Christ.

A Hanging in Detroit: Stephen Gifford Simmons and the Last Execution under Michigan Law (Wayne State University Press, Detroit, MI, 2003) by David G. Chardavoyne provided, among other things, information on the rituals of public executions. The third edition of Roger Hood's *The Death Penalty—A Worldwide Perspective* (Oxford University Press, Inc., New York, 2002) provided a wealth of information about the scope and application of the death penalty in different countries.

The news feature service, Human Rights Features (New Delhi, India), and Forum 90, an abolitionist group that monitors capital punishment in Japan, provided information on the imposition of the death penalty in Japan ("Japan Hanging on to Death Penalty," [2003], and "The Hidden Death Penalty in Japan," [2001], respectively).

In *FYI: Rights of Survivors of Homicide* (1999) the National Center for Victims of Crimes (Washington, D.C.), a nonprofit organization that supports victims' rights and promotes victim assistance, describes some state statutes and policies that allow victims' families to witness executions. Other information about victims' families as execution witnesses comes from *Who Owns Death? Capital Punishment, the American Conscience, and the End of Executions* (William Morrow, New York, NY, 2000) by Robert Jay Lifton and Greg Mitchell.

Polls taken by the Gallup Organization (Princeton, NJ) and Harris Interactive (New York, NY) were also used in this book.

INDEX

Page references in italics refer to photographs. References with the letter t following them indicate the presence of a table. The letter f indicates a figure. If more than one table or figure appears on a particular page, the exact item number for the table or figure being referenced is provided.

Due process
 Callins v. Collins, 108
 Federal Death Penalty Act (1994), 7–8
 newly discovered evidence, 30–31
 notification of death sentence
  contemplation, 29–30

E

East, John P., 111
Eberheart v. Georgia, 23
Eddings v. Oklahoma, 35
Educational attainment of death row
 prisoners, 69
Eighth Amendment. *See* Cruel and unusual
 punishment
Einhorn, Ira, 12
Electrocution, 46–47, 56
*An Empirical Analysis of Maryland's Death
 Sentencing System with Respect to the
 Influence of Race and Legal Jurisdiction*
 (Paternoster et al.), 82–83
Enmund v. Florida, 24–25
Equal Justice Initiative of Alabama, 74
Error
 Curran statement, 114–115
 Feingold statement, 113
 rates in capital cases, 81
Estelle v. Smith, 38–39
Evidence
 newly discovered, 30–31
 suppressed, 31–32
Executions
 international statistics, 11
 juvenile offenders, 35–37, 54
 McVeigh, Timothy, 2, 3, 58, 91, 105,
  106–107
 media witnesses, 58–59
 military, 5
 minimum age, 54*t*
 numbers of persons executed, 61, 62*t,* 63*t*
 televising, 58
 victims' family as witnesses, 57–58
Exoneration
 DNA testing, 8, 76–77
 McMillian statement, 118
 statistics, 75*f*
 studies, 74–77
Extradition, 12

F

"The Failure of the Death Penalty in Illinois"
 (Armstrong and Mills), 73–74
*The Fair Defense Report: Analysis of
 Indigent Defense Practices in Texas*
 (Texas Appleseed Fair Defense Project),
 82
Federal death penalty
 appeals, 7
 capital crimes, 3
 costs, 85–86
 East statement, 111
 first federal execution, 2
 in non-death penalty states, 4
 racial bias, 79–81
 reversals of convictions or sentences, 82
Federal Death Penalty Abolition Act
 (proposed), 113–114

Federal Death Penalty Act (1994), 7–8
*Federal Death Penalty Cases:
 Recommendations Concerning the Cost
 and Quality of Defense Representation*
 (Subcommittee on Federal Death Penalty
 Cases), 85
Federal Death Penalty Resource Counsel
 Project (FDPRCP), 3
*The Federal Death Penalty System: A
 Statistical Survey* (Justice Department),
 79
*The Federal Death Penalty System:
 Supplementary Data, Analysis and
 Revised Protocols for Capital Case
 Review* (Justice Department), 79–81
Federal executions
 Garza, Juan Raul, 3–4
 Jones, Louis, Jr., 4
 McVeigh, Timothy, 3, 58, 91, 105,
  106–107
Federal judges, 27–28, 47–49
Federal statutes, 53*t,* 55
Fein, Bruce, 109
Feingold, Russell, 113–114
Fierro v. Gomez, 46
Fifth Amendment, 38–39
Firing squads, 55–56
First Amendment, 58–59
Florida
 electrocution, 46–47
 execution of insane persons, 39–40
 imposition of the death sentence, 15
 judge sentencing, 19
Food and Drug Administration (FDA), 45
Ford v. Georgia, 44–45
Ford v. Wainwright, 39–40
Foreign nationals, 95–96
Forum 90, 98
Foster v. Florida, 21
France, 12
Franklin, Benjamin, 1
Furman v. Georgia, 5, 13–14, 51, 117–118
Furrow, Buford, 90
Future threat
 jury consideration, 15
 psychiatric testimony, 15, 37–38
 race/ethnicity, 45

G

Gabrion, Marvin, 4
Garza, Juan Raul, 3–4, 91
Gas chamber, 46
Gender
 death row inmates, 68–69, 70(*t*7.3)
 executions, 61, 63
Genocide, 93
Georgia
 bifurcated trials, 14–15
 electrocution, 47
 execution of mentally retarded persons,
  54
 Furman v. Georgia, 13–14
Germany, 96
Germany v. United States of America, 96
Gideon v. Wainwright, 73
Gilbert, Kristen, 4
Gilmore, Gary, 5

Gingrich, Newt, 111
Ginsburg, Ruth Bader
 double jeopardy, 21
 legal representation, 10
Godfrey v. Georgia, 25–26
Godinez v. Moran, 42
Gonzalez, Henry B., 117
Greeley, Horace, 2
Green River killer case, 11
Gregg v. Georgia, 14–15
Guilt. *See* Innocence and guilt

H

Habeas corpus review
 Antiterrorism and Effective Death
  Penalty Act (1996), 5, 47–49
 delay of execution, 27–28
Hanging
 constitutionality, 45–46
 state statutes, 56
*A Hanging in Detroit: Stephen Gifford
 Simmons and the Last Execution under
 Michigan Law* (Chardavoyne), 57
Harmless error, 6–7, 28–29
Hatch, Orrin, 75, 103–104
Heckler v. Chaney, 45
Helms, Jesse, 107
Herrera v. Collins, 30–31
The Hidden Death Penalty in Japan
 (Takahashi and Mariadason), 98
Hitchcock v. Dugger, 24
House Judiciary Committee hearings, 74–75
Hyde, Henry J., 107
Hynes v. Tomei, 53–54

I

Illinois
 moratorium, call for a, 8
 racial makeup of death row, 78
Indigent defendants, 39
 See also Counsel, right to; Ineffective
  counsel; Legal representation costs
Ineffective counsel
 court cases, 26
 state statutes, 73–74
 testimony and statements, 116, 119–120
Innocence and guilt
 exonerations, 74–77
 guilty pleas and mental competence, 42
 Keating statement, 105–106
 miscarriage of justice claims, 31
 Moseley-Braun statement, 118
 public opinion, 91
 Scheidegger testimony, 104–105
 Stewart statement, 106
"Innocence and the Death Penalty:
 Assessing the Danger of Mistaken
 Executions" (Death Penalty Information
 Center), 74–75
*Inquiry into the Justice and Policy of
 Punishing Murder by Death* (Rush), 1
Insanity
 execution of insane persons, 39–40
 psychiatric diagnosis, 39
Intent, 24–25
International Court of Justice, 96

International Covenant on Civil and Political Rights, 93–94
International issues
  abolitionist countries, 97t, 98t, 99t, 100t
  extradition, 12
  juvenile offenders, countries with death penalty for, 100–101
  retentionist countries, 94–99, 95t
  trend towards abolition, 11
  United Nations resolutions, 93–94

J

Japan, 97–98
Johnson, Gary, 10
Johnson, Sam, 107
Johnson v. Texas, 37
Jones, Louis, Jr., 4
Jordan, Samuel, 116
Judaism, 115
Judge sentencing
  Alabama, 19–20
  Florida, 19
  jury recommendations, 19–20
  Ring v. Arizona, 6–7
Jurek v. Texas, 15
Juries
  "death-qualified," 16–17
  future threat consideration, 15
  lesser charge consideration, 17–18
  parole ineligibility information, withholding of, 18
  presumption of malice, 29
  racially-based peremptory challenges, 44–45
  sense of responsibility, 18
  sentencing recommendations, 19–20
Jurisdiction and death penalty imposition, 83–84
Jurors
  exclusion of based on death penalty beliefs, 16–17
  racial attitudes, 42–44
Jury sentencing
  Apprendi v. New Jersey, 20
  Ring v. Arizona, 6–7, 20–21
  state statutes, 52
  Walton v. Arizona, 20
Justice Department studies on racial bias, 79–81
Juvenile offenders
  countries with death penalty for, 100–101
  execution of, 35–37, 54
  minors tried as adults, 35–37
  public opinion on death penalty for, 89, 89t

K

Katz study, 110
Keating, Frank, 105–106
Kennedy, Anthony, 37
Kentucky, 79
Kidnapping, 23, 51
Kinsella, John J., 8
Kliesmet, Robert B., 111
Kopp, James Charles, 12
Kyles v. Whitley, 31–32

L

Latzer study, 81–82
Legal representation costs, 84–86, 85t
Legislation
  Anti-Drug Abuse Act (1988), 3
  Antiterrorism and Effective Death Penalty Act (1996), 3, 5, 47–49
  execution of mentally retarded persons, 54–55
  federal death penalty laws, 53t
  Racial Justice Act (Kentucky), 79
  state statute changes, 51–52
  Terrorist Bombings Convention Implementation Act (2002), 3
  Texas Fair Defense Act, 82
  United Nations resolutions, 93–94
  Violent Crime Control and Law Enforcement Act (1994), 3
Lethal gas, 46, 56
Lethal injection
  FDA jurisdiction, 45
  Scalia, Antonin, 108
  state statutes, 55, 56
Liebman study, 81
Life imprisonment without parole
  Anders statement, 111
  public opinion on, 88
Lindh, John Walker, 90
Lockett v. Ohio, 16, 23
Lockhart v. McCree, 17
Louisiana, 16, 52–53

M

Maine, 2
Malice, presumed, 29
Malvo, Lee Boyd, 4
Mandatory death sentences
  Louisiana, 16
  North Carolina, 15–16
Marshall, Thurgood
  Eighth Amendment, 14
  exclusion of jurors opposed to the death penalty, 17
  ineffective counsel, 119–120
  jury responsibility, 18
Maryland
  death penalty imposition study, 82–83
  moratorium, call for a, 8–9
  sniper shootings, 4
  victim impact statements, 32
Massachusetts
  federal death penalty, 4
  reinstatement bills, 5–6
McCleskey v. Kemp, 43–44
McFarland v. Scott, 27–28
McMillian, Walter, 118
McVeigh, Timothy, 3, 58, 91, 105, 106–107
Media witnesses to executions, 58–59
Mental competency, 42
Mentally ill persons, 89, 89t
Mentally retarded persons, death penalty for
  court challenges, 40–42, 54–55
  culpability, 40–42
  public opinion on death penalty for, 89, 89t
  Virginia, 6, 36, 41–42, 55
Methods of execution
  constitutionality, 45–47

numbers executed by method, 66, 66t
  state statutes, 51–52, 55–56
Mexico, 96
Mexico v. United States of America, 96
Michigan
  abolitionism, 2
  costs of federal cases, 85–86
  federal death penalty, 4
Minors tried as adults. *See* Juvenile offenders
Miscarriage of justice claims, 31
Mistrials due to suppressed evidence, 31–32
Mitigating circumstances, 23–24, 35–37
Moratoria
  Jordan statement, 116
  lifting of, 5
  public opinion, 91
  state calls for, 8–9
Moseley-Braun, Carol, 118
Muhammad, John Allen, 4, 58
Murder
  intent, 24–25
  of law enforcement officers, 51–52
  presence at the crime scene, 24–25
Murray v. Carrier, 31
Murray v. Giarratano, 27

N

National Institute of Justice, 79–81
National Jewish/Catholic consultation, 115–116
Native Americans, 5
Nebraska, 83–84
New Hampshire, 6
New York
  costs of the death penalty, 84
  death penalty statute, 53–54
Newly discovered evidence, 30–31
Non-death penalty states, 85–86
North Carolina
  costs of the death penalty, 84
  death penalty study, 83
  mandatory death sentences, 15–16

O

O'Connor, Sandra Day
  age as mitigating circumstance, 36, 37
  execution of mentally retarded persons, 40
  innocent defendants, 10
  intent, 24, 25
Oda, Shigeru, 96
Oken, Steven, 8–9
Oken v. State, 9
Oklahoma City bombing, 3
Outcomes of death sentences, 70–71, 73t

P

Paraguay et al. v. Gilmore, 95–96
Parole ineligibility, 18
Patterson, James Earl, 8
Payne v. Tennessee, 32–33
Penry, Johnny Paul, 40–42
Penry v. Johnson, 41
Penry v. Lynaugh, 37, 40–41, 54
Peremptory challenges, 44–45